CHARLES DICKENS'S AMERICAN AUDIENCE

CHARLES DICKENS'S AMERICAN AUDIENCE

Robert McParland

LEXINGTON BOOKS
A division of
ROWMAN & LITTLEFIELD PUBLISHERS, INC.
Lanham • Boulder • New York • Toronto • Plymouth, UK

Published by Lexington Books
A division of Rowman & Littlefield Publishers, Inc.
A wholly owned subsidiary of The Rowman & Littlefield Publishing Group, Inc.
4501 Forbes Boulevard, Suite 200, Lanham, Maryland 20706
http://www.lexingtonbooks.com

Estover Road, Plymouth PL6 7PY, United Kingdom

British Library Cataloguing in Publication Information Available

Library of Congress Cataloging-in-Publication Data
McParland, Robert.
    Charles Dickens's American audience / Robert McParland.
       p.   cm.
    Includes bibliographical references and index.
    ISBN 978-0-7391-1857-3 (cloth : alk. paper) — ISBN 978-0-7391-4841-9 (electronic)
    1. Dickens, Charles, 1812–1870—Appreciation—United States. 2. Dickens, Charles,
1812–1870—Influence. 3. Books and reading—United States—History—19th century.
4. United States—Civilization—19th century. 5. Popular culture—United States—
History—19th century. I. Title.
    PR4592.A54M37 2010
823'.8—dc22   2010013846

Printed in the United States of America

Contents

Acknowledgments   vii

1	Seeking Charles Dickens's American Audience	1
2	Charles Dickens and the American Community	11
3	Dickens and American Publishers	43
4	Charles Dickens's First Visit to America, *American Notes*, and *Martin Chuzzlewit*	67
5	Dickens and Library Reading	83
6	Learning from Fiction and Reality	101
7	Dickens in a House Divided	121
8	Civil War Reading	141
9	Theatricality	159
10	The Public Readings and the American Reconstruction of Charles Dickens	173
11	The Afterlife of Charles Dickens	193

Bibliography   215

Index   235

Acknowledgments

THE BICENTENARY OF CHARLES DICKENS'S BIRTH in 2012 is cause for celebration of what his work continues to mean for us in the twenty-first century. What Dickens and his work meant to his contemporary readers in America is the subject of this book. Their voices, in all of their variety, will, I hope, come across in these pages.

My foremost note of gratitude is to Jonathan Rose, whose professionalism, kindness, and high standards provided me with an exemplary model of scholarship. I am grateful for his insight and encouragement in moving this project along. Chapters were read at various stages by Jonathan Rose, Robert Ready, and C. Wyatt Evans.

My scholarly debts are many. I am particularly thankful for the work of Richard Altick, whose work on *The English Common Reader* is inspiring and enduring and to Robert L. Patten, whose *Dickens's Publishers* remains a pivotal work. The list of Dickensians who have made heroic efforts to better our understanding of Dickens is distinguished and long. Many of their names appear in the bibliography. I am also indebted to the transatlantic studies of Robert Weisbuch, Kim Sturgess, and others, and to the cultural studies of readers and book history studies by Ronald Zboray, Jonathan Rose, Kate Flint, Robert Darnton, Christine Pawley, Charles Johanningsmeier, and others. We are all served by the advances made by the Society for the History of Authorship, Reading and Publishing (SHARP) and the Reading Experience Database (RED) in Britain.

While writing and research can be a long and solitary process, this was also an adventure in community. I received the assistance of some generous people on the SHARP listserv. There were those who listened to portions of this manuscript at conferences at University College in Cork, Ireland, SHARP-Minneapolis, Dickens in Italy in Genoa, Italy, Research Society for Victorian Periodicals conferences, Victorian Studies Association conferences, Drew University colloquia, and the Princeton Center for the Book. My thanks for the attentive and helpful staffs of the New York Historical Society, New York Society Library, and Onondaga Historical Society in Syracuse, New York, to Susan Hamburger of the Penn State Libraries for her assistance with the Mortlake Collection, and the staffs and resources at Drew University, New York Public Library, Cornell University Library, Cortland Historical Society, Princeton University Library.

I am grateful for the support of my family, and offer my heartfelt thanks to John Kudlak for our cross-country conversations, to Debbie Cariddi for her moral support and endurance with my many hours of talking about Dickens, and to my colleagues at Felician College in New Jersey.

1

Seeking Charles Dickens's American Audience

ALTHOUGH CHARLES DICKENS WAS ONE OF THE MOST POPULAR British authors of the nineteenth century, on both sides of the Atlantic, the American audience for Dickens's novels and public readings has never been carefully examined. An investigation into the reception of his texts by ordinary Americans, those who were not professional literary critics but who were reading Dickens's writings solely for personal pleasure or use, can give us valuable insights into nineteenth-century American culture. Because Charles Dickens was so pivotal and popular an author, it is important to understand this fascination of nineteenth-century readers. His sentiment, his caricatures, his social panoramas, his humor, and his melodrama interacted with the lives of his American audience. During a time when the American nation was emerging, the novels of a British author, Charles Dickens, contributed significantly to the making of American culture.

Observing that the decoding of cultural texts is influenced by fields of discourse, this study will suggest that elements of popular culture, including theater, predisposed reader reception to Dickens's fiction. This study will also look at how the Dickens novel acted as both a vital "amusement of the people" and as a space for his readers to meet, as an extended family, or "imagined community." His novels thus acted as a home-like point of stability in a rapidly changing society.

This is a study of how Charles Dickens's American audience, 1837–1912, in their great diversity, coalesced into a reading community around the sentiments, characters, images, and themes of this one significant author. In discussing Dickens's reception, it is important that our inquiry be not only a matter of reviewing the critical response to his books, as George Ford has done.[1] One must also assess the popular reception. Those who were not professional literary critics or editors, but rather, workers, homemakers, immigrants, former slaves, and businesspeople, as well as writers, clergy, or teachers, were the readers who made these books popular. They also need to be included in this assessment. This study attempts to begin to reclaim the forgotten voices of a significant public: the diverse American audience of one of the most popular novelists of the nineteenth century, Charles Dickens. It asserts that the wide consumption and reproduction of Dickens by American audiences shaped the development of American literature and culture. The market for Dickens launched imitations, circulated socially shared themes and caricatures, and promoted business. Through shared sentiment and melodrama, it prompted a unifying American character.

The excellent recent work on common readers provides useful methodological models. We may ask, how far can we recover middle-class and working-class readers' responses and did these differ from each other? It is also useful to compare responses of males and females, blacks and whites, immigrants, and people of different classes and occupations. In addition, possible regional variations in the audience of Dickens are explored: his audience in rural areas of the Northeast, the South, and the West. However, a history of an audience cannot be limited to readers alone. One must include theater patrons, listeners to public readings, publishers, people who were read to, or who heard of Dickens's characters second-hand.

This study focuses upon Dickens's contemporaries and their immediate successors. It concludes with the Dickens centenary in 1912, because literary modernism may have subsequently complicated the question of reception. In Virginia Woolf's view, culture changed "on or about December 1910," with the exhibition of the post-impressionists in London. The 1913 Armory Show in New York soon followed. The generation of Mencken, Fitzgerald, and Hemingway debunked their predecessors and championed a different aesthetic from that of Dickens and his contemporaries. What was valued in writing likewise shifted. The twentieth century may be taken as a point of transition in American culture, as well as in Anglo-American relations. The First World War, disrupting Victorian notions of stability, further emphasized this divide.

Dickens's stories emerged at a time when "an older, more communally centered culture [was] being subverted by the mass regimentation of industrialism" (Keating 8). In 1833, Peter Gaskell, in *The Manufacturing Population of England* (1833), observed what he referred to as "the separation of families, the breaking up of households, the disruption of all those ties which link man's heart to the better parts of his nature" (92). The condition of England

and the condition of America were at stake in the nineteenth century. Thomas Carlyle wrote: "We call it a Society; and go about professing openly the totalest separation, isolation. Our life is not mutual helpfulness; but rather, cloaked under due laws of war, named 'fair competition' and so forth; it is mutual hostility. We have profoundly forgotten everywhere that Cash-payment is not the sole relation of human beings; we think, nothing doubting, that it absolves and liquidates all engagements of man" (*Past and Present* 143). Dickens's writing was, in part, a response to overcome such isolation. Through sentiment and melodrama, Dickens provided entertainment within the family circle and to other groups of readers and listeners. Reading Dickens acted as an enlivening, awakening, and emancipatory practice, "education in the widest sense" (Rose 3). Dickens, as humorist, entertainer, and social critic, sought to preserve the "amusements of the people," give voice to society, and restore the deepest sense of "home": the imagined community with a heart of mutual sympathy.

The humane radicalism of Charles Dickens enabled his American audience to discover much that was relevant to their individual lives. Dickens was highly attuned to popular culture and to his audience, as Paul Schlicke and others have demonstrated, and he sought to contribute a sense of community to his broad audience. Dickens, says Schlicke, "chose to commit himself to public service" (245). Or, as William Axton notes: "His ultimate aim was to awaken his reader to the vital significance of his ordinary experience" (162). Reinhard Wittmann observes that the need for an author to connect with his or her readers led to "a spiritual community created by the book" (Wittmann in Cavallo and Chartier 300). Ronald Zboray asserts that "Fiction played a part in building a sense of social solidarity based upon the printed word, a fragile republic of letters. Within that fictive, ever shifting and elusive, largely imaginary community, the modern portable sense of American self was born" (80). What is sought here is how this sense of "imagined community" may have emerged in contact with and resistance to British authors, specifically Dickens.

Until recently it was thought impossible to recover the ordinary reader in history. However, the work of Jonathan Rose, David Vincent, Kate Flint, Ronald Zboray, and others has increasingly shown that it is possible. The field is new and open and rich with possibilities. Instead of emphasizing the writer, this reverses the lens, to focus upon the reader. Likewise, while Charles Dickens's critical reception has been frequently assessed, his popular audience—the one that in market terms and in social terms most counted has not.

The study of Victorian readership and audiences in recent times began with the pioneering work of Richard Altick in *The English Common Reader—A Social History of the Mass Reading Public, 1800–1900* (1957). While George Ford, in *Dickens and His Readers* (1955), explored the critical reception of Dickens's novels, the investigation of his ordinary readers, who represent the thousands of every day persons who read and responded to his work, has only recently begun. Jonathan Rose (2001) has explored working-class readers, including Dickens's working-class readers in Britain.

There has never been an exploration of Dickens's common readers in America. This study, while it deals with a broader American audience, including writers, editors, ministers, and political figures, is intended as a movement in that direction. Statistical data in Robert L. Patten's *Dickens and his Publishers* (1978) provides quantitative measures and discussion of the production and circulation of Dickens's novels. Records of Harper Brothers, G.P. Putnam, and Carey and Lea's cost books are referred to here to supplement Patten's findings, along with Michael Winship's focus upon the publishing economics of Ticknor and Fields. Library records are also consulted as an indicator of the American reading public.

This study follows the lead of Ronald Zboray, who has investigated the American nineteenth-century community of readers in *A Fictive People: Antebellum Economic Development and the American Reading Public* (1993). Zboray sees the printed word as "the primary avenue of national enculturation." He addresses antebellum publishers' confident use of technological innovations and their use of trade papers, book auctions, periodical depots, and traveling book agents. His study inquires into how books mediated between the individual and the expanding society and devotes attention to community change. This study, like his, theorizes that as traditional relations between people and locales shifted, the printed word served through fictive bonds to connect readers with the larger structure of the nation and that the printed word became "a primary tool of community building." Fiction provided for "affectional needs formerly fulfilled locally" and mediated "between the self and the threat of cultural disorder" (xxi). It "would also help the individual cope personally," providing "the way toward self-construction" (80). These propositions are tested here in connection with Dickens.

The context in which books were read is a concern of William Gilmore's *Reading Becomes a Necessity of Life* (1992) and Christine Pawley's *Reading on the Middle Border: The Culture of Print in late Nineteenth Century Osage, Iowa* (2001). Inquiry here into regional differences in Dickens's audience takes its cue from these studies on reading communities. Seeking the role of reading within a broader history of New England mental processes, perception, and consciousness, Gilmore locates a specific, coherent social and cultural subregion: the Windsor District of Vermont. The concept of human habitats guides his inquiry into factors shaping daily life within which knowledge and print circulates. Gilmore analyzes the type of community, its placement in the communications network, its household occupations and sizes, consumer economic participation, literacy, family libraries and what was thinkable in that place and time. Pawley inquires into reading as a social practice to "uncover the social meaning of print" (3). She examines the sources and contexts of reading: schools, libraries, churches, voluntary associations, newspapers, and case studies of readers. Exploring the everyday uses of print information by people in Osage, Iowa, she takes "an ethnographic approach to print use in a historical community" (7). Her goal is to "describe and analyze the interaction these ordinary townspeople had with print" (8), including local attitudes toward reading and how print materials were acquired. She asks: What role did print have in a reorientation from a local to a more national perspective? Was reading principally a solitary activity, or did people read in the company of others? How did reading and the myths embodied in stories support the establishment of values and self-definition?

Likewise, Paul Johnson explores the influences of religious revival on antebellum reform in a specific locality. He investigates the interconnections of social, economic, political, and religious tradition in Rochester, New York. This kind of microcosmic look at Dickens's readers in specific locales can begin to tell us about their reading habits and Dickens's impact upon them.

This study of Dickens's readers, following these scholars, looks briefly at cultural sub-regions and their place in the communications network. It considers the social meaning of print, viewing reading as a collective activity that did indeed support values and self-definition, as well as national construction. This study offers the view that Dickens was often read in the company of others, in families and literary societies, and that this use of print aided in the construction of local communities of readers and the broader "imagined community" of the American nation. It points, in part, to a specific local community, Syracuse, New York, as an industrial town in which Dickens's novels were distributed and read. Dickens's 1868 visit to this area makes it a key site for examining audiences. Syracuse, where Dickens's readers went to Weiting Hall to hear him read, was built upon the expansion of trade that followed the completion of the Erie Canal. It was a town in which print was circulated from both major American publishing centers, Boston and New York City. Syracuse was situated within a region notable for antebellum abolitionist and women's rights efforts, where Dickens may have been perceived by some as a social reformer. Reception in Syracuse is perhaps indicative of the response to Dickens in similar towns across the United States that became crossroads where industrial and agricultural pursuits intersected and print sources were multiplying. Dickens's visit made a memorable impact on many Syracuse residents, resulting in the formation of reading circles later in the century that are useful in examining the responses of common readers to Dickens.

Syracuse newspapers and the Onondaga Historical Society actively sought the responses of Dickens's readers to his public readings. It is interesting also to compare Dickens's critique of Syracuse in 1868 with his earlier comments on small towns in America in his 1842 *American Notes*. While Dickens's public comments in 1867 suggested a new, welcoming attitude toward America, his personal letters, with respect to Syracuse and rural America, did not. Syracuse is a place in which we can see the continuing ambivalence of both the author toward America's developing areas and of Dickens's audience toward the author.

The study of this town in upstate New York shows that the reading of Charles Dickens's stories in nineteenth-century America was a social practice that contributed to the development of American society and social awareness. As Pawley has indicated, print technology helped in "refocusing American consciousness from a local to a national horizon" (1). The same point has been made by Zboray, who has argued for the notion of "a fictive people." Stated in another way, the circulation of print materials, like Dickens's novels, may be said to have performed a role in the development of what Benedict Anderson has called "imagined community," a nation "conceived as a deep, horizontal comradeship" (7). Anderson notes "In fact, all communities larger than primordial villages of face-to-face contact (and perhaps even these) are imagined" (6). He points out that "print-languages laid the bases for national consciousness in three distinct ways":

1. They created unified fields of exchange and information.
2. Print gave a fixity to language.
3. Print capitalism "created languages of power of a kind different from the old administrative vernaculars." (44–45)

The circulation of Charles Dickens's novels performed the role of creating unified fields of exchange and information. They contributed to written and spoken language and created a different kind of language of power: an empowerment of people through the expression of sentiment in reading, writing, or personal theatricality. In serial periodical publications, in cheap and expensive editions, in theater productions and adaptations, the writings of Charles Dickens entered the unique situations of American readers. While each reader approached Dickens's fiction in his or her own way, the shared experience of reading or hearing references to Dickens's characters acted as a reference point for them all. The Dickens novel created a field of discourse, a common ground for communication. It was a source of shared symbols, images and phrases, a melodramatic meeting ground for social sentiment.

Dickens contributed to "imagined community," which Anderson says is intended to connote the shared discourse and cultural reference points that enable people to imagine and conceive of their personal connection to the nation and to persons whom they might not personally meet. The community suggested here, however, is one of readers who share common texts, although they may not share the same politics. This community of readers is one of people interacting with the distribution of communication and discourse. This circulation of print affected consciousness; it had an impact upon how people viewed their relationship to each other. For a community may be defined as a mutuality of concerns among people who also express differences. It is an interacting assemblage of unique personalities with some common interest, shared discourse, or frame of reference. In this case, that frame of reference is the Dickens novel, or essay. As Americans appropriated and took ownership of Dickens's texts, these widely circulated texts provided a means for his audience to become a community of readers.

The serialization of Dickens's novels and the corresponding social nature of Victorian reading practices is the subject of Linda K. Hughes and Michael Lund's study *The Victorian Serial* (1991), as well as Jennifer Hayward's *Consuming Pleasures* (1997) and Patricia Okker's *Social Stories* (2003). Several Dickens scholars, such as Kathleen Tillotson and John Butt, have closely examined Dickens's working practices as a serial novelist. The studies by Hughes and Lund, Hayward, and Okker devote attention to his audience, often approached through reviews. Here emphasis is placed upon Dickens's American readers, discovered through their journals and letters and in the accounts of libraries and reading circles. Meredith McGill's study of the culture of reprinting and Charles Johannigsmeier's investigation of newspaper syndication of fiction, likewise, draw attention to the contexts in which stories by Dickens appeared and were read in America. This includes the nationalistic context observed by Robert Weisbuch and Kim C. Sturgess in which English authors were appropriated by American audiences. This study seeks to supplement their findings with the voices of Dickens's audience.

In the search for the female reader of Charles Dickens, the work of Kate Flint, *The Woman Reader 1837–1940* (1993), Sally Mitchell's *The Fallen Angel: Chastity, Class and Women's Reading, 1835–1880* (1981), and Janice Radway's *Reading the Romance* (1984) raise questions about whether reading preferences were gender based and how publishers targeted female readers. The evidence in this study corresponds to the findings of Christine Pawley, Ronald Zboray, and others who indicate that women and men read the works of Charles Dickens in equal numbers.

Dickens's American audience included those who heard his fiction read aloud, or saw it enacted in plays. This study asserts that the reception of

Dickens's audience was predisposed by theater. The significance of William Shakespeare for American culture has been recently examined by Kim C. Sturgess in *Shakespeare and the American Nation* (2004). Dickens also had a considerable impact, as his works were adapted into a variety of cultural forms, including plays and films. Deborah Vlock, in *Dickens, Novel Reading and the Victorian Popular Theatre* (1998) asserts that theater and melodrama created a context for reception of Dickens's novels. Vlock's work helps us to look at how the theatricality of Victorian society is reflected in the texts of Dickens, whose theater interests are noted by William Axton, Robert Garis, and others. This theatricality can be seen in autobiographical writings of Dickens's readers, who imitate Dickens's style or see Dickens's characters in everyday life. Dickens's public readings underscore this theatrical context for reception. Paul Schlicke's suggestion that Dickens felt that the work of popular entertainment was purposeful and that he had a specific social role as a writer is also emphasized here. In *Dickens and Popular Entertainment* (1985), Schlicke writes that because Dickens "cared genuinely about the imaginative health of his fellow human beings" the public readings were "the culmination of his lifetime's dedication to the cause of popular entertainment." Through them, Dickens was "enacting the values which his fiction and journalism had propounded" (245). In connection with the variety of audience response indicated here, I point to Mikhail Bakhtin's notion of dialogism and heteroglossia in the novel. This helps us to consider the many-voicedness of nineteenth-century society embodied both in Dickens's texts and in the texts of the readers of Dickens as they respond to his novels.

To recover the response of Dickens's audience and their point of view, the following methods have been used: An inquiry into memoirs, autobiographies, and letters of Dickens's American readers from the period of 1835–1912, as well as letters to the editors of newspapers and major journals. Nineteenth-century American reading circles, particularly those of the latter part of the nineteenth century in New York State, are explored through each group's records and minutes, obtained at historical societies. Quantitative data has been obtained from public library circulation records. The publishing statistics provided by Robert L. Patten in *Charles Dickens and his Publishers* (1978) are supplemented with material from publisher's archives. The collections of New York Public Library and New York Historical Society special collections have been consulted for autobiographies and other relevant texts, as well as the New York Society Library's circulation records and catalogs of several other nineteenth-century libraries. The New York libraries have provided access to nineteenth-century newspapers and journals. Historical societies' records of reading circles were obtained by correspondence. Publishers' records at the Princeton University Library (Putnam) and Columbia

University Library (Harpers), as well as useful sources at the Morgan Library (Dickens collection, Miscellaneous American collection), Onandaga (Syracuse) Historical Society, Mortlake Collection at Penn State University Library and Cornell University Library have also been consulted. On-line autobiographies, letters, and books from the University of North Carolina, and the University of Michigan and Cornell University *Making of America* collection were also useful. In these collections are autobiographies, letters, or other materials in which Dickens's audience mentions the author or his texts. Creative writers, book and sermon-writing ministers, educators, reporters, and people who recorded meeting Dickens are among the writers of these texts. The members of the SHARP-L listserv have also offered invaluable assistance in locating some relevant material. Newspaper accounts of Dickens's public readings in various American cities have been examined to locate audience members' recollections.

These sources remind us that home and hearth are at the center of Dickens's sentimental world. The hearth is symbolically at the center of fancy and imagination, while reading and story provide a shared experience in familial life. The metonymic house of Dickens's *Household Words, Bleak House,* Satis House, and his other settings and the inversion of this into what Freud called the *unheimlich*, or the uncanny, appears to connect Dickens's concerns with the American experience of the Civil War period. Community and home were shattered at that time in a house divided. In this investigation of an actual audience involved in popular culture, Dickens's panoramic and polyvocal books are viewed as having made a contribution to the creation of a heterogeneous culture. I propose the view that the intersection of Charles Dickens and his American audience helped to forge a reading community.

Note

1. See George Ford, *Dickens and His Readers: Aspects of Novel Criticism Since 1836* (Princeton: Princeton UP, 1955).

2

Charles Dickens and
the American Community

C HARLES DICKENS'S STORIES INFLUENCED THE LIVES of a diverse American audience and contributed to the development of the American character.
As his novels crossed the Atlantic, they also crossed class, gender, racial, occupational, and national boundaries. Dickens's fiction, as a common reading
experience, participated in a dialogue in which sentiment, melodrama, and
theatricality were bound up with the development of American democracy.
The American appropriation of Dickens occurred in a context of nationalistic
resistance to British culture that helped to define American distinctiveness.
In America, Dickens's characters circulated through people's lives and homes
and in the public sphere, and became for his readers familiar personages
through which they could reflect upon their lives. According to a book note
in the *U.S. Democratic Review* in 1847, "In this country, the writings of Dickens have been extensively read, and are, perhaps, as popular as in England"
(*U.S. Democratic Review* [March 1847]: 54). Reading Dickens was a social and
participatory act by which Dickens's American audience, involved with his
stories amid the busy context of life, negotiated the national imagination and
their personal experience.[1] Through the circulation of his texts, by private or
public readings, Charles Dickens, a British author, contributed to the making
of the imagined community of America.

The influence of Charles Dickens upon the American reading public has to
be considered contextually. Clearly, Dickens was only one of many influences
upon their awareness and upon discourse. Readers were reading many different books, pamphlets, and periodicals. These intersected with their reading of
Dickens, whose work came to them in a variety of forms and within a wide

array of social and cultural frameworks. Dickens reading occurred within a variety of contexts. However, because Dickens's writings were so popular, they contributed to discourse in America, in all regions of the country.

During the American Civil War Dickens was read, North and South, across the division of two embattled regions. It is important to note this because the emphasis in this study is to be distinguished from the political sense of "imagined community," which Benedict Anderson believes arose from shared print culture.[2] The American "community" is diverse and it is not always in agreement. The intention here is not to suggest that reading Dickens caused the nation to cohere in a *political* sense. Economic and social factors are perhaps more considerable than the exchange of print in forging a nation. However, the reading of similar texts creates sociability, the capacity to discuss common characters and ideas. It creates what Ronald Zboray has called "a fictive community." Dickens's stories provided this sense of common ground, whatever ideological sense his readers brought to their reading. There will always be regional differences among readers and differences across race, class, and gender which are interesting to explore. Even so, the wide popularity of Dickens led to the awareness that others were also reading Dickens's novels. Readers shared a familiarity with his characters and plots. Reading Dickens's fiction in family parlors and in small groups in public places brought people together in a shared conversation. This is what is primarily meant here by "a community of readers." For all of their social and political differences, these readers shared a familiar narrative and vocabulary, and were familiar with the images and characters that they found in Dickens's work. Reading Dickens became a common practice, one shared across the considerable diversity of the nation.

An authentic community, today as well as then, reflects this diversity. It is plural and varied. It shares a dialogue but does not necessarily arrive at an easy consensus. The intention here is to suggest that print culture did make a contribution to social awareness across the United States and that Dickens was part of the conversation. Dickens was read everywhere and he brought people together into discussion about his fiction. People consumed the same Dickens materials, even if they were politically and regionally divided and read Dickens in different ways.

In reading Dickens, readers had differing interpretations. Opinion about Dickens himself was divided. However, his books were bought everywhere and his stories circulated steadily in all regions. For example, *A Tale of Two Cities* appeared from May to December 1859 in *Harper's Weekly*, which had reached a circulation of 200,000. *Harper's* was distributed in Richmond, as well as in New Orleans, before the war. The story was popular North and South, regardless of political disagreement.

Dickens's writing was popular, available, and widely talked about. Readers responded to the tales through their own social and political discourse and this variety of response is precisely the point. It is not public opinion of Dickens the man that matters here. It is that his books circulated and entered the minds and imaginations of people that matters. Dickens's role in the stimulation of the American publishing business, print circulation, and library reading is significant. It is in this respect—and within a wide context of other reading experiences—that Dickens contributed to American culture.

In the production and reception of popular literature, the audience found entertainment and instruction. War, politics, and regional ideology served to shape readers' responses. A reader's involvement in a Charles Dickens novel inevitably involved this reader in a cultural exchange and a creation of the "fictive affective bonds" that Ronald Zboray has asserted.[3] In this respect, there were many similarities between northern and southern readers of Dickens. However, this sharing of reading habits or literary sensibilities does not indicate a shared *political* culture. Southern readers, for example, repeatedly read Dickens within their own perspectives on the institution of slavery. This is particularly evident in their responses to Dickens's *American Notes*. Their letters and journals express a political difference that is distinctive of southern literary culture. As Alice Fahs has pointed out, while print culture supported affective bonds, it also produced imagined differences. Further, the economic practices of print capitalism worked within a communications circuit in which northern publishers could market volumes and periodicals more freely during wartime than was the case in the South. In the North, publishing activity continued in vigorous fashion. In the South, once the war began, production and distribution was problematic. In Fahs' view, literature in the Civil War period expressed a new relationship between individuals and the nation. Fahs argues that war poems suggest the connection of individuals to a unified regional purpose. As the war went on, literature began to provide support less for an abstract idea of nation as for the recognition of individuality and individuals.[4]

Dickens's reputation was subject to these trends. America passed through many changes from Dickens's initial impact in the late 1830s and early 1840s to the 1860s. While Dickens was read differently in different regions, he was read familiarly. Political differences did not keep people from reading Dickens, or from his having an impact upon their awareness in their immediate communities. Dickens's work was read widely and remained part of the consciousness of the age.

Indeed, "there are a diversity of reading communities at any one historical moment," as Stephen M. Colclough points out (39).[5] Zboray's observation that a "fictive community" emerged in America holds true in America after mid-century, even as the nation further divided sectionally. A "reading community," in the sense that this term is used here, is expressed by Reinhard Wittmann, when he speaks of "a spiritual community created by the book" (301). In this community of readers, an individual reader "was compensated by his awareness that reading made him part of a community of like-minded people" (296). It is important for us to recognize that nationalist feeling and ideological bonds produced a political difference among readers. Yet, across political differences, we see some affective similarities in Dickens's readers' responses to his fiction. They are a "reading community" that shared in their common humanity an interaction with Dickens's texts. The concern here is with seeking actual readers in specific reading communities on the local scale. It is not with making any broad claims about America's national development. Rather, how might we begin to recover the reading practices of Dickens's contemporaries and how they read Dickens?

Dickens's texts, which were more widely read in America than those of most American authors, became highly desirable property for American publishers and contributed to the commercial development of the American publishing industry. Insofar as print circulation fosters what Benedict Anderson has called "imagined community," Dickens's writings, in a variety of formats, was involved in the emergence of American popular culture and democracy. While print indeed played a role in fostering American readers' national awareness, the point here is that Charles Dickens's fiction fostered conversations, small reading circles, and public "types." What emerged around Dickens's works, a "fictive community," occurred in spite of the ways in which regional, ethnic, or political differences affected readers' attitudes and interpretations.

Dickens, while English, was a myth-maker read by Americans during a period of social myth-making and nation building. Widely acclaimed and embraced as a friend, Dickens was caught in an antagonistic model of Anglo-American relations by which Americans defined their uniqueness and difference. American nationalist rhetoric opposed British influence, or "the burden of Britain," Robert Weisbuch notes (8). Pointing to American literary attempts "to refuse and refute English models" (26), Weisbuch suggests that during this period "American writers tend to fix on one or another Englishman as The English Spokesman [...] and they tend to fuse the qualities of a literary work with an idea of the national character" (22). Robert Spiller argues that lacking neo-classicism as an enemy of their romanticism, American romantics "found their opposition in the British literary hegemony" (344–53). Kim Sturgess, speaking of Shakespeare, writes of the irony that "while calling for native writers with the capacity to create a literature commensurate with the country they also turned to a foreign author and, by accommodating him to their own necessities, claimed him as their own" (iv). Dickens, likewise, was popularly acclaimed and converted into an American product. This appropriation of Dickens had a significant impact upon American culture.

The absence of copyright protections for British authors encouraged the publication of British texts in America. Reprints enhanced economic gain for publishers, since they did not have to pay for the use of these texts. This and the cultural legacy of Britain in the United States led to a close connection between the literature of the early American republic and Britain. As William J. Gilmore notes: "nearly 75 percent of all reading matter through the mid-1820s consisted of British and, to a lesser extent, European works" (25). Timothy Dwight in his *Travels* (1821) stated that for Americans "every art, science, and path of literature" came from British writers (ibid.). James Fenimore Cooper in his *Notions of Americans* (1828) said that "compared to the books that are printed and read, those of native origin are few indeed" (Weisbuch 4). Charles Brockden Brown wrote, "Our books are almost wholly the productions of Europe and the prejudices which infect us are derived wholly from this source" (6). Walt Whitman argued in *The Brooklyn Eagle* in 1847 that there would be no American future "as long as we copy with a servile imitation, the very cast-off literary fashions of London" (Whitman in Miller 187).

Charles Dickens's writings influenced how people saw the world and sometimes how they expressed themselves in it. As part of the thought and conversation of Americans of all classes, regions, races, and sexes, Dickens provided them with a common language, a cast of characters, clichés, and images that entered the public mind. At a time when Americans were setting forth a set of values and a vision of life amid their domestic and commercial activities, the widely read stories and characters of Charles Dickens provided them with ways of coding strangers, ways to cast their fleeting impressions of people, their appearances and mannerisms. Dickens's cast of British characters enabled Americans to consider their own difference from these British models. Whether embraced or resisted, Dickens gave his American readers ways of seeing the world and themselves and models for how they might tell their own life stories.

As one American Dickens reader, Frances E. Willard, an educator and temperance crusader, wrote in 1860:

> Dickens writes strange, startling histories, and your pulse beats faster as you follow the fearful destinies that he reveals; but I suppose you never thought that our own Bridget, in the kitchen, and John, at the stable, have histories scarcely less full of right and wrong forever warring, of passion, and of pain. And we ourselves, if but our strange life out of sight were known, are hardly what the world calls prosaic. (Willard 154–58)

This visceral impact of Dickens's fiction, those moments during which the 'pulse beats faster,' is recognized here. Willard's response suggests that common readers—Bridget and John—have discovered their secret lives and passions in Dickens's characters. They too have dramatic histories. In Willard's view, some of Dickens's common readers are much like David Copperfield. They realize that they are the heroes of the stories of their own lives—and Dickens has affected them profoundly. Such lives have destinies; they are filled with ethical and emotional conflicts and crises. Willard's perspective encompasses the common reader of Dickens and suggests that readers may see their lives in his fiction.

Autobiographies, journals and letters demonstrate that the fiction of Charles Dickens influenced American readers. Even so, we are faced with questions about how readers like Mrs. Willard understood Dickens's novels. Were American readers different from British readers of Dickens? What were the effects of empathy upon the reading process of a common reader, or upon this particular reader's memory and self-concept? Robert Darnton has pointed out that, as we look at texts from the past, "our relation to those texts cannot be the same as that of the readers in the past"(First Steps, 155). If reading is a process of "struggling to name," as Roland Barthes has suggested, what is Mrs. Willard attempting to name here? (S/Z, 92) How did Dickens name for her that "strange life out of sight" that she believes is vibrantly at work in the lives of common folks like Bridget and John?

Dickens welcomes the common reader into *David Copperfield*. Reversing the C.D. in his own name, he begins his novel this way:

> Whether I shall turn out to be the hero of my own life, or whether that station will be held by anybody else, these pages must show. To begin my life with the beginning of my life, I record that I was born (as I have been informed and believe) on a Friday, at twelve o'clock at night. It was remarked that the clock began to strike, and I began to cry, simultaneously.

Who were Charles Dickens's American readers, who picked up this autobiographically based novel and perhaps identified their own lives with it? We may meet this interesting "unknown public" of Charles Dickens's audience in out of the way places: in autobiographies, personal correspondence, publisher's archives, marginalia in first editions of Dickens novels, extant records of nineteenth-century reading circles, library circulation records, or newspaper accounts of audience response at Dickens's public readings. The data is often sketchy—the briefest mention by a reader of having read or heard a Dickens story, often with little further elaboration upon this. But even these brief jottings by Dickens readers begin to tell a story.

For example, we may meet readers of Dickens in interviews with common readers. When Richard E. Broome, a farmer in South Carolina who became a lawyer and state assemblyman, was interviewed by the Federal Writer's Project in the early 1930s, he recalled his late-nineteenth century childhood:

> One day mother came by as I was intensely reading a copy of The Tale of Two Cities by Charles Dickens. She smiled and said she was happy because I loved to read books. (Broome *Federal Writer's Project* 3)

The intensity of Broome's reading reflects his deep engagement with Dickens's story. He recalls the supportive recognition of his reading by his mother. His interest in Dickens's novel and the praise of his mother merge to create a memory that remains vivid for him many years later. As Jonathan Rose has asked, "how do texts change the minds and lives of common readers?" Is not Broome's comment about his experience the beginning of an answer to this provocative question? (Rose, *Reading the English Common Reader*, 48).

Dickens is mentioned in journals, like that of Samuel Shelton Gould, a Harvard graduate born in 1843, who wrote on June 26, 1865, while in the navy and at sea:

> John Forster (Dickens biography), DeQuincey, Macaulay, Shakespeare, Tennyson, and Dickens have formed my leisure reading, if that time which I have stolen from my sleep can be called leisure. (Gould in Higginson 405)

For Gould, even a busy life at sea offers a few moments in which to read Dickens and other British authors. Gould not only reads Dickens's fiction, he reads about Dickens also. Dickens is regarded as "leisure reading": a break from the demands of life.

We hear of Dickens in travelogues, like the 1851 essays of Native American writer George Copway, a Methodist convert, who was known as "Firm Standing" in the Ojibwa tradition:

> I leave the city in company, among others, of a gentleman who seemed to have a very unfavorable opinion of America and Americans, having got most of his information from writers of the Trollope and Dickens school, of which there are plenty. (127)

Copway's meeting with this gentleman recalls a notorious chapter in Dickens's own experience of America: his first visit to America, which he recorded in *American Notes* (1842). Copway has had a direct encounter with this reader, who has apparently spoken at length about Dickens's views, or what he takes Dickens's views to be. Copway's additional remark, however, suggests that he was aware of many other people who took their views about America from Dickens's *American Notes.*

Dickens is spoken of in letters by famous Americans like Washington Irving, who wrote to Mrs. Storrow in October 1841:

> What do you think? Dickens is actually coming to America. He has booked passage for himself and his wife on the steamboat for Boston. (Irving in Hotten 39)

He is also mentioned by the forgotten, like Austin Ward, a Mormon, who could find Dickens's novels in a Mormon library in Utah in 1857:

> [T]here was little poetry, and less light literature, though a few standard novels were there, among which I particularly noticed the works of Dickens and Marryat. (267)

Ward's testimony affirms that, by 1857, Dickens's novels had made their way west, across the American countryside. It also reminds us that Dickens's work was responded to by many common readers: ones who were not professional authors, editors, or critics. While there was not much poetry or fiction for Austin Ward to read in the Utah library, there were novels by Marryat and novels by Dickens. The distribution of these novels, inland and far west of the Mississippi River, is significant. Dickens's novels had been brought by water routes as far west as California and they had also been brought by the Mormon community to Salt Lake City. His novels were available for Mormon readers, even though poetry and "light" reading were virtually absent from the Mormon library.

These examples and many others confirm that Dickens's stories, widely reproduced and circulated, had impact in the United States. As Dickens's characters became familiar to his readers, they came to think of these characters as living people and wrote letters to the author expressing their concerns about what future installments might bring. As Martyn Lyons notes, "A new relationship was created between the writer and his or her public. American readers, it was reported, crowded the docksides to greet the ship bringing the next installment of Dickens's *The Old Curiosity Shop,* so eager were they to learn the fate of the heroine, Little Nell" (314). This popular response to the serialization of his fiction answered for Dickens what Reinhard Wittmann has called the need for an author to connect with a reading public. This need led to "intensive contact" with these readers, "leading to a spiritual community created by the book" (Wittmann 300).

The American community was, in part, forged through sentiment and melodrama, which created affective ties between people. Sensibility, as a virtue, enhanced conversation and affected written communication, as Richard L. Bushman points out (81–83, 91–92). Dickens's texts, read collectively and serving as a model for written communication, were at the center of this phenonemon. In America's drift toward a consumer and mass-media society, Dickens's theatrical stories and character types stirred laughter or pathos among his American audience, generating public responses and at times creating a collective catharsis. For example, Dickens's sentimental story of Little Nell's life and death in *The Old Curiosity Shop* was a significant culture text for American readers, for hardly a family was untouched by child death or by infant mortality.[6] Indeed, as Ann Douglas and others have shown, there was a fascination with death and mourning and a domestication of death and the afterlife (Douglas 200–226).

Thousands of readers read this:

> It was very peaceful in the old church, and the village children soon grew to love Little Nell. At last Nell and her grandfather were beyond the need of flight. But the child's strength was failing, and in the winter came her death. Dear gentle, patient, noble Nell was dead. The traces of her early cares, her sufferings, and fatigues were gone. She had died with her arms round her grandfather's neck and "God bless you!" on her lips. (OCS)

The death of Little Nell caused a sensation. One playwright, Edward Sterling, couldn't bear to see Nell die and gave Dickens's story his own ending in which Nell lives happily ever after. Meanwhile, Nell became a major social mythological figure. She became, for example, suggested for a figure in a wax museum. The writer of *Sketches and Recollections of Lynchburg* (1858), Margaret Cabell, who called herself "the oldest living inhabitant" of that town, says that she would add to Lynchburg, Virginia's Charles Llewellen's wax works the figures of George Washington, Sleeping Beauty, and Little Nell: "and in the background, the sweet pensive face of dear little Nell by the side of her grandfather" (Cabell 277).

Cabell would immortalize Little Nell alongside George Washington, a founding father of America, and Sleeping Beauty, a classic fairy tale figure. The mythical status of Little Nell in America is clear from this statement. Nell, whose goodness met death in Dickens's *The Old Curiosity Shop*, should be forever preserved, as a model of lasting value alongside these figures.

Little Nell became an icon for a culture in which "sentimental people wept easily at suffering" (Bushman 81). American culture produced sentimental poetry about Little Nell. For example, Celia Thaxter writes:

> She filled her shoes with fern-seed
> This foolish little Nell
> And in the summer sunshine
> Went dancing down the dell
> But she was filled with such delight
> This foolish little Nell (142)

In Rebecca S. Nichols' poem on Nell, written sometime between 1840–1850, we read:

> Autumn came! The leaves were falling
> Death, the little one was calling
> Pale and wan she grew, and weaker
> That to us she seemed still dearer
> As the trial hour grew nearer (79)

Nell became a figure in which sentiment and ritualistic expression of grief was focused. Mary Abigail Dodge, a popular mid-century poet, writes: "Little Nell felt it all / Felt how bright it was and fair / Laughing, puzzling Little Nell" (131). Fanny Fern (1811–1872), writer of the popular *Ruth Hall* (1855) and *Fresh Leaves* (1857), pictures Nell as a deprived child:

> How distinctly I was made to understand that Nell was not to speak above a whisper or in any way infringe upon the rights of her uncombed, unwashed, unbaptized, uncomfortable little Griffins. Poor little Nell, who clung to my gown with childhood instinctive appreciation of the hard face and wiry voice of our parlor [....] I say, old Ink Stand, look at Nell now! (Fern, *Fresh Leaves* 102–105)

With gestures of melodrama and sentiment that instinctively drew upon popular entertainment, Dickens appealed to readers' emotions.[7] Lydia Marie Child, author and abolitionist, was one reader who observed the impact of Dickens's characterizations on human feeling. To her friend Sarah Shaw, she wrote on March 23, 1856: "I have admired several of Bulwer's heroines, but I never loved one of them and hugged them to my heart as I do Little Nell, and Esther, and Little Dorrit. Dickens is the great Apostle of Humanity. God bless him" (212).

Affective responses like this to Dickens's fictional characters can be found in the memoirs of his readers. Mrs. Jane T. H. Cross, a southern author, remarks in 1860: "I will read now, I will lose, in the pathetic story of 'Oliver Twist', a sense of my own miseries. It is one of the few novels I can read; there are some touches of deep feeling in it" (155). Kate Wiggins, who met Dickens as a child on a train during his American reading tour, points to her family's response to the sentiment in *David Copperfield* and *A Christmas Carol*:

> "Do you cry when you read out loud too?" I asked curiously. "We all do in our family and we never read about Tiny Tim or about Steerforth when his body is washed on the beach on Saturday nights for fear our eyes will be too swollen to go to Sunday school." "Yes, I cry when I read about Steerforth," he answered quietly. (21)

Readers often repeated the memorable line from *Oliver Twist*, "Please sir, I want some more." In the first chapter, Oliver appears with a bowl in his hands, asking for more gruel:

> He rose from the table and, advancing, basin in hand, said, somewhat alarmed at his own temerity, "Please, sir, I some more."
> The master was a fat, healthy man, but, he turned very pale. He gazed in stupefied astonishment on the small rebel and then clung for support to the copper. The assistants were paralyzed with wonder; the boys with fear. "What!" said the master at length, in a faint voice.
> "Please, sir," replied Oliver. "I want some more."

Widely read, Dickens entered the American vocabulary. Oliver Twist's "Please sir, I want some more" and Mr. Micawber's assertion that "something will turn up" became familiar slogans among Americans. From Union Army Headquarters, Ulysses S. Grant, thinking of politics, refers to Mr. Micawber in a letter of August 16, 1864 to E.B. Washburne:

> I have no doubt but the enemy are exceedingly anxious to hold out until after the presidential election. They have many hopes from its effects. They hope a counter-revolution: they hope to elect a peace candidate; in fact, like Micawber, they hope for something to turn up. (McPherson 295)

Dickens made a character tag of Mr. Micawber's phrase. We meet Micawber in *David Copperfield*, where he appears as a loquacious, somewhat eccentric but endearing fellow. "Mr. Micawber's difficulties were an addition to the distressed state of my mind," says David Copperfield.

> I have known him come home to supper with a flood of tears, and a declaration that nothing was now left but a jail, and go to bed making a calculation of the expense of putting bow-windows in the house "in case anything turned up."

Later, we read:

> "And then," said Mr. Micawber, who was present, "I have no doubt I shall, please heaven, begin beforehand with the world, and to live in a perfectly new manner if—in short, if anything turns up." (148)

In Chapter 12, Mrs. Micawber says that her family believes that something might be done for a man of ability like Mr. Micawber. "Mr. Micawber is a man of great talent, Master Copperfield," she says. David affirms this and Mrs. Micawber now uses the familiar phrase: "That he may be ready, in case of anything turning up" (151). As we read on, Mr. Micawber again takes up the phrase:

> "My dear friend," said Mr. Micawber, "I am older than you; a man of some experience in life—and of some experience, in short, in difficulties, generally speaking. At present, and until something turns up (which I am, I may say, hourly expecting) I have nothing to bestow but advice." (154)

Mr. Micawber's phrase was used to describe the growth and hopes of American towns and cities. Mr. Josiah Gardner Abbott (1814–1891) of Boston, in the Massachusetts State convention debates of May 4, 1853, uses the phrase, claiming that his opponents do not have good reasons for their report. "What is the reason they give? It is the old argument that was ever potent with Wilkens Micawber—waiting for something to turn up" (*Proceedings* 429). The next year, Harriet Beecher Stowe uses the phrase:

> [Y]et still I find myself easy to be entreated, in hopes, as Mr. Micawber says, that something may 'turn up,' though I fear the difficulty is radical in the subject. (*Sunny Memories* 317)

By the time of the Civil War, Mr. Micawber's phrase was particularly pervasive and perhaps resonant for a society hoping that something would soon turn up. For America, Dickens's phrase echoed a kind of cultural expectancy, a sense of the promise of the vast continent. Panhandlers and miners of the West hoped that the something that would turn up would be gold. James Fowler Rusling, a New Jersey lawyer and brigadier general, in 1877, writes: "Individual miners and the lighter companies seemed mostly to have suspended or like Mr. Micawber to be waiting for something to turn up" (82).

Orestes Brownson, the transcendentalist philosopher, used Dickens's phrase in support of a more ethereal view:

> But under them all I saw the same spirit, the spirit of the age [....] Something, as Micawber was to say, "might turn up" and out of the seeming darkness, light might at length shine. (111)

Oliver Twist, like the wildly popular *Pickwick*, also became a culture text.[8] One phrase on the lips of people who had read or heard of the book was "Please, sir, can I have some more." However, it is by no means certain that all of the Americans who made use of Oliver's famous phrase read the novel. Oliver is the subject of many peculiarly negative associations for people who know the popular phrase, or who had an idiosyncratic reading of the story. For example, we might consider what acquaintance the following people had with Dickens's novel:

In Catherine Ann (Ware) Warfield's fiction we hear:

"Yet all alike," I repeated. "In vain alike, I mean flatter their vanity ever so little and they are at your very feet asking 'for more' like Oliver Twist; more bread for amour propre, the insatiable!" (303)

Oliver appears to have gained a bad reputation here. Now he has an "insatiable" appetite. What might Ms. Warfield's attitude toward society be as she recalls Oliver's request for food?

Poor Oliver doesn't fare any better in postal employee James Holbrook's diary. There Oliver becomes feline. In New England, January–February 1854, Holbrook tells us, there were lots of money-letters in the post office. It was like getting through a maelstrom, he says.

And the lion, whoever he was, had an insatiable and indiscriminating appetite, for he consumed supplies coming from three or four neighboring counties in the State, and like a feline Oliver Twist, continually "asked for more." (122)

For Robert Barnwell Roosevelt, a one-term Congressman and uncle to Theodore Roosevelt, Oliver becomes an unfortunate mink who got into the eggs on a farm: "We killed that mink. Like Oliver Twist, he returned for more, and met his fate. I had him stuffed" (135).

Indeed, it is natural to wonder if these people read Dickens's story, or derived their knowledge of Oliver from public conversation or hearsay. Oliver is given little sympathy by these writers and is used as a metaphor for vain people, voracious consumption, and hungry minks. Clearly, the process of reading "involves reader's constructions, such as mental representations, changes in attitude and belief, or affective reactions," as David S. Miall observes (296). Readers are interpreters, paraphrasers, constructors of meaning who, as Roger Chartier has asserted, "read between the lines" and "subvert the lessons imposed upon them" (Miall 294). This is certainly true of Dickens's American audience, who interpreted Oliver in various ways.

There are, of course, a variety of archival records from many readers who clearly did read Dickens. Hinton Rowan Helper (1829–1909), author of *Compendium of the Impending Crisis of the South* (1860), certainly knows Dickens's story when he compares convicts with Bill Sykes:

Low brows, heavy features, and cold steel-gray eyes, gave them the expression with which Cruishank has pictured Sykes in his illustrations of *Oliver Twist*. They were Australian convicts, brutal wretches, whose hands were red with blood. (257)

Oliver Twist was put to a wide variety of uses by Dickens's contemporaries. Mrs. Elizabeth Sweet, a spiritualist, identified with Oliver, as she recalled a

Quaker (Society of Friends) school in Poughkeepsie on Church Street, where she was sent by her father when she was a child: "Obediently, I went, reported myself at the desk, and, like Oliver Twist, wanted to know what was coming next" (172). As Mrs. Sweet writes her autobiography, she turns to a well-known, sympathetic reference: Oliver Twist. Identifying with Dickens's character, Mrs. Sweet recalls a phase of her own life, her time as a child in school. Looking back, she recalls herself as a young girl who was then looking forward, with anticipation, wondering what the future would bring. Perhaps, in her own experience of reading Dickens's *Oliver Twist*, she was both identifying with Oliver and anticipating how the story would unfold. As David S. Miall points out, studies indicate that "Readers of literary texts often appear to draw more explicitly and frequently on their active personal feelings: a literary text may speak to an individual through its resonances with that individual's experience" (304, *Book History* Vol. 9).

Recalling *Oliver Twist* led to different associations for other readers. For instance, Dickens's Oliver and the Artful Dodger were matched with real life scenes of New York City's poor children. Junius Henri Browne, a popular magazine writer, looking at poor children in the city in the 1870s writes:

> Not a few are pale and haggard, and sad-eyed, reminding you of Smike, Oliver Twist, Little Nell, with the promise of better things in them. With education and training, they would be intelligent and worthy men and women. Their eyes look appealingly at you [....] Each one was furnished with a little bowl and spoon, and it was interesting to see how quickly the bowl emptied in most cases, and like Oliver Twist, they called aloud for more. (194)

The connection between Dickens and the urban poor is clear. This American journalist here associates the children of New York with Dickens's fictional children of London. In this way, he puts out a call for public response that can ensure the potential that these deprived children may have. The image Brown presents is that of the injured Smike, the outcast Nell, and Oliver, holding out his bowl for food.

"Oliver was born in the workhouse, and his mother died the same night," begins Dickens's novel. The workhouse system looms large: "All relief was inseparable from the workhouse, and the thin gruel issued three times a day to its inmates." Recalling the novel, Margaret Cabell, in 1858, compares a local workhouse-like building to Oliver Twist. It too has been abandoned and orphaned:

> The workhouse has long since been destroyed—the spacious dwelling house alone remaining to attest the folly of the builder. Mrs. Williams occupied but a short time, and then the building, like Oliver Twist was let out to anyone whom they could get to take it. (333)

In Cabell's account, Oliver is the abandoned, the cast off building. She immediately associates the workhouse with *Oliver Twist*, a novel in which the workhouse is one of its central settings. One might expect Ignatz Leo Nascher, a New York social worker writing in 1909, to also point to *Oliver Twist* in this way. Instead, he uses Dickens's novel to address the issue of crime in the city:

> The term *Fagin*, after Dickens' notorious character in Oliver Twist is now generally applied to one who induces of children to become pickpockets and shoplifters. (49)

These public references to Oliver Twist, or the popular use of Micawber's phrases, suggest the pervasive impact of Dickens in America across gender, class, and region. Perhaps they suggest colloquial usage more than reading practices. However, the circulation of these phrases probably began with the reading of Dickens's texts. American writers recognized that their own reading audiences were likely to know their references to Dickens's characters. They knew that from page to stage, across geography, ethnicity, class, and race, Dickens's fictional world was widely distributed among nineteenth-century Americans.

Dickens's American audience included people from a variety of ethnic backgrounds. There were German-American readers, like Professor Karl Rosenkranz, who pointed out in 1872 that

> When Boz in his *Nicholas Nickleby* exposed the horrible mysteries of an English boarding school, many teachers of such schools were, as he assures us, so accurately described that they openly complained that they he had aimed his caricatures directly at them. (6)

There were Jewish-American readers like Ellen Mordecai, who wrote from Raleigh, North Carolina, in 1860: "If you want to read an interesting story, get *A Tale of Two Cities*. Dickens, you know. I have just read it" (16). There were also African American readers like Willie Parker, who in "The Freedman's Story" in *The Atlantic* (1866) said, "It is reserved to some black Shakespeare or Dickens to lay open the wonderful humor, pathos, poetry, and power which slumber in the Negro's soul" (152). Indeed, as Riverside Press editor Arthur Gilman observed in 1876, "Charles Dickens addresses today a more numerous and varied circle of readers than any other author" (191).

The comments of these readers show that Dickens's stories and caricatures made a great impression on the imaginative life of nineteenth-century Americans. People saw Dickens characters everywhere. Dickens provided a lens through which his readers took many verbal pictures of ordinary people.

In their memoirs, they are continually comparing people with Dickens's characters. Their lives are filled with Pickwicks, Dombeys, and David Copperfields. For these Dickens readers, people who appeared in some way striking or unusual were Dickens characters. Of an old man in an Indianapolis carpenter's shop "where Mr. Worrall taught," William Robeson Holloway (1836–1911), who would one day manage the Indianapolis railroad and later serve as President McKinley's consul to Russia, writes in 1869: "[H]e might have sat for delineation of the old schoolmaster in the Curiosity Shop" (62). Mrs. Eliza Moore Chinn McHatten Ripley (1832–1912) in her recollections of New Orleans, published in 1912, writes of earlier days in New Orleans: "Billy McKean, as the irreverent called him, was a picture of Pickwick" (68). Of an associate, Joseph Glover Baldwin (1815–1854) writing of life in Alabama and Mississippi in 1860 says: "He was the proudest man I ever saw: he would have made the Warwicks and the Melvilles, not to say the Plantgenets and Mr. Dombey feel limber and meek" (112).

The pride of Mr. Dombey is clearly delineated by Dickens in the first unforgettable pages of his novel. The story begins: "Dombey sat in the corner of the darkened room in a great arm-chair by the bedside, and Son lay tucked up warm in a little basket bedstead." Soon this father's proud connection with his newborn son is broadened to suggest Dombey's megalomania and his sense of his male child as "a destiny":

> The earth was made for Dombey and Son to trade in, and the sun and moon were made to give them light. Rivers and seas were formed to float their ships; rainbows gave them promise of fair weather; winds blew for or against their enterprise.

Dombey wears a "blue coat and stiff white cravat" and a "pair of creaking boots" and "a loud ticking watch," suggesting tightness in his personality and a time-driven orientation to his life. We learn that "Dombey and Son had often dealt in hides, but never in hearts." Of his wife, we hear that he was "content to bind her broken spirit to the dutiful and meek endurance of the present" (D&S 3). It is no wonder that Joseph Glover Baldwin compares "the proudest man" he ever saw to Mr. Dombey.

Dickens's Pickwick and Dombey move through the imaginations of his readers, as they point to people in their lives. For Mabel Louise Nassau of Elmira, New York, the author of a neighborhood study of Greenwich Village in 1913, there is just something Dickensian about a woman she has interviewed:

> Mrs. Q. is English. She came to America when thirty-eight, and is now over sixty, still she hasn't grown at all American, and seems to have walked straight out from the pages of a Dickens novel. (52)

This pattern of people referring to Dickens's characters continues steadily throughout the nineteenth century, into the first decades of the twentieth century. Whether they are farmers, teachers, or lawyers, as they come to write their memoirs, Dickens's readers have his characters indelibly etched in their memories. For example, John Ludlum McConnel (1826–1862), a career soldier, recalling his school days, remembers cringing at a schoolmaster's flute playing:

> In David Copperfield, Dickens describes a certain flute-playing tutor by the name of Mell, concerning whom, and the rest of mankind, he expresses the rash opinion, "after many years of reflection," that nobody ever could have played worse. But Dickens never saw Strongfaith Lippincott, the schoolmaster, and he therefore knows nothing of the superlative degree of detestable playing. (308)

McConnel points to Mr. Mell, whose flute playing is encouraged by the old woman of Salem House:

> "Have you got your flute with you?"
> "Yes," he answered.
> "Have a blow at it," said the old woman coaxingly. "Do!"
> The mater, upon this, put his hand underneath the skirts of his coat, and brought out his flute in three piece, which he screwed together and began immediately to play. My impression is, after many years of consideration, that there never can be anybody in the world who played worse. He made the most dismal sounds I have ever heard produced by any means, natural or artificial. (76)

Likewise, poet and author Mary Abigail Dodge, writing as Gail Hamilton in 1866, refers to a character

> who with her causeless pugnacity, his harsh tones, and her theatric hard-tossed snovels, seemed a character just stepped out of Dickens rather than like a flesh and blood woman going to husband and children and sitting room and supper. (150)

The appearances and the mannerisms of people trigger these readers' associations with Dickens's characters. For them, a Dickens character is sharply drawn, a caricature with exaggerated outward features or attributes. Often an individual's quirks, tone, or eccentricities appear Dickensian. People are Pickwickian, Dombey-like, or theatrical. Sometimes the Dickens characters they see in daily life come in pairs. For example, Mary Clemmer Ames (1839–1884), a noted socialite and writer in Washington, D.C., writes in 1874 of young newlyweds who reminded her of Dora and David Copperfield:

> The groom often seems half to deprecate your sudden glance, as if, like David Copperfield, he was afraid you thought him "very young" and yet he invites you

to glance again by his conscious air and proud possession, which says: "Behold!
I may be young-very. But I have gotten me a wife." (155)

Ames refers to David Copperfield's own sense of his youth, or to her sense of
how young this character is. There is a sense of pride in Ames's David Copperfield, especially in his relationship with Dora.

Dickens's Cheeryble Brothers of *Nicholas Nickleby* (1839) come to mind for
Americans who see them in brothers or in twins. The Boston Colored Citizens
in *Triumph of Equal School Rights* in Boston, meeting December 17, 1855,
refer to "brothers Henry I. and William I. Bowditch, each pair like Dickens's
brothers Cheeryble" (BCC 8). The Harper Brothers were compared by many
people with the Cheeryble Brothers, according to J. Henry Harper (152). Isaac
T. Hopper, an abolitionist in Woodbury, New Jersey, reminds Lydia Marie
Francis Child, his biographer, of Dickens's Cheeryble Brothers. Child assumes
that her readers will have read Dickens and will recognize her reference to a
personality type expressed by the Cheeryble Brothers.

> The roguery of his boyhood subsided into a love of little mischievous tricks; and
> the physical tone of humor, that rippled through his conversation, frequently
> reminded me of the Cherryble [*sic*] Brothers so admirably described by Dickens.
> (364)

Dickens's descriptions of the Cheeryble Brothers stirred Lydia Child's social
imagination. The "physical tone" of the laughter she finds in Hopper reflects
the humor that she finds in Dickens's characters. Frequently, we see readers, like
Child, saying that people in their lives remind them of Dickens characters.

What these readers share is Charles Dickens's fiction, which pictured and
gave voice to ordinary persons like themselves. In their accounts of their lives,
the memory of a Dickens story is sometimes brought to bear upon one's own
personal experience. For example, when Mrs. John Farrar (1791–1870), in
1865, reflects upon the issues of divorce in her autobiography, she turns to
Dickens's *Hard Times*. Mrs. Farrar summarizes Stephen Blackpool's struggle
to get a divorce from his alcoholic wife. She cites Mr. Bounderby's response
that Stephen could never afford a divorce and his insistence that such a divorce for a working-class man was improper (89). Mrs. Farrar here is clearly
using Dickens to try to say something about her own struggle with the divorce
laws of her time. In Dickens's novel, she has read this:

> "Now, a' God's name," said Stephen Blackpool, "show me the law to help me!"
>   "Hem! There's a sanctity in this relation of life," said Mr. Bounderby, "and—
> and it must be kept up" [...] "Now, I tell you what!" said Mr. Bounderby, put-
> ting his hands in his pockets. "There *is* such a law."

Stephen, subsiding into his quiet manner, and never wandering in his attention, gave a nod.

"But it's not for you at all. It costs money. It costs a mint of money."

"How much might that be," Stephen calmly asked. [...]

"[...] I suppose from a thousand to fifteen hundred pounds... perhaps trwice that money."

"There's no other law?"

"Certainly not." (Chapter 11, 73)

In her autobiography, Mrs. Farrar appears appalled by this. In her authorship, she continues to refer to herself by her married name.

Nathaniel Parker Willis, one of the most popular magazine writers of the mid-nineteenth century, wishes that Dickens were present so the world might be able to hear through his reports the stories of a man whose father was a physician. His statement suggests that he sees fiction as a kind of mimetic reflection of the world and that the person he has met is surely as entertaining as any Dickens character. Lacking the presence of Dickens, Willis becomes the writer, releasing the story of this unknown person in upstate New York. He writes in 1862:

He sees no company except himself, and as I sit at table with him, and listen to his conversation, exceedingly rich, varied, and extraordinary as it is, I mourn that Dickens is not here to take his picture for the world. (495)

The vivid quality of Dickens's depictions is admired by Willis, who perhaps wishes that he could describe this man's character as well. Willis's comments suggest that Dickens's audience matched the people they saw in daily life with characters they read about in Dickens's books. Dickens's characters were alive in people's imaginations in both the North and the South. His caricatures acted as a mirror, a model for representing the people that they encountered. For example, Sidney Andrews in *The South Since the War* (1866) writes of the Confederate vice-president:

I saw Alexander H. Stephens today—a little old man with the most marvelous eyes, looking not so much like a human being as like a character from one of Dickens's stories. (358)

Whitelaw Reid, the *Washington Tribune* editor who would become Benjamin Harrison's running mate in 1892, sees at a parade in Beaufort, South Carolina, in 1862 a gathering of Negroes:

A keen-eyed lady on the platform, the owner of a particularly showy turban, and lo! beneath its dazzling colors looked forth, in befitting black, the very face of Mrs. Gummidge, the "lone, lorn creatur" of David Copperfield's early acquaintance. To the very whimper of the month, and the watery eyes, and last particular of desolate and disconsolate appearance, it was Mrs. Gummidge's self, as Dickens made her immortal. (118–19)

Dickens's character Mrs. Gummidge is certainly viewed in a negative light by Myrta Lockett Avary, the wife of a Confederate officer, looking back on the Civil War years in 1903. Apparently feeling inconvenienced on a journey, she characterizes one of the travelers as a Mrs. Gummidge:

> I sat, almost frozen, huddled up in the one shawl that answered for a shawl, blanket, and rug, and tried to keep my teeth from chattering and myself from hating that whining Mrs. Gummidge of a woman [....] Of course, Mrs. Gummidge got the best room. (80)

With David Copperfield, readers encounter the continually perturbed Mrs. Gummidge:

> I soon found out that Mrs. Gummidge did not always make herself so agreeable as she might have been expected to do, under the circumstances of her residence with Mrs. Peggoty. Mrs. Gummidge's was rather a fretful disposition, and she whimpered more sometimes than was comfortable for other parties in so small an establishment. (43)

For Dickens's audience, striking images of "keen-eyed" or "whining" women, or ones with "theatric, hard-tossed snovels" are characters who have stepped out of his novels. Americans see these theatric Dickens characters all around them, even when they travel overseas. For example, Mary Ann Howitt (1854), an American art student in Munich, writes of Madame Thekia and Fraulein Sanchen: "A pity it is that Dickens never saw her, for then of a truth, she would have been immortalized, with her oddity, her faithfulness, her good nature, and her crossness" (461). Howitt brings her reading of Dickens to Europe with her and it acts as a lens though which she sees: "We live not so far from the Palace, at a sort of curiosity shop, which Dickens would love to describe" (3). She then describes this place, modeling her description on Dickens.

Reading Dickens helped some travelers far from home to pass the time and to stay connected with the human community. Among these readers of Dickens, one could hardly be farther away from civilization than Isaac Israel Hayes, a sailor at sea in the Arctic. For Hayes, a volume of Dickens was among his most precious possessions:

> Upon leaving the brig I had selected from the narrow shelf which held the little library that I learned to love so well during the last long winter, three small

books, which I thrust into my already crowded clothes bag. They were the before mentioned volume of Dickens, the "In Memoriam," and a small pocket Bible; all parting gifts from kind friends to me when leaving home; and all doubly precious, for themselves, and for the memories which they recalled. (208)[9]

These books, embodying memories of loved ones at home, were soaked and torn, Hayes says, and their backs were loose. Yet, they served both a practical purpose and an emotional one. So he held to them as one would hold to a tether to something precious and secure: "I kept them under my head as helps for a pillow and for their companionship" (ibid.).

For Americans like Hayes, Dickens provided a memory of home and a resource for self-construction. His writing entertained them and served as a model for their own self-expression in letters and diaries.[10] When a Dickens story was read aloud on a ship, in camp, or at home, it was a common amusement, a space where the wide world came in and sentiment and theatricality was shared. His popular texts were sites of connection.

Charles Dickens's immense popularity in America springs, in part, from his ability to communicate effectively with his readers by suggesting a direct personal contact while writing for a mass audience. Their responses suggest that during Dickens's time it was possible for an often sentimental and theatrical writer like Dickens to forge bonds of connection with his or her audience. Dickens's ability to do this may be attributed, partly, to his storytelling gifts. His lively caricatures, winding plots and resolutions, and his narrative voices offered an abundant panoramic world and suggested the immediate face-to-face encounters he later actualized in his public readings.

Dickens's readers had regular contact with the author and his works through the serial form of their publication. They were involved in the ongoing process of a story within the busy context of life. Texts intersected with their lives, arriving in installments, unfolding alongside their own personal life stories and activities. As Hughes and Lund have pointed out, that "context complicated and enriched the imagined world when the literary work was resumed" (8–9). This may have contributed to an overlapping of the outer world of the reader and the fictional world of the text.[11]

The process of serialization in the nineteenth century appears to be similar to that of a prime time television program today, or to a soap opera, as Jennifer Hayward has indicated (5–6). The serial creates an ongoing interest in the characters of a story and forges a connection between the audience and this cultural product. Characters become familiar and shared by the audience. Thus, audience and producer begin to forge a common imaginative culture of fictive persons who work through identifiable crises and concerns. These characters and their situations become the stuff of the dreams of popular culture.[12]

The reading of Dickens's novels, in serial publication, was a social ritual practiced in many homes and discussed in public arenas. The regular appearance of his stories promoted a bond of connection with his readers, as Kathleen Tillotson and John Butt point out:

> To the author it meant a larger public, but also a public more delicately responsive, who made their views known during the progress of a novel both by writing to him and by reducing or increasing their purchases. Through serial publication an author could recover something of the intimate relationship between storyteller and audience which existed in the ages of the sagas and Chaucer; and for an author like Dickens, who was peculiarly susceptible to the influence of his readers, this intimate relationship outweighed the inherent disadvantages of the system. (21)

Critics have pointed out that the serial promoted a vital "intimacy between reader and story" (Hughes and Lund 11). Arriving in a particular material and visual context, the serial created a sense of shared experience in a national event, and generated a collective anticipation of a story's outcome. "Indeed, a story's characters could come to seem a part of readers' own extended family or circle of friends," Hughes and Lund add (10). Dickens's novels unfolded in this climate, month by month, encouraging an active imaginative relationship between reader, text, and writer.

For example, when the ladies of the Wednesday Club of Syracuse, New York met to discuss Dickens, Mrs. H. R. Hare noted: "Charles Dickens, whose tales are household words in every home where the English tongue is heard, was a novelist of the highest rank and the greatest humorist of this century." While this mention of Dickens's stories as "household words" plays upon the title of Dickens's own publication, it also appears to be quite consistent with the interests of these women who listened to Mrs. Hare's lecture. For the group's secretary adds: "Dickens domestic life was discussed by Mrs. Curtis and several members of the club." The domestic concern of these women is emphasized by the presence among them of a Household and Economic Club, members of which wrote a "Help Booklet" (Wednesday Club Minutes; February 24, 1892; Onondaga Historical Association).[13]

Dickens's readers who gathered in groups like this shared common texts, stories they read together, often as these stories unfolded in serial installments in the pages of a periodical. These readers were involved in what Hughes and Lund have referred to as "creating a home" and "living in history."[14] For Americans at this time not only faced the question of what it meant to be an American, they also were facing changes in their experience of community, time, and work. Between 1820–1860, with urban growth, the national population increased and residence in cities increased 226 percent (Haltunnen 35). In small towns and rural locales, the traditional community, a social web of face to face encounters, was unwinding. In the past, most people had known each other by sight and by name. In this somewhat insular social network, family, home, and church served as a center. But now the forces of industrialization and modernity were causing demographic shifts, a movement to urban centers, and breaking down traditional forms of community. In both the United States and Great Britain, it became more necessary to "create a home" and to forge imagined community. One way in which the affective bonds of home could be realized was through expressive communal reading and spirited discussion. Dickens, as a source of sentiment that could be shared, provided a vision of connection amid fragmentation, a way to "live in history" and to imagine one's place within the vast social panorama of modern life.

Dickens's stories often start from the experience of displacement and lead to the discovery by characters of their home, or their bonds with others. For example, Oliver Twist is orphaned, tossed into a workhouse, and journeys through Fagin's den and the London streets toward the recovery of his inheritance. Little Nell is cast out upon the road and her journey results in her sad passing. Perhaps, some critics say, this theme of displacement often arises because Dickens himself felt displaced when he was sent to work at a blacking factory as a child. But displacement was also the collective experience of many people in the early to mid-nineteenth century. In the nineteenth century, the growth of the city drew people interested in new economic opportunities from their homes in the countryside. It was claimed by some that this movement toward the city was destroying old family bonds and undermining stable family life. Dickens's readers could regain some sense of home and imaginative connection through their shared experiences of reading his stories. As Christine Pawley writes:

> An important aspect of the inseparable development of the middle class and of institutions was the establishment of certain dominant values, often expressed through myths-stories that express key values. Myth construction was one process by which middle and upper middle classes defined themselves as separate from the working class. It was also a means, *mutatis muntandis*, by which the working class defined itself and was defined, as well as part of the process of establishing institutions such as schools and libraries. (6–7)

Dickens's texts aided American readers in this work of self-definition. The popular texts of this period—advice manuals, tales of the self-made man—suggest that people, during this time of upheaval were trying to pin down their places in society.

Texts, like those of Dickens, marked out social types, ways to describe how a good businessman could best function, or how a domestic housewife could best fulfill her role. Dickens provided his readers with models, or caricatures, that enabled them to identify features of the world in which they were living. In a sense, perhaps Dickens was still putting labels on the bottles of the blacking factory, or creating signs as did Nicholas Nickleby. Dickens never stopped naming things and he helped his readers to name them. For now the factory was a turbulent, lively society.

Charles Dickens's stories, as they arrived serialized in magazines, also enabled readers to "live in history." In the opinion of Dickens reader Henry Copee, an educator speaking in 1873, "Dickens's delineations are eminently historical and present a better notion of the period than the general history itself " (455). Along with this, the serial form in which Dickens's stories appeared, reflected the historical consciousness of the time and often suggested a sense of passage and personal development, as Hughes and Lund have pointed out. They suggest that a serial, with its "space between numbers," forced readers to pause in their encounter with the narrative and promoted an anticipation of the future. In reference to Dickens's *A Tale of Two Cities*, they write:

> Being within each number was for installment readers living in history, a fictionalized past in which one was not completely sure where all events lead; being between numbers or at the end of the entire text was inhabiting one of those moments at which one glimpses or creates larger patterns, fixing oneself more securely within a scheme of history. (61)

Dickens's readers, living in a transitional period, were dealing with a shift in their awareness of space and time. An increasing pace of life, compression of time, and rate of transition changed perceptions of the individual in relation to the wider society. The change from a nation of predominantly stable agricultural units to an increasingly industrial society caused some dislocation and disorientation, or a need for adjustment and adaptation.[15] Family time proceeded at a different pace than the business clock and railroad schedules. Print served as a means of connection as commercial enterprise urged movement to new territories, scattering family and friends throughout a region, and the roads and rails moved people on new journeys. One way people countered the separation caused by these changes was by gathering in associations, such as reading circles. As George Lunt (1803–1885) of Massachusetts, U.S. district attorney during Zachary Taylor's presidency and the writer of a dozen books, said in 1873:

> Hence family and friends were more closely drawn. The better feelings of our nature were, I think, deeper than when scattered over a wide but thin social surface; just as the water in a well is more concentrated than if diffused in the basin

of a pond. To some extent therefore, wholesomely isolated besides the ordinary round of not very formal visiting parties, there were reading circles, for those who were prompted by intellectual yearnings, frequented by young ladies and gentlemen, married or single, at which passages from the better class of books were read aloud by such male members as felt competent to the exercise, by turns. (142–43)

Reading Charles Dickens brought people together socially, emotionally, and imaginatively. Circles of readers made Dickens a central part of their small communities, reading him aloud and discussing his stories across several months. For example, at the Wednesday Club in the growing city of Syracuse, New York, on a snowy Thursday, February 4 in 1892, the all female reading circle heard one of their members read from *Dombey and Son*. The secretary reports:

> The afternoon of Thursday, February fourth found the ladies of the Wednesday Afternoon Reading Circle quite ready for their sleigh-ride into the country to the pleasant house of Mrs. Barrett where, after a nice ride they were received with graceful hospitality and a steaming cup of chocolate. There were [...] twenty members and four guests. As it was Dickens' day, the ladies [...] all suspended to roll call with quotations from that author. (Wednesday Club Minutes, February 4, 1892; Onondaga Historical Association)

We see here the graceful hospitality of the parlor theatrical in which warmth and cultivated conversation contrasts with the cold winter outside. It is not noted which quotations were put forth to the group. However, it appears that they made Dickens their topic of discussion at least three times during the 1890s. With a strong interest in Dickens's biography, the women connected Dickens's life with their own concerns. Dickens was portrayed as a self-made man. The secretary writes that

> Mrs. Barrett gave a very interesting history of Charles Dickens, following him from a boy through all the trials and hardships of poverty and toil on to a great and distinguished success of wealth. (ibid.)

Along with this theme of self-made success and wealth, the Wednesday Club secretary immediately adds that Dickens was married in 1838 and he and his wife were separated in 1858. "He had five sons and two daughters," she says. Her selectivity here suggests that marriage and family were among these women's central concerns.

The secretary notes that "Mrs. Klock read from *Dombey and Son*, the birth and death of Paul Dombey, which selections were fine examples of the pathetic description of those scenes which are constantly occurring in the houses of men, 'The old-old fashion, Death!'" Mrs. D.H. Gorving, taking the notes of this meeting, writes that the speaker noted Dickens's childhood writings and his early love of books:

> Being a very delicate child he sought companionship of books, his father had a small collection, out of which Dickens said, came a glorious host to keep him company. (ibid.)

The women listening to this lecture on Dickens also heard passages from Dickens's fiction. The reading circle focused on Dickens's *A Tale of Two Cities* and on the French Revolution on November 18, 1896. Descriptions of the drama of the revolution were offered to the group. The secretary writes: "Especially thrilling was the storming of the Bastille, The flight, imprisonment and death by the guillotine of the helpless King." She adds that "Mr. Trowbridge pleasantly filled an intermission" with piano playing "which was followed by Mrs. Barrett reading selections from Dickens's *Tale of Two Cities*. History here becomes a "thrilling" spectacle: a melodrama of flight, imprisonment, and death "pleasantly" filled out by parlor piano playing (ibid.).[16]

In Cortland, New York, the Truxton Club, formed in the winter of 1886, included several individuals who had read Dickens when they were children. The minute book indicates that on February 2, 1886: "Subject for the evening Cardinal Woolsey [sic]. Miss Emma Jones read the Chapter on the Great Cardinal in Dickens *Child's History of England*." Opening Dickens's history today, we can find some of what Miss Emma Jones must have read. Cardinal Wolsey appears in Chapter 27, where Dickens calls him King Henry VIII's "most powerful favourite and adviser." Dickens tells his readers that Wolsey has "a name very famous in history for its rise and downfall" (218). He calls Wolsey a "stately priest" and provides Wolsey's background, as the son of a butcher from Ipswich. Dickens notes that Wolsey could "dance and jest, and sing and drink." Dickens writes, "He was wonderfully fond of pomp and glitter, and so was the King" (218–19). King Henry appears ruthless by comparison:

> For many such reasons, the Cardinal was high in estimation with the King, and, being a man of far greater ability, knew as well how to manage him, as a clever keeper may know how to manage a wolf or a tiger, or any other cruel and uncertain beast, that may turn upon him and tear him at any day. (219)

The Cortland group consisted of husbands and wives who, along with their interest in history, had a theatrical taste for Shakespeare as well as for Dickens. On November 23, 1891, eight members met at Mrs. Kenney's to read the fourth act of *Romeo and Juliet*. According to the minutes:

The committee had decided that reading should be the main feature of the meetings. Each one present voted by ballot for three authors whose works they preferred. "Dickens" received the most votes, eight. They then balloted for a choice of his works and *Pickwick Papers* was chosen. Each member to read ten minutes at a time. (Truxton Club Minutes, February 2,1886; Cortland Historical Society)

Comedy and tragedy intersected as the group followed the drama of Shakespeare by reading Dickens's *Pickwick Papers*, beginning on December 7, 1891, and continued the reading of *Pickwick*" on December 22.[17] One can imagine the members of this club picking up their volumes of the *Pickwick Papers* and beginning to read:

The first ray of light which illumines the gloom, and converts into a dazzling brilliancy that obscurity in which the earlier history of the public career of the immortal Pickwick, would appear to be involved, is derived from the perusal of the following entry in the transactions of the Pickwick Club, which the editor of these papers feels the highest pleasure in laying before his readers, as a proof of the careful attention, indefatiguable assiduity, and nice discrimination, with which his search among the multifarious documents confided to him has been conducted. (1)

The common social reading experience of these literary circles in Syracuse and Cortland parallels a Michigan group's interest in Dickens in the early 1870s. At that time, the reading of the works of Charles Dickens by "a half dozen ladies" was central to the formation of the Jonesville Library in Michigan.

In the Spring of 1873, a half dozen ladies who had been reading Dickens' works, formed a plan whereby they might obtain the reading of several desirable books at the cost of one. The names of 23 ladies were taken, who each purchased one book for the club. The books were exchanged every two weeks. The next year two clubs were in operation, and the idea of a ladies' library was developed. (*Michigan Centennial* 602)

Similarly, The Ladies' Library Association of Kalamazoo, Michigan, in weekly meetings in 1888, discussed *Bleak House, Pickwick,* and Dickens in America (Stanley 284). Dickens was also read in the 1890s by the Pickwick Society of Deposit, New York, which took its name from a Dickens novel. The group met in the library from 1893 to 1899 to discuss public topics and read fiction, including Dickens's *Pickwick* (Records of Pickwick Society [1893], Deposit Public Library, N 21).

The presence of these reading circles demonstrates that reading Dickens aloud served as a communal reading experience both in Dickens's lifetime and afterward. The gathering of these readers shows that Dickens's fiction, through a variety of versions, reached readers of all backgrounds, across thousands of miles. How many other authors of the time besides Charles Dickens could capture the popular imagination from Deposit to Kalamazoo? How many reached across class and race, gender and lifestyle, location and occupation? Year after year brought an expansion of Dickens sales in America. His work was published, reprinted, and given away. The novels of Charles Dickens, under different covers and formats, through a variety of publishers, became mass-market items. They put identifiable characters, images, and phrases into circulation in America. People at a distance from each other shared the same laugh or dwelled upon the same sorrow, as they encountered the same Dickens story.

Like David Copperfield, Dickens's readers were engaged in a process of living in history, actualizing their potential as "heroes of their lives." With Dickens as a model, one could tell his or her own story and recognize his or her self in time. Like Oliver, who regains his inheritance, or Esther Summerson, who discovers hers, Dickens's readers, each in his or her own way, could grow and learn lessons.

For this audience, like the characters of Dickens's fiction, dwelled in time-conscious worlds. For readers of *Great Expectations*, Miss Havisham, reclusive in her cobwebbed room, has attempted to stop the flow of time. But the serial form of the story itself insists upon time's unceasing flow. In *Bleak House*, readers encounter, as they begin to read, a vision of the prehistoric past, an antediluvian creature arising from the mud and muck and the fog of London, casting its shadow over the modern world, conveying the sense that alongside progress is regression. In a world mired in law and fog, Lady Dedlock is haunted by a ghost, trapped in a liminality of the past not resolved and the future not yet realized. In reading, as in life, Dickens's audience experiencing similar liminality awaited the realization of each phrase of the story as it was presented to them. The fiction serial, like a train passing through several stops, was itself suggestive of the age's sense of motion and progress, expansion and transition.

One Dickens reader, the author A.D.T. Whitney, creates in her own fiction a character who carries a Dickens novel on a train journey, yet never quite gets around to reading it. She prefers to watch the scenery:

My first introduction to her [...] was in the little east parlor of the Giant's Cairn at Outledge House. I was going to take the 6:30 train down to Boston. I came into the parlor ten minutes before the whistle to pick up my bag and shawl and was safely off in a big armchair in the Pullman car, with any parcels all put up, and my novel in my lap waiting till I was tired of other things and wanted it; which case I have never yet come to in a railway journey, though the novel is

always there [....] A railway is such a good chance to read things that are not
printed [....]

   She was handsome to begin with[....] There came an electric perception of
freshness all over, with just looking at her. As Mrs. Gradgrind, or a more cheerful person, might have said, there was a face in the room pink and smooth with
good rest, and cold water, and the pleasantness of a morning blaze, and you
didn't know whether it was somebody else's or yours. (2)

Dickens's readers were ones who picked up and read the book, even as
the landscape hurtled by. Life beyond the window, that large landscape of
America, had its own enchantments. However, as the American nation grew
larger, according to one critic, print had to supply "some of the affectional
needs formerly fulfilled locally" (Zboray 80). Fiction, including Dickens's
portraits of groups of people interacting, his cast of many characters, offered
people images of human interconnection. These fictional relations could act
as a reminder of the dimensions of mutual life that people lived within. The
self-constructing readers of Dickens's novels appear to have used Dickens's
novels as a mirror in which they saw the people around them, especially the
more eccentric and curious characters they encountered in their lives. It was
often these persons, or images of people seen through the lens of Dickens,
who struck their imaginations and found their way into the pages of their
recollections and autobiographies.

Notes

   1. The term "national imagination" here is reflected in studies on the American
character such as David Potter's essay "The Quest for the National Character" in *The
Reconstruction of American History* (1962), Henry Steele Commager's *The American
Mind: An Interpretation of American Thought* (1950) and the investigations of Alexis
de Tocqueville in *Democracy in America*.
   2. Dickens's friend Wilkie Collins wrote in *Household Words* in 1858 of "the
unknown public" of some three million readers who were "right out of the pale of
literary civilization." They didn't buy books or take out library subscriptions but they
did purchase inexpensive serial fiction and supported the new sensational novels that
were spinning off of these presses. Collins said that "the future of English fiction may
rest on this unknown public, which is now waiting to be taught the difference between
a good book and a bad." Collins wished to dispel the illusion that "the great bulk of
the reading public in England was composed of subscribers to this journal" or were
"the customers of the eminent publishing houses, book clubs and circulating libraries, the purchasers and borrowers of newspapers and reviews and penny journals."
Dickens's American audience appears to have been comparable. Benedict Anderson,
Imagined Communities, London: Verso, 1991.

3. Ronald Zboray, *A Fictive People: Antebellum Economic Development and the American Reading Public.* New York: Oxford UP, 1993.

4. Alice Fahs addresses the sentimentalization of war literature and mourning in *The Imagined Civil War—Popular Literature of the North and South 1861–1865* (Chapel Hill and London: University of North Carolina Press, 2001) in "The Sentimental Soldier," (93–119). Robert L. Patten, emphasizing an increase in sales, repeats the story that inquiries were made about the fate of Little Nell (110). See also Wayne Booth, *The Company We Keep* (Berkeley: University of California Press, 1988).

5. Stephen M. Colclough, "Procuring Books and Consuming Texts," *Book History,* Vol. 3 (2000): 21-44.

6. Ann Douglas points to a "fascination with death and mourning" and the growth of consolation literature, such as that of Lydia Huntley Sigourney (1791–1865), as a popular genre (Douglas 201). See Douglas's chapter "The Domestication of Death," (200–226) in *The Feminization of American Culture* (New York: Alfred A. Knopf, 1977).

7. Theater and sentiment in Dickens's texts met an American audience predisposed by melodrama and a daily theater of sentimental expression. Paul Schlicke writes of Dickens that "as readers have long recognized, his intimate familiarity with the theatre of the day infuses his art at every level" (46). Caricature is present in Dickens, in part, because, as Schlicke says, "Dickens's methods of comic characterization attribute essential significance to external appearance, so too acting practice of the age was based on the audience's acceptance of gesture as a true expression of inner disposition" (77). See Paul Schlicke, *Dickens and Popular Entertainment,* (London: Allen and Unwin, 1985). This is echoed by Karen Haltunnen in her discussion of the function of sentiment in society and middle-class attempts at refinement and expressing emotional honesty in a genteel theater of home parlor behavior. Ann Douglas, writing of the sentimentalization of northeastern middle class culture, states: "Involved as it is with the exhibition and commercialization of the self, sentimentalism cannot exist without an audience" (244).

8. Paul Davis, in *The Lives and Times of Ebenezer Scrooge* (Yale UP, 1990) refers to Dickens's widely circulated works, like *A Christmas Carol* (1843), as "culture texts." These texts, transposed in many different forms from theater to film to comic books and presented across generations in multiple print versions have had a lasting impact upon American culture

9. From Hayes's account of life at sea in 1853, it can be inferred that reading aloud was a hopeful pastime of these sailors. Hayes does not say which Dickens novel was tucked under his pillow. However, it is likely, that the sailors shared his friend Bonsall's copy of *Waverley* and his own copy of Dickens until they docked at Rensselaer Harbor. There the sailors wore mittens, making turning book pages rather difficult. Hayes writes: "The circumstances were too depressing for us to feel our ordinary interest in reading aloud, or in listening, and the time was passed mostly in silence" (Hayes 209).

10. Jonathan Rose points to the use of Dickens as a model by autobiographers. He writes that "most working people had to struggle with the art of recording their lives, and they cited Dickens, more than anyone else, as the man who got it right" See

Jonathan Rose, *The Intellectual Life of the British Working Classes* (Yale UP, 2001), 111–12.

11. See Linda K. Hughes and Michael Lund, *The Victorian Serial* (Charlottesville: University Press of Virginia, 1991) and Jennifer Hayward, *Consuming Pleasures—Active Audiences and Serial Fictions from Dickens to Soap Opera* (Lexington: University Press of Kentucky, 1997).

12. Patricia Okker has written that "reading magazine novels provided individuals with an opportunity to connect with a community of disparate members and, at the same time, to reshape the community itself" (27–28). See Patricia Okker, *Social Stories* (Charlottesville: University of Virginia Press, 2003). Also considering this exploration of what a society or nation was, Ronald Zboray has argued that fiction served as a surrogate community through mimesis. "As the individual redirected the self from the locale to the nation, that larger community had to supply some of the affectional needs formerly fulfilled locally. Fiction, evoking emotional responses and attempting to create the illusion of life [...] pointed the way toward self-construction" (80–81). See Ronald J. Zboray, *A Fictive People: Antebellum Economic Development and the American Reading Public,* (Oxford UP, 1993). Anne C. Rose asserts that social construction was achieved through play in company with others. In contrast with an increasingly complex public sphere, leisure was a space for testing "elective relations" or "an open field for social expression." Thus, Victorians turned to communal entertainments, including reading aloud and "they read to each other to build bonds of sentiment by savoring literature together" (123). See Anne C. Rose, *Victorian America and the Civil War* (Cambridge UP, 1992).

13. Hughes and Lund extensively discuss *Dombey and Son* (1848) and Mrs. Florence Dombey as a domestic angel (15–58).

14. The phrases "creating a home" and "living in history" are derived from Hughes and Lund's discussion of the fiction serial. These phrases title the chapters in which they consider Dickens's *Dombey and Son* and *A Tale of Two Cities* as examples.

15. Rapid economic and social changes between 1820 and 1850, according to Edwin C. Rozwenc, "deranged the previously established bases of personal identification and social status" (xii). He stated that "then we can assume that the American in the Jacksonian generation had a peculiar problem of self-identification and self-esteem" (Rozwenc in Haltunnen 191). In her conclusion to her inquiry into the social history of this period *Confidence Men and Painted Women* (Yale UP, 1982), Karen Haltunnen speaks of the person "plagued with anxiety concerning his social identity." She says of the American of 1830–50 that "he occupied no fixed position within a well-defined social structure, and his vague sense of restlessness and dread spring from his liminality, his betwixt and between social condition" (Haltunnen 192). Dickens's stories addressed these issues, offering recognizable character types and images of individuals acting within society.

16. These comments may suggest the theatricality within this reading group and how they are drawn to Dickens's theatricality and the dramatic *agons* of history. Both the Syracuse and Cortland reading groups noted here showed a strong preference for reading history, as well as Shakespearian drama and Dickens. Their attention is given to Dickens's biography. The Wednesday Club focused upon the same texts that

Hughes and Lund discuss in their reflections of "creating a home" (*Dombey and Son*) and "living in history" (*A Tale of Two Cities*). In the century's final year, Syracuse residents gathered to hear British photographer H. Snowden Ward and his American wife Catharine Weed Barnes Ward speak about Dickens. The couple showed about 120 lantern slide photographs taken in Britain of Portsmouth, Chatham, Rochester, London, and Dickens's home at Gads Hill. The objective of the lectures was to give people images of the local atmospheres that figured in some of Dickens's stories. Again, the focus of this lecture was on Dickens's biography and on connecting his fictional world with the factual every day world of experience. "The Real Dickens-Land" provided a portrait of Dickens, centering upon this geography: images of Dickens's birth-place, the church where he was christened, a house in Chatham where the Dickens's lived. The lecture described his neighbor George Stronghill as the original for Steerforth in *David Copperfield.*

17. The minutes record that the Truxton group's reading was interrupted by "a long interval on account of sickness," resuming January 25. On February 8 and 22, the group met "and read a few chapters of *Pickwick.*" On March 7, 1892, "Mrs. Muller kept the time for the reading," again of Dickens's *Pickwick* (Minutes of Truxton Club, January-March 1892; Cortland Historical Society).

3

Dickens and American Publishers

CHARLES DICKENS'S WORKS WERE AT THE CENTER OF THE CONTEST over international copyright that became one aspect of a testing ground for creating a distinctly American literature. Dickens's works were widely read and commercially desirable property that reached American readers through both his British publishers and through less official American publishers' efforts to gain access to his works. Dickens was not only a British import. In the 1840s, the reprinting and circulation of his novels, often without payment to Dickens, became an American industry.[1] The fiercely competitive production of Dickens's stories by American publishers and their circulation throughout the United States contributed to a conversation among common readers and reviewers that promoted America's project of nation building and what Benedict Anderson has called "imagined community."

The wide distribution of Charles Dickens's novels throughout nineteenth-century America may be analyzed by following Robert Darnton's model of the communications circuit for the production, dissemination, and reception of print.[2] This model recognizes the many people involved in the movement of texts from publisher or printer to bookseller to buyer and reader (Darnton, *Lamourette* 65–83). Darnton's model provides us with a way to examine print culture as a dynamic process. As Darnton has said, "books do not merely recount history; they make it." Dickens's novels, in particular, appear to be books that made a difference in this way. Projected toward a public, they entered a process by which they engaged readers, acting as an agency of social change.

Dickens's fiction was received within an ideological context of American nationalism and the imperatives of business competition. The Dickens text as a commodity in America was subject to economic forces and cultural pressures specific to the United States. As social objects and social resources, Dickens's texts appeared in a variety of forms ranging from periodicals and cheap publications to books to theater adaptations. The material form in which the story appeared and the movement of each Dickens story through various cultural frames affected how it was read. Dickens novels were reprinted in variously priced editions to meet the needs of different audiences. In the passage from publisher or printer through shipper to bookseller and on to the reader, messages were transmitted; signs, symbols, discourses underwent transformations as they passed from Dickens's pen through the communications circuit. Publishers had to consider printing and production costs, physical transportation, including geographical distance, and the need for middlemen such as agents and booksellers, in their efforts to match supply with demand. This affected the appearance, availability and pricing of print products and how they were received. Darnton points out that we can study "each phase of this process and the process as a whole, in all its variations over space and time and in all its relations with other systems, economic, social, political, and cultural" (111).[3]

Commercial competition over Dickens's works intertwined with the development of American culture and national identity. From his first appearance with the *Pickwick Papers* in 1837, Dickens was both a popular celebrity and a contested commercial property. Reprinting Dickens for profit, publishers engaged the reading public. *The Pickwick Papers* became a widespread publishing phenomenon.[4]

The reprint culture of antebellum America, as Meredith McGill notes, "offered a model of national identity." The appearance of Dickens's fiction, or other author's serialized stories and essays and news in newspapers and periodicals, created what McGill calls

> a sense of near-simultaneity that was crucial to the imagination of the federal form of the nation [....] The prominence of reprinting in antebellum newspapers offered a syncopation of the national imaginary that fortified the principles of a states rights' federalism, providing both the homogeneity crucial to a sense of national belonging and constant reassurances of a saving heterogeneity (107–8).

In this decentralized printing environment, the circulation of Dickens's texts participated in what Benedict Anderson has called "that remarkable confidence of community in anonymity which is the hallmark of modern nations" (36).

Park Benjamin's *New World,* a cheap, large-format story paper, held that the reprinting of Dickens's texts was an act of democracy. In his view, this asserted that these texts were common property, making them more national in outlook. American publishers like the *New World* promoted democratic and nationalistic principles while dependent upon foreign texts. They appropriated these texts within their own formats, making them American products. As McGill notes, "The editors assume that political aims and market mechanisms are mutually enabling, and attach national ideals not to texts or authors, but to publishing formats and methods of distribution" (23). The reprinting of foreign texts without payment to foreign authors was described as a way of protecting American business interests and a democratic means of illuminating the public.

Charles Dickens's *American Notes* (1842), for example, was reprinted at one-fortieth the cost of the British two-volume version. The text appeared under the *New World* banner depicting Columbus's discovery of America and was absorbed amid the nationalistic texts of the paper. The *New World* emphasized reprinting as an act of democracy in its appeal to "the unrestrained dissemination of learning among the people," as McGill has indicated (22).

The view that appropriation of foreign texts was indeed an act of democracy and public education supported intense opposition to the idea of international copyright. The first of several international copyright bills proposed by Henry Clay in Congress (1837, 1838, 1840, 1842, 1843) was opposed in memorials to Congress by a ratio of three to one (Barnes 66; McGill 83). As McGill points out, debate on tariff rates, the banking system and transportation, and the extension of slavery into the territories was connected with resistance to international copyright (83). In each case, issues of states' rights and commercial liberties existed alongside the Federalist impulse toward centralization. Lawmakers emphasized the protection of American producers against foreign competition by placing high tariffs on foreign goods. These concerns about "protection" of American interests existed side by side with the publishers' unpaid use of British intellectual and cultural property.

While it is clear that international copyright was not part of a specific agenda for Dickens's American visit in 1842, he famously addressed the issue. It remained a contentious issue among American publishers who remained firmly opposed to international copyright and writers and publishers with opposing views. Philadelphia publisher Henry Cary claimed that words and ideas were common property. Publisher Abraham Hart (1810–1885) lobbied against copyright legislation for English authors. Henry Clay took up the cause but legislative action on international copyright met with resistance and delay in Congress.

Without copyright restrictions, the story papers furiously reprinted any popular British fiction they could get their hands on. The papers sold widely and made a profit for their publishers. The *New World* and *Brother Jonathan* were joined by the *New York Herald* and *The Sun* and many other firms in the practice of reprinting Dickens's works. *Brother Jonathan*, called a "mammoth weekly" because of its large format, was the first story paper to print *American Notes* at twelve and a half cents. The *New York Herald*, a city newspaper with a wide circulation, printed 50,000 copies in two days (Patten 131). *The Sun*, a New York daily which intently followed Dickens's 1842 tour of America, also put out a version (O'Brien 74–75).[5]

There appears to be a strong connection between the downturn of the American economy with the Panic of 1837 and the rise of the cheap fiction story papers in the late 1830s. Likewise, one can see a connection between the stagnant economy and the refusal to pay for reprints of British publications. Ever since the early days of the Republic, it appeared resourceful to some to gather fiction at no cost in order to ensure one's profitability. Now, an editorial in *The New World* on February 12, 1842 asserted that Dickens's popularity in America had much to do with reprinting and a lack of international copyright:

> Has Mr. Dickens yet to learn that the very absence of such a law as he advocates, he is mainly indebted for his widespread popularity in this country. To that class of his readers—the dwellers in log cabins, in our back settlements—whose good opinion he says is dearer to him than gold, his name would hardly have been known had an international copy-right law been in existence. (*New World* [February 12, 1842]: 18)[6]

The American publishers of Dickens, producing Dickens in story papers, in simple brown wrapper volumes, and in other cheap formats, brought the English writer's fiction to the firesides, swamps, and forests of America, as Dickens himself recognized (Dickens, *Pilgrim Letters* 1:230). They capitalized on Dickens's popularity in America, which emerged as a lively response to his humor, his sentiment, his accessible style and the ways in which his texts interacted with the lives of his readers.

Dickens's appeal to British authors for support on the issue of international copyright arrived to him at Niagara Falls as a "memorial" with twelve signatures. A copy was sent to William Cullen Bryant at the *Evening Post* and was published there on May 9. James Fenimore Cooper wrote to Rufus Griswold, "I see that [Bryant] begins to fire a little at Dickens [....] This country must outgrow its adulation of foreigners, Englishmen in particular, as children outgrow the rickets" (Exman 157). Cooper, in a letter of August 6, 1842, complained to the (New York) *Evening Post* that Charles Dickens had cited him as a signer of a petition to Congress on the copyright issue when he was not. Cooper said that while he supported Dickens's views on copyright, he never signed such a letter. He added that he did not like being connected to documents of which he knew nothing (Cooper Letters IV: 302–05).

In 1843, supporters of international copyright and opponents of it squared off like soldiers on a battlefield. This simile was used by the *Southern Quarterly* in a way that seems almost prescient with respect to the civil war that lay in America's future. The *U.S. Democratic Review* and the *Southern Quarterly* took different sides on the issue. The *U.S. Democratic Review* wrote nationalistically:

> The English author—Mr. Dickens, for instance, since he appears to stand at the head of this movement, has written his book for the large and liberal reading public of his own country, under the rights, for his compensation and protection conferred upon him by its institutions and laws; how is he injured by the reproduction and diffusion of the same in another country three thousand miles across an ocean, a distinct political body? He has certainly been richly enough paid at home.

The *U.S. Democratic Review* asked: "May I not, he asks, light my candle at my neighbor's lamp, without wrong to him, or to my conscience, if I can do so without intrusion upon him in the process, or inconvenience him and his?" (*Democratic Review* [May-June 1843]: 120) The *Southern Quarterly Review*, in response, cited these comments in July 1843. It agreed with the notion of neighborly exchange, but qualified this, calling the *Democratic Review*'s argument "more specious than profound" (30). It said:

> War is waged in this country and England on the subject of International Copyright. There has been a regular declaration of hostilities through the press, and the contest presents a singular anomaly in the bellicose proceedings, being partly a civil and partly a foreign war. The combatants are English and American authors against American publishers and American readers: American authors and writers against each other, and American publishers in the same category in respect to their brethren. In this region we are quite remote from the theatre of contest. New York, Philadelphia, and Boston are the great battlegrounds. (*Southern Quarterly Review* [July 1843]: 1)

This disagreement between the *U.S. Democratic Review* and the *Southern Quarterly Review* highlights the nationalistic and competitive threads that run through the issue of international copyright and the culture of reprinting Dickens and other British texts. Amid this competition, some critics insisted that the commercial imperatives of publishers were to be balanced with their didactic or moral role in society. For example, when Wiley and Putnam started their "Library of Choice Reading," *The American Review* hailed their project and called it one aspect of "a new era in publishing history." The editors of *The American Review* also insisted that the publisher had a significant social and cultural role as educators of the public. They wrote:

> Publishers are school-teachers, and the books they print and circulate, the lessons they teach [....] Books educate the people, and publishers are responsible for the mental and moral training they impart. To make money is not the sole motive of the publisher, and the reckless profession with which cheap works of

doubtful morality have been sent abroad, will meet with its reward. (*Putnam's Monthly* (Vol. 1): 521)

If any publishers believed in their didactic or cultural purpose, this was inevitably intertwined with commercial goals and nationalistic motives. Whether America could develop its own literature in these circumstances was a salient issue for some. One reader of Dickens, the famous New York judge William Kent, later described the times in a speech in Albany in 1854:

> Of American writers we scarcely had any. Irving was only commencing his brilliant career [....] Books were not so cheap formerly as now. They were not rained down on you at railroad stations, nor could you then pass a morning's conversation with the fertile genius of Dickens, or moralize with Thackeray.

Kent himself held converse as a reader with Dickens, Thackeray, and Walter Scott. He read *Ivanhoe*, *Rob Roy*, and the *Waverley* novels. He said, "I confess that I feel for Walter Scott the debt immense of gratitude (sic)" (21–22). Kent's words remind us that the works of British authors like Dickens, Thackeray, and Scott met America during a time of considerable change among America's publishers and writers. A state of alienation among American writers and intellectuals during the Jacksonian period is described by Arthur Schlesinger, Jr., who says that they were unable to "find enough sustenance in the established order" (369). Thomas Bender points to a divide between the literary culture of the legal gentry, the wealthy lawyers and business proprietors of New York and the cultivated elites of Boston, on the one hand, and a growing democratic popular mass audience of newspaper readers on the other (118).[7] Some American publishers, particularly those of Boston classed with the gentry, were inclined toward *belle lettres*. Others were commercially oriented, seeking profit from the market for popular fiction. Dickens appealed across class lines to both groups; Dickens's name remained at the center of the international copyright debate. He claimed that the wide availability in America of inexpensive and non-copyrighted works by British authors like Scott and himself was inhibiting the development of American literature. Richard Henry Dana, the author of *Two Years Before the Mast* (1840), disagreed. He believed that American literature was essentially the same as English literature and should remain so and that Dickens's work itself was a good example of the literature the nations should share in common. Upon returning from a conversation about Dickens over dinner at publisher George Ticknor's house in Boston, Dana wrote in his journal: "All think Dickens's books entertaining and clever" (Dana Journal I, 102). Dana then asserted that American literature was "duly English" and in a letter, he told George Palmer Putnam so: "You are not going to put in a spade to help dig the ditch (which some in our city are so hard at work upon) between our literature and that of the Fatherland" (Dana *Letters*, 178; Ziff 48). In Dana's view, America ought not to drive a wedge between English and American literature but must seek quality. The "best readers," he said to Putnam, would not stand for less and "commonplace will beget commonplace" (Dana, ibid.).

Meanwhile, "democrats" like Evert A. Duyckinck, the son of a bookseller, began a search for this distinctive American literature. Focused upon a literary nationalism, he began meeting with fellow writers in his large library room at 20 Clinton Place in New York, discussing the prospects for homegrown writing that was unique to life in the United States. The men began a literary journal, *Arcturus*, which ran for eighteen months, December 1840 to May 1842. Duyckinck joined in this publication with William Alfred Jones and Cornelius Mathews, one of those "grotesque, swaggering [...] after dinner orators" who, the *New World* on June 25, 1842, complained, had loudly taken up Dickens's cause of copyright. *Arcturus* addressed American culture and city life, with a call for literary nationalism. Duyckinck became advisory editor for Charles Wiley and George Palmer Putnam for their "Library of Choice Readings."[8] G.P. Putnam enthusiastically supported Duyckinck's dreams of an "American Library." The quest for an American literature had begun in earnest.

When Charles Dickens's novels began to reach America in 1837, America was a sizable and largely untested market for publishers. Seeing Chapman and Hall's success with the *Pickwick Papers*, Carey and Lea of Philadelphia in November 1836, issued 1500 copies of the first part of *Pickwick Papers* at a cost of $207.26. Suspending trade courtesy, or their payments for advance sheets and agreements with overseas authors and their publishers, and initially not paying Dickens, Carey proceeded to reprint *Pickwick* papers in five parts. Henry Charles Carey on June 14, 1837, wrote to "Mr. Saml. Dickens" to offer twenty-five pounds via the publishing firm's Liverpool bankers W. and I. Brown and Company for the parts of *Pickwick* they had printed. Eugene Exman notes that Carey sent Dickens fifty pounds for *Pickwick*, noting his success with it (59). Carey later claimed that publishing a young and untested writer, like 'Boz,' was uncertain and risky. "The author was unknown and the enterprise doubtful," Henry C. Lea wrote years later in the *American Literary Gazette*, on May 15, 1867, rationalizing the endeavor.[9]

The publishing firm of Lea and Blanchard assumed Carey's 'rights' in publishing Dickens's works. Dickens wrote on October 26 of his "great pleasure to hear of the popularity of the *Pickwick Papers* in America—a country in which [...] I take a high interest which I hope one day to become better acquainted" (Dickens, *Pilgrim Letters*, 1: 322). Dickens agreed to Carey's publication of *Oliver Twist*, stating, "I shall be happy to enter into any arrangement with you for transmission of early proofs" (Dickens, *Pilgrim Letters*, ibid.). Dickens wrote to the firm on November 22, 1839, of Chapman and Hall's willingness "to treat with you for the transmission (at such times as will enable you to publish in America on the same day as we publish in England) [...] and with of each number of my new work in parts, including the plates" (*Pilgrim Letters* 1: 604). After February 5, 1840, John Miller, the English agent for Lea and Blanchard, arranged for early proofs of each number.

Next, arrangements were also made for *Barnaby Rudge* and the *Old Curiosity Shop*. Lea and Blanchard invited Dickens to be their guest when he arrived in Philadelphia. Dickens told the publisher that he would put off any commitments until after his arrival "on your side of the Atlantic" (*Pilgrim Letters,* 2: 425). Dickens later declined an offer of "around 100 pounds" from Lea and Blanchard for *American Notes* (Patten 132). Twice this amount was paid for sheets for *Martin Chuzzlewit* says R. Shelton Mackenzie in *The Life of Charles Dickens* (New York: T.B. Peterson, 1870, 404–405). The popular success of *Pickwick* in Britain in 1837 provided some measure of the novel's potential before Carey undertook this seemingly doubtful enterprise. Patten points out that in offering trade courtesy "Carey hoped to forestall all rivals, and could have looked to his fellow publishers for support in defending his claims" (98).[10]

"Boz," as Dickens was then called, arrived in America as a celebrity, the author of *Pickwick,* the creator of Oliver Twist and the beloved Little Nell.[11] America's publishers, for the most part, at first greeted Dickens on an amicable note. On February 18, 1842, Dickens was given a public dinner in his honor in New York at which 800 people were present, many from publishing and journalistic establishments. Washington Irving, the author of "Rip Van Winkle" and "The Legend of Sleepy Hollow," among other stories, presided over the dinner.

However, Charles Dickens was soon at the center of a piracy struggle among competing American publishers in the 1840s. "Friend" to some, he was "enemy" to others, competitor or foil, as America searched for its literary voice and commercial independence. Dickens was appropriated to American purposes. The downturn in the American economy from 1837 led to economic constraints for America's publishers and to competition from the "mammoth weeklies." In effect, a culture of reprinting emerged and courtesy of the trade was abandoned. On Cliff Street, Dickens's work was embraced by Harper and Brothers, a company that would soon become one of New York's leading commercial publishers. In the absence of international copyright, Harper and Brothers put out *American Notes, Martin Chuzzlewit, The Christmas Books*, and *Dombey and Son.* The company's first official effort with Dickens's works was *American Notes for General Circulation,* which, despite the depression lingering over America, Harpers brought out in November 1842 in plain brown wrappers at 12½ cents.

The Harpers' volume, a reprint from British sheets, ran in two columns across ninety-two pages. It carried Dickens's dedication on the first page, followed by the Contents, noting eighteen chapters. Reprint publishers with nationalistic aims made use of foreign texts, like Dickens's *American Notes*, to provide an image of the United States, even one that was, as in Dickens's case, critical of American habits and mores. A dependency upon British texts by American publishers for income and by audiences for reading material is clear. "Americans looked to Dickens and to other foreign travelers to represent a nation that was fragmented and rapidly changing," notes McGill. This led to "The consequent importance of foreign opinion to American's understanding of themselves" (24).

This becomes clear as we observe how Dickens's text appeared as a newspaper "extra" in the *New World*, under its masthead banner of Columbus and his ships colonizing the new world. Drawing attention to the relation of text and format, McGill has noted that the publication was "an exercise in colonial dependency" (21–24). Dickens's text was co-opted and set within "a nationalistic framework that defies British authority even as it conscripts it for purposes of national description" (22). Harper's competitor, the *New World*, proudly declared in the left column heading of their publication that this was the "First American Edition." The *New World* publication of *American Notes* appeared in forty-six pages at a price of twelve and a half cents each. This cost, like Harper's price, was one-fortieth the cost of the two volume, 614 page original British edition (McGill 23).

Before Dickens, Frederick Marryat had urged copyright protection and royalties for British authors whose works were printed in America. Indeed American writers, including Washington Irving and Nathaniel Hawthorne, like Dickens, argued that the practice by publishers of issuing British reprints at little cost stifled the production of a native American literature. But publishers like Park Benjamin and the Harpers held out against proposals for international copyright, sometimes arguing their commercial interests in nationalistic terms. In John Tebbel's view, putting British fiction into the American market at cheap prices raised literary standards (544). McGill, on the other hand, suggests that the problem was one of a literature that operated on different principles: native authors had to compete with foreign reprints circulating independently of "authorial control or national purpose" (20). An American literature had to break with the use or imitation of British products to be distinctive. American publishers' reprints of foreign texts expressed nationalistic goals and through their formats and commentary they were able to "refract an image of the nation as a whole that was seemingly impossible to produce by domestic means alone" (McGill 20–21).

Like the *New World,* several American publishers claimed that their distribution of foreign literature was a kind of American democracy in action. While the *New World* editors claimed that reprinting was "the unrestrained dissemination of learning among the people" and was a means to reach a broad public, the Harpers pointed out that increased costs for paying for foreign copyrights would affect labor, book production, and the book trade. While their re-printings expressed a colonization of this literature, it is evident that there was also a dependency upon it. There is some credibility in the view that a dependency on foreign reprints did not allow American authors to be published and allow American literature to find its own voice and to grow independent of British influence. Since American writers had to receive payment, it was more economical for publishers to print foreign works. Consequently, the voices of American writers were less often distributed and heard. However, as McGill observes, "We need to see reprinting as a culture, something more than an obstacle to the development of an authentic national literature" (ibid.).

Unauthorized printings of the works of Dickens in different formats reached into America's audiences alongside many other British works, like those of Bulwer-Lytton. They also emerged, as McGill has pointed out, next to "scandalous texts" like Eugene Sue's *The Mysteries of Paris,* politically partisan texts like Epes Sargent's *Life and Public Services of Henry Clay,* and domestic texts like Frederika Bremer's *The Home: or, Family Cares and Family Joys.* In newspapers, they appeared alongside news of the day, notes on fashion, and political commentary. Dickens's fiction, in the midst of this complex crossing of texts and people, intersected with public and private life. Foreign fiction, like Dickens's, participated in America's struggle for nationhood and self-understanding as part of a larger field of foreign influence. However, Dickens, as we shall see, was a particularly popular and resonant force among the American public.

The impact of foreign writers like Dickens included texts critical of America, like *Martin Chuzzlewit* which was begun in January 1843 in seventeen numbers, with the bound book coming out in July. Harpers' edition put it in direct competition with Lea and Blanchard's supposed "rights" to Dickens and with other publishers who were producing and distributing Dickens. The international copyright dispute grew heated at the time that copies of *Martin Chuzzlewit* appeared in New York. The novel sold about 20,000 parts per month. According to Patten, "The sales figures do not entirely support a conclusion that the *Notes* were a failure [....] But there is much truth to the argument that the hostile, or,—even worse, condescending—critical reception of the book affected the public's feeling about Dickens" (136). Patten points to a lull in publishing production and sales because of "financial uncertainties, political unrest, and the sort of general depression that feeds upon itself to intensify its effects" (ibid.). The maximum monthly circulation of *Martin Chuzzlewit* in New York was about 23,000 copies (ibid.). Dickens's publisher Chapman and Hall gave him a 5 percent commission, or a stipend of about 200 pounds a month that amounted to 400 pounds a number after printing expenses.

Publishers' payments to foreign authors only returned as the American economy began to grow in ways that supported the growth of the publishing industry. In the midst of these developments, American publishers turned to *belles lettres* as a market consistent with public interests and consumption patterns (Greenspan 75). By 1846, British publishers had jumped into the publishing game in America with cheap fiction editions. Bradbury and Evans, Dickens's new publishers in Britain, responded to reprint competition in America by producing the Cheap Edition of Charles Dickens, which American distributors imported from England beginning in 1847. These volumes included *Dombey and Son* in its Library of Choice Reading.[12] As Greenspan observes, Dickens was "the case of one writer whose fiction would have been an obvious choice" for publication in these series, if not for the perilous conditions created by printers who could issue cheaper editions (183).

Dombey and Son was a best seller both in Britain and in America. In the final years of the decade (1847–1849), there were eight such books, of which Dickens's novel was one. Patten points out that sales of *The Personal History of David Copperfield* (1850) were not as strong as those of the preceding novel, *Dombey and Son* (208).[13] Bradbury and Evans began to limit their press run of *David Copperfield*, the novel Dickens called his "favorite." By 1861, "the numbers of *Dombey* in print exceeded those of *Copperfield* by 212,500, or over 10,000 complete copies" (Patten 188).

David Copperfield, beginning in May 1849 and continuing through November 1850, was, however, a hotly contested property among American publishers. Dickens, by mid-century, had become a highly profitable and competitive business and was a source of intense competition. The novel was a pivotal work in Dickens's canon, a *bildungsroman* that echoed Victorian themes of progress, growth, and change. It was seized upon by more than a dozen publishers in New York alone, where, between the 1840s and 1860, the publishing trade was the city's fastest growing business enterprise. Without international copyright, Dickens, along with some other popular authors, could in effect build a publisher's profits, although profit margins were limited by the fact that other publishers could bring out a competing edition.

Dickens's British publishers countered the overseas competition with their own "cheap editions." Dickens could be found in triple-decker novels, "library" editions, "people's" editions, "Charles Dickens" editions and in newspaper and magazine reprints. Along with the Dickens book trade there was the reprinting of Dickens's stories in parts in periodicals. As Dickens began his own periodical *Household Words* in Britain in 1850, several American companies rushed to reprint his stories or his articles from it. The most prominent of these were the Harper brothers, who decided to reprint Dickens in their new monthly magazine.

Everyone wanted a piece of Charles Dickens. In 1850, the British author remained at the center of intense disputes between American publishers seeking rights to his work. Some publishers paid Dickens for his stories, while, as in the past, others grabbed and reprinted them. Dickens volumes from his British publishers were distributed by Ticknor and Fields and Little, Brown of Boston and he was "published" (reprinted) by T.B. Peterson and Lippincott of Philadelphia. In New York, his work was issued by Harper and Brothers, G.P. Putnam, and D. Appleton and a dozen other companies. The "Editor at Large" in *Putnam's*, September 1854 edition wrote:

Here we sell Dickens, in a hundred editions, at every railway station. In brown covers, in yellow covers, in every possible species of cover. We gloat over his *Bleak House*; we devour his *Hard Times* (*Putnam's Monthly* [September 1854]: 36).

As American readers devoured Dickens's novels, *Harper's New Monthly* and *Putnam's Monthly* became at this time locked in what Ezra Greenspan has called a "cultural clash" (294) and rivalry. *Putnam's,* a periodical printed in double-columned pages, was an image-maker. It frequently printed comment on Dickens and other writers. With a circulation ranging from 12,000 to 20,000, it projected life in New York to the rest of the nation. George Palmer Putnam described *Putnam's*, edited by George William Curtis, Charles Briggs, and Parke Godwin, as a publication intended to "combine the popular character of a magazine, with the higher & graver aims of a Quarterly review" (Putnam Letters, October 1, 1852; Putnam Collection, Princeton University Library).

Along with its aspirations to appear as a journal, *Putnam's* had a political edge and at times carried a nationalistic tone. As Thomas Bender observes, "*Putnam's* provided the medium for the development of the cluster of political principles that gradually defined Northern political opinion, the ideology of the Republican Party, whose platform, as we have already noted, was drafted by (Parke) Godwin, using very much of the very language of his *Putnam's* articles" (167). If so, its readership may be seen as a particular "community" in contrast to the readership of *Harper's* or other periodicals like Littel's *Living Age,* or the *Southern Quarterly.*[14]

Harper's Monthly Magazine, like *Putnam's,* developed a wide readership between 1850–53. However, unlike *Putnam's, Harper's Monthly* did not seek to become a journal; its columns and articles suggest the magazine's efforts to reach and cater to a popular audience. Its audience, perhaps was more "democratic" in its sympathies than that of *Putnam's* and *Harper's* was widely distributed to the southern region in the years before the Civil War. And while *Putnam's* only reported on appearances of Dickens's novels, *Harper's* reprinted them. In its inaugural edition in June 1850, *Harper's Monthly Magazine* mentioned that it would carry stories by Dickens, as well as those of other British authors. In "A Word at the Start" the editors said, "The magazine will transfer to its pages as rapidly as they may be issued all the continuous tales of Dickens, Bulwer, Croly, Lever, Warren, and other distinguished contributors to British Periodicals." Of these authors, Dickens, in particular, found other periodical outlets, as *Harper's* noted: "Dickens has just established a weekly journal" [*Household Words*].[15]

Harper's printed Dickens's stories in 1850 with attributions. However, as Eugene Exman has observed, short pieces from Britain by lesser-known authors were printed without attribution and as the magazine concluded its first year only a few attributions from British works were being listed. All attributions to Dickens's *Household Words* soon vanished from the pages of *Harper's*. Dickens's name continued to be mentioned, no doubt in part for his name recognition and sales value (Exman 310). However, by 1854, *Harper's* was "transferring" Dickens's *Hard Times* directly from its serial publication in *Household Words*, making that story increasingly available to its American readers, with no acknowledgment of Dickens as the author (ibid.).

While Harper and Brothers continued to reprint British work without payment or attribution, in general, understandings with foreign authors were beginning to be honored. As in the past, Dickens did not always get paid for American reprints of his stories. However, a bill in Congress generated a ray of hope for British authors in 1850. It also heated up debate among American publishers on the issue of international copyright.

For example, Henry Carey's opposition to copyright legislation was published at this time. *Putnam's Monthly Magazine* disagreed with Carey's anti-copyright position, arguing that the lack of international copyright meant competition for American authors from abroad and severely limited the development of American literature. *Putnam's* insisted that the United States needed a law "to protect our intellectual labors from the destructive competition of not cheap labor, but pirated manufactures" (*Putnam's* [January 1854]: 103). In 1854, an Anglo-American copyright treaty supported by Presidents Fillmore and Pierce was rejected by the Senate (Barnes 49–94).

In 1854, Carey, while criticizing Dickens, provided his estimate of current book sales. Of Dickens, he wrote: "The most active advocate of international copyright is Mr. Dickens, who is said to realize $50,000 per annum for the sale of works (that are) little more than amusement for his leisure hours." He added, "If the sale of books were as great in England as they are here, English authors would be abundantly paid" (Carey in *Putnam's* [January 1854]: 100). Of American authors, Carey said that "there is no one of whose books so many have been circulated than those of Mr. Irving." He pointed to sales figures he estimated at "some hundreds of thousands" and mentioned "the edition recently issued by Mr. Putnam," that is selling for $1.25 per volume, noting that the sale of this "has already amounted to 144,000 volumes." Of *Uncle Tom's Cabin*, he recorded a sale of 295,000 copies to date. Carey provided a table of his estimates of sales:

> Of the works of Hawthorne, Longfellow, Bryant, Sedgwick, and numerous others, the sale is exceedingly great; but, as not even an approximation as to the true amount can be offered, I must leave it to you to judge of it by comparison with those of less popular authors above enumerated (Carey in *Putnam's* [January 1854] 102).[16]

Carey does not specify where he obtained these figures.

An estimation of Dickens's total circulation in America at mid-century is likewise difficult to approximate because of the number of competitive publishers producing his work and the variety of forms in which his stories appeared. While Patten expertly tracks Dickens's production of *Household Words* and *All the Year Round*, he points out that after 1847, most of Dickens's income derived from approved reprints from his British publishers. This does not account for Dickens volumes reprinted by America's less "official" publishers. In addition, in America, Charles Dickens's stories also circulated in periodicals or newspapers other than *Household Words* and *All the Year Round*.

Dickens's fiction was circulated within a periodical universe saturated with an emerging literary nationalism. When *Harper's Monthly Magazine* began printing serialized English fiction, the competing *Graham's Magazine* criticized *Harper's* for using British sources as "anti-American." Two years later, in the opening statement of its first issue, the popular *Putnam's Monthly Magazine* suggested its own nationalistic platform. Declaring that it would open their readers to the universe, Putnam's editors, proposed that "in the rapid life of this country [....] A man buys a magazine to be amused—to be instructed, if you please, but the lesson must be made amusing" (*Putnam's* [January 1853]: 6).

Asserting the distinctiveness of an American literature, apart from British influence, was a keynote of *Putnam's* first editions. "Cooper is no more an imitation of Scott than is Bulwer or Dickens," the editors wrote. "Has Mr. Dana a prototype? [....] Bryant is wholly American [....] Whom does Emerson imitate? Carlyle!" However, Emerson's work is "superior," the editor says (*Putnam's* [January 1853]: 28).

A direct comparison of America's promise with Britain's production of print and literacy appeared in the next issue, with "A Letter to John Bull" (*Putnam's Monthly* [February 1853]: 221–29). The writer said, "I do not think there is an American family in the land which does not take in some newspaper or magazine." The writer attests to the "almost universal circulation" of newspapers and magazines in America and criticizes London papers, which "all are too costly to be taken by the poorer classes." He says that he has no book trade statistics at hand but that he believes that "the circulation of books is on a level with that of periodicals." For, he says:

> No really valuable work is published in England which is not reprinted here: the works of our own authors are widely read; the trade of bookmaking is lucrative, and that of book publishing more so. One publishing house, the Harpers, issue on the average a book a day, the sales of which vary from five to fifty thousand copies. (*Putnam's Monthly* [February 1853]: 221–29)

Putnam's and *Harper's* frequently commented on Dickens and reached thousands of American readers. Single copies had several readers and were read multiple times. *Putnam's* in 1853 printed 20,000 copies in January, then 22,500–25,000 in February. This increased to about 35,000 copies per month by the summer (Greenspan 295). Harper and Brothers' annual income from sales in 1853 was estimated at two million dollars, despite two fires that swept their printing plant. Because of the destruction of many records, statistics for Harpers' releases, including its run of Dickens's *Bleak House* in 1852–53, are difficult to obtain. However, those records which do remain indicate that sales increased from the mid-1840s to 1853, as the depression subsided (Exman 165).

Bleak House (1852–53) first appeared in America in *Harper's New Monthly Magazine,* which sold for twenty-five cents a copy. According to Harper and Brothers records, in 1852 Rufus Griswold attempted to obtain the first proofs of *Bleak House.* He authorized one of his associates at the *International Monthly Magazine* who was going abroad to give Dickens a $2,000 advance for the sheets to his next novel. News of this was printed in the New York *Evening Post* (Exman 310). The Harper *Priority List* indicates that *Harper's* paid 360 pounds ($1,728 by Exman's estimate) for proofs of *Bleak House.* Serialization in *Harper's* began in April 1852. The story was published in book form, in two volumes on September 21, 1853.

In a letter Charles Dickens wrote of *Bleak House* developments:

> The story has taken extraordinarily, especially during the last five or six months, when its purpose has been gradually working itself out. It has retained its immense

circulation from the first, beating dear old Copperfield by a round ten thousand or more. I have never had so many readers. (Dickens, *Pilgrim Letters*, 4: 483)

A serial in 34,000 copies suggests "striking popularity," Patten states. He points out that "In 1852 an edition of 1,000 copies was probably still standard for many works." Drawing upon the work of Michael Sadlier, Patten adds that "First printings of yellowbacks ranged between 1,000 and 5,000 copies" (227).[17] The Dickens trade was not seriously affected by the economic trends that affected the American publishing business in the mid-1850s. The *Ladies Repository* reported the wide circulation of *Bleak House* in 1852–53, noting that it generated advertising income:

> *Bleak House*, which appeared in monthly numbers, had so wide a circulation in that form that it became a valuable medium for advertising, so that before its close the pages of the tale were completely lost in sheets of advertisements which were stitched to them. (*Ladies Repository* [May 1854]: 44)

As Harper and Brothers became one of the most visible of the magazine publishers of reprints of Dickens, the firm of T.B. Peterson at 306 Chestnut Street in Philadelphia became one of the most visible book publishers of Dickens. T.B. Peterson had assumed the rights to publish Dickens and were known as Dickens's publishers, making use of the stereotype plates from Carey (Lea and Blanchard). The company had also made a deal with Harper and Brothers for the plates of Dickens's recent novels. Following Carey's practice, they claimed to provide trade courtesy to Dickens, although they had no contractual agreement with him. By 1867, T.B. Peterson had issued twenty-three editions of the novels; this increased to twenty-five within the next two years (Tebbel 247). In *Philadelphia and Its Manufactures* (1858), Edwin T. Freedley wrote:

> T.B. Peterson's have in their possession the stereotype plates of about six hundred different books, small and great, principally novels. They have invested about $50,000 in Dickens's works alone, of which they print twenty-nine different editions: the only complete series in the United States. The sales annually average 50,000 volumes. (166)

Harper's agreement with T.B. Peterson was generally respected. However, other firms also sought to print Dickens's fiction. In one case, T.L. McElrath in 1854 put out an American edition of *Hard Times*. Harpers responded by issuing the book at one-half McElrath's price. McElrath complained in the *Empire City*, an ephemeral newspaper, that Fletcher Harper had caused his business to fail. Horace Greeley of the *New York Tribune* may have been inclined to agree, says Exman. Thomas McElrath, son of the publisher, was his associate at the *New York Tribune* (Exman 89).

Dickens's entire catalog continued to be published in Britain and shipped to the United States. In January 1856, Chapman and Hall sent 1,898 volumes of *Oliver Twist* to New Orleans and 468 volumes to New York (Patten 403). The *Pickwick Papers* were then sent to New York in 1855–57. Bangs, an American distributor, carried 1,638 volumes of the novel in 1856 and 507 volumes of it in early 1857. Chapman and Hall issued 1,275 numbers of *Christmas Books Cheap Edition*, in one volume, that were sold in New York. By December 1856, some 975 numbers of the *Christmas Books* were sent to America. Of these, "75 dozen" were sold to Bangs, New York (ibid.).

"By 1864, the Dickens competition in America was intense," notes John Tebbel. "Twelve publishers, at least, were printing him, ignoring courtesy of the trade, but Dickens himself was getting as much as $5,000 for advance sheets of a single novel" (Tebbel 1: 411). In the months following the war, Appleton received 250 sets of Dickens before December 1865. Another 480 volumes, or twenty sets, were sent to Little Brown and 600 volumes in cloth, or twenty-five sets, went to the Philadelphia publisher Lippincott, which issued a standard edition of Dickens (Tebbel 1: 376). In December 1865, Scribners was sent 277 volumes (Patten 389n.). The year 1866 saw four American publishing firms distributing Chapman and Hall–produced copies of Dickens. These firms sent their books out through agents and distributors to booksellers throughout the country. In Tebbel's view, Dickens "sold better in America than they did at home." Dickens reissues appeared "to have no end" (Tebbel 1: 544–45).

The Dickens productions of Harper and Brothers, G.P. Putnam, and T.B. Peterson made their way from New York and Philadelphia across the United States through a variety of distributors and book agents, notably including James Cephas Derby, one of the leading distributors of Dickens and other print material from East Coast publishers. Dickens's novels were also distributed out of Boston by Ticknor and Fields, a highly respected publisher of *belles lettres.*

As their trade expanded, publishers were locked in a dispute over priority to Charles Dickens. A "triangular contest" was described by the *New York Times*, May 18, 1867. Harpers, T.B. Peterson, and Ticknor and Fields all were claiming Dickens.[18] Harpers claimed a prior arrangement with Dickens, one that Dickens consented to abide by. T.B. Peterson claimed an arrangement with Harpers for reprinting from advance sheets of the Dickens novels. Ticknor and Fields asserted that Dickens had signed a contract with them. A compromise was struck in which Ticknor and Fields would print Dickens stories in book form and the Harpers would serialize his stories in their magazine. However, this arrangement did not please T.B. Peterson, who also claimed priority "rights" to Dickens, based upon its purchase of Lea and Blanchard's plates and catalog.

As Ticknor and Fields put out its "Diamond Edition," T.B. Peterson's publicly expressed upset with what they believed was Ticknor and Fields' intrusion on their claim to Dickens. Before 1850, they had begun to pay for advance sheets run as serials in *Harper's Weekly* and *Harper's Monthly*. On March 16, 1867, in an advertisement in the *Boston Transcript* they asserted:

> T.B. Peterson and Brothers, Philadelphia, in connection with Harper and Brothers, are the only Publishers in America of the works of Charles Dickens, that have ever paid anything for the manuscripts advanced proof sheets of his various works, so as to enable Harper and Brothers to publish them in America. (Moss 215)

The company also placed ads in the *New York Tribune* on April 6, 1867: "3,250 pounds sterling was paid for the advance sheets of Charles Dickens's last three works." In the *American Literary Gazette*, T.B. Peterson listed their twenty-two editions of Charles Dickens's works (Moss 215–17).

The *American Literary Gazette* reported:

> Ticknor and Fields Diamond editions have had an immense sale; so have Petersons' […] and now Hurd and Houghton are in the field with three [sets of Dickens]. (ibid.)

The Nation inaccurately asserted that Dickens "had never received anything from this side of the water for his books" (*The Nation* [April 25, 1867]: 328). The *Chicago Tribune* said on October 24, 1867:

> the public are already so familiar with the various editions of Charles Dickens's works […] now issuing from the press of Ticknor and Fields […] that the mere announcement of each new series is all that is requisite. (Moss 222)

Meanwhile, we can see the development of international copyright in statements like one from the *New York Tribune*, which defended Ticknor and Fields' rights to Dickens and criticized T.B. Peterson:

> The Boston firm says in effect to Mr. Dickens: "We make money off the product of your brain, and it is only honest that you should have a part of it." The Petersons say: "Somebody is sure to take your book; let us take it first and we will give you so many dollars." To pretend that a payment like this is in the nature of a copyright, and that Mr. Dickens, having sold the advance sheets of a book to one house, has no right to consent to its subsequent publication by another is simply absurd. (*New York Tribune* [October 30, 1867]: 96)

In the years before an exclusive publishing agreement was established between Dickens and Ticknor and Fields, the Boston firm, by arrangement with Chapman and Hall, distributed a Library Edition of twenty-six volumes from 1858 to 1861. Some 3,500 volumes were sent to them at two shillings per volume in January of 1858. There were 2,000 more volumes sent by December 1858. Fields imported 5,700 copies in 1859. The Boston firm was sent 100 volumes each of *Pickwick*, I and II by December 1860 and in December 1863 made available 1,650 volumes.

James Fields "had long been ambitious to get Dickens on his list" (Fields *Yesterdays* 196). As of 1866, he began actively seeking Dickens, offering him his company's sponsorship of a reading tour of American cities and a 10 percent royalty. As the reading tour was beginning in 1867, Fields negotiated a deal for 1,000 pounds for a short story, "A Holiday Romance" for *Our Young Folks: An Illustrated Magazine for Boys and Girls*. Clearly, Fields saw a market for young readers. Ticknor and Fields began 1867 with 300 volumes of Dickens without illustrations. By December, there were another 26,000 volumes. Paying $1,000 to Dickens, Fields also published Dickens's short story "George Silverman's Explanation" in three installments in *The Atlantic Monthly*.

Ticknor and Fields' volumes of Dickens's works appeared in three editions: deluxe, moderate, and cheap. They absorbed much of the Dickens trade for the next few years. According to Tebbel, "these sets sold in the thousands" (402). The firm also published *Readings from Charles Dickens, as condensed by himself*, in 1868, with selections including: "Bob Sawyer's Party," "The Story of Little Dombey," "Bardell and Pickwick," and "David Copperfield," with illustrations by Sol Eytinge, Jr. In addition, the firm published Edwin Whipple's studies of Charles Dickens and James Fields's recollections, *Yesterdays With Authors*, which devotes a long chapter to Dickens.[19]

In 1867, Hurd and Houghton followed with its own collection of Dickens's works. In response to Dickens's reading tour, Appletons, in 1868–70, likewise felt compelled to produce an eighteen-volume set. Ticknor and Fields responded with a letter to Dickens, saying that Appleton's volume of *Edwin Drood* had done "incalculable damage" (Stern 22). By 1873, Dickens was published by Appletons in a half dozen different editions, including, according to its catalog, its "best cheap edition" the seventy-five cents per copy, fourteen-volume cloth "Handy Volume" edition (Stern 22–23). Harpers, meanwhile, issued the illustrated "Household Edition" in sixteen volumes and Lippincott produced deluxe and standard editions of Dickens and Thackeray (Tebbel I: 376). J. Applegate, following the demise of George Conclin Publishing of Cincinnati, succeeded that firm by issuing 10,000 copies of Dickens's works in two volumes. Tebbel claims, "it was so easy to sell" Dickens (Tebbel, 1: 483).

American publishers invested considerable effort in distributing and selling Dickens. While the constant reprinting of Dickens's works makes it difficult to quantify the overall circulation of Dickens in America, it is obvious that his works became a site of intense commercial competition. In 1837, the public response to the serialization of the *Pickwick Papers* indicated the emergence of a mass readership that would revolutionize publishing in America. Within the tensions of competitive commerce and American nationalism, the fiction of Charles Dickens earned a wide and lasting readership and had a profound impact upon American life. Despite the attacks upon Dickens's character by some American newspapers and the backlash against his *American Notes*, Charles Dickens remained one of the most popular authors of works distributed in America. The fierce competition among publishers over Dickens's works reflects the extraordinary popular demand for Dickens's fiction. In the 1840s, men like George Palmer Putnam, James Cephas Derby and the Harper brothers looked toward Dickens's works to enhance the financial potential of their publishing businesses and to meet the rising demand and social promise of America's growing readership. The novels of Charles Dickens, so popular among American readers, launched by many publishers in a variety of ways, had certainly fulfilled that promise.

Notes

1. Dickens's income and official circulation is well represented in Robert L. Patten's study *Dickens and his Publishers* (Oxford UP 1978). Patten carefully accounts for the works produced and distributed by Dickens's publishers Chapman and Hall and Bradbury and Evans. He also includes a record of Dickens's books that were sent to America by his British publishers and distributed by American publishers. However, more difficult to track are the reprints of Dickens's stories appearing in American magazines, newspapers, cheap editions of books, book "library" series, and inexpensive volumes issued by a variety of American companies. Patten offers some measures of the Dickens trade in America. For example, he states that when the serialization of *Bleak House* began in April 1852, some 118,000 copies a month were sold in America. He notes that according to Henry C. Carey, at least 250,000 copies were "supplied to American readers, through newspapers and magazines, and in the book form" (Patten 233; Carey, *Letters on International Copyright* 59). However, because of the constant reprinting of Dickens's works, the overall circulation of Dickens in America is quite difficult to quantify or even approximate.

2. Reviews may act as one indicator of the reception of Dickens in America; however, they need to be supplemented by the response of common readers and by publisher's records. One might follow the manner of Alexis Weedon or Michael Winship by looking at the material context in which his fiction was produced and distributed: production costs, prices set, or advertising accompanying its distribution to readers. There is a crucial connection between an author and the economic system in which he or she works. See Alexis Weedon, *Victorian Publishing* (Aldershot: Ashgate 2003), 1–2. Likewise, the search for common readers in work by Jonathan Rose,

David Vincent, and others gives us insight into a valuable and previously unheard array of voices whose understandings and uses of fiction may differ from that of the professional critic.

3. In *Literature and the Marketplace* (1995), John O. Jordan and Robert L. Patten, who have both written extensively on Dickens, argue that distribution was not always a linear movement from one step to the next and may have involved many agents. They encourage an approach that recognizes all factors in the communications circuit as interdependent, or what they call "polyvocal" and decentered (11–12).

4. The success of *Pickwick* John Feather calls "one of the legends of the history of literature and the book trade alike" (Feather 152). Norman Feltes, among others, has examined the production of *Pickwick* in some detail. Norman Feltes, *Modes of Production in Victorian Novels* (Chicago: Chicago UP, 1986).

5. To George Palmer Putnam, Benjamin wrote that he was to "procure early sheets of novels from their British publishers for reprinting in the magazine," notes Greenspan. *Barnaby Rudge* was among three works that Benjamin mentioned in a letter to Putnam that appeared in the *New World* in 1841 (Greenspan 117).

6. Frank Luther Mott credits Dickens's popularity to the pirates who gave him "such an audience as no single author had in any country." "Pathos and sensationalism, along with comedy, were required to make a brew which Americans found intoxicating in the Dickens novels they loved best" Frank Luther Mott, *Golden Multitudes—The Story of Best Sellers in the United States* (New York: R.R. Bowker, 1947), 85.

7. Dickens was received by both literary gentry and by the "democrats" in New York, a city that was fast becoming a network of newspapers and a seedbed of literary nationalism. While the gentlemanly literature of publications like Lewis Gaylord Clark's *Knickerbocker* catered to a well-educated, upper-class readership, the *Democratic Review*, Bender states, espoused nationalism and had more of a mass public for popular writing in mind. Frederick Law Olmstead, who assisted in the editing of the new *Putnam's Monthly,* was one of the writers of the gentry. Others of the genteel tradition were Bayard Taylor and Richard Stoddard. All of these men, at one time or another, wrote about Dickens in their autobiographies.

8. Encouraged by Evert Duyckinck's search for American voices and subjects, publisher George Palmer Putnam began to seek American writers. Meanwhile, he also sought out works by Dickens. In January 1834, Putnam had begun his monthly register of new publications, *The Bookseller's Advertiser.* After 1836, as a partner in the firm of Wiley and Long, he assisted Park Benjamin in procuring Dickens's early works. Ten years after beginning his partnership with John Wiley, Putnam and Wiley published Dickens's *Dombey and Son,* in 1848. It became a best seller. Despite his later support for international copyright, initially Putnam did not pay for Dickens's works. In seeking Dickens, Putnam pursued the commercial potential of the works of an author who appears to have crossed boundaries between all social classes.

9. In February 1837, Carey and Lea issued 1,200 copies of *Sketches by Boz* at a total cost of $177. They cost fourteen cents each in sheets and twenty cents each to bind. Carey, Lea and Blanchard then produced an issue of 2000 copies of *Oliver Twist* (*Talrumble and Twist*) at a cost of $434 (thirty-five cents each) in 1837 by using sheets from *Bentley's Miscellany* (Patten 130).

10. In 1837, Carey faced stiff competition from the Harper Brothers. The economic depression that set in that year affected Carey's business. The firm shifted its emphasis from fiction and foreign reprints to professional books in the medical and technical fields. As economic depression deepened, story papers like *New World,* edited by Park Benjamin, and *Brother Jonathan,* edited by John Neal, moved in to fill the gap.

11. The sentimental and melodramatic tale of Little Nell made her a beloved figure for Dickens's American audience. Dickens noted that mothers wrote to him to tell him of their own little girls who had died, as Edgar Johnson has put it: "how good she was, and how, in this or that respect, she resembled Nell." While there are reports that Dickens received letters in which readers begged him to spare Little Nell, Dickens's practice of burning his fan mail makes verifying this difficult. What is clear is that, while he discussed alternatives for his story with his friends, Dickens reached his own decision about the fate of Little Nell. Jennifer Hayward implies that the fiction serial disempowers or controls the audience, which waits in anxiety and expectation for the next installment. She also claims that this audience may influence the writer: "By involving a community of readers in collaboratively interpreting and to some degree shaping a text, serials incorporate a space for critique and thus defuse the text's potentially coercive power," she writes (31). Because Dickens burned his letters from his public it is difficult to gauge how, or if, he responded to suggestions from them. However, in the *Old Curiosity Shop,* Dickens was his own final arbiter. He ultimately went his own way, against the wishes of his audience to keep Nell alive.

12. It was not until the 1848 issue of *Dombey and Son* that Dickens's sales again regained their earlier stride. Patten records that this novel had gross sales numbers of 667,359 in its British publication and earned Dickens 9,165 pounds (Patten 188). He also mentions *Dombey's* best-seller status in America with sales "above 175,000 in various editions." Patten, *Dickens and his Publishers,* note 25, 197. Patten points to Eugene Exman, *The Brothers Harper* (New York: Harper and Row), 281, who also cites Frank Luther Mott, *Golden Multitudes.*

13. In the 1840s, a book that sold 175,000 copies would be considered a best seller. Frank Luther Mott in *Golden Multitudes* gauges a best seller as a book that achieves sales of about 1 percent of the U.S. population. Harpers published five of the eight best sellers: *Home Influence, Jane Eyre, Wuthering Heights, Vanity Fair, and The History of England.* The other best sellers were Andersen's *Fairy Tales* [Wiley and Putnam] and John Greenleaf Whittier's *Poems* [B.B. Mussey] (Tillotson 128). This list accounts for the books of 1848 only. The sales of *Dombey and Son* exceeded those of Dickens's next novel, *David Copperfield* (Patten 226). Chapman and Hall's accounts in 1849 "were substantially lower than for the previous year," notes Patten (ibid.). A "Cheap Edition" of *Oliver Twist* was issued in 1850.

14. Did *Putnam's Monthly* or *Harper's New Monthly* create a "community" of readers? Patricia Okker says that the "ability of readers to influence a magazine novel suggests that rather than being passive consumers, at times they functioned as collaborators in the creation of magazine novels." It is often difficult to hear the voice of *Harper's* readers through that of Donald Mitchell, or that of George Curtis in "Editor's Drawer." The inclusiveness of *Harper's* "Editor's Drawer," a regular column in the magazine, may have been developed, in part, as a commercial strategy for gathering

and involving readers rather than allowing them to dictate or change the magazine's content. Subscribers are only in the broadest sense a "community." The allegiance of magazine readers to a particular magazine may also be questioned. It is difficult to determine what kind of a community of readers, if any, the readers of Dickens's stories in *Harper's* were.

15. When Volume I, Number I of *Harper's New Monthly Magazine* appeared in June 1850, there were 7,500 copies circulated. There were 50,000 copies of each edition in circulation by the end of the year. The publication was produced in 144 pages of two columns and cost twenty-five cents (Exman 69–70).

16. Alongside the appearance of *Bleak House* were other popular works. By Carey's count, as of January 1854, Susan Warner's *Queechy* and *Wide, Wide World* had sold 104,000 volumes at about eighty-eight cents per volume; Fanny Fern's *Fern Leaves* had sold 45,000; I.K. Marvel's *Reveries of a Bachelor* had sold 70,000 volumes; Northrup's *Twelve Years as a Slave* had sold 20,000. Other books on Carey's list include: Fanny Foster's *Alderbrook* (33,000); Novels of Mrs. Hentz (93,000 across three years); *Western Scenes* (14,000); Seward's *Life of John Quincy Adams* (30,000); *Salad for the Solitary* (200,000); *Young's Science of Government* (12,000); *Encyclopedia Americana* (14 volumes, 280,000); Griswold's *Poets and Prose Writers of America* (21,000); Barnes's *Notes on the Gospels and Epistles* (300,000); Downing's *Rural Essays* (3,000). Carey's estimates should be measured alongside publisher's records.

17. Robert L. Patten says, "But the popular success of *Bleak House*, measured by sales rather than reviews, was markedly greater than any of the monthly serials written during the 1840s. Furthermore, *Bleak House* inaugurated a sustained increase in Dickens's circulation" (216). Circulation of *Little Dorrit* opened with 38,000 copies, *Our Mutual Friend* with 40,000, and *Edwin Drood* with 50,000 (ibid.). *Bleak House* also stimulated advertising (220). Patten records 180,000 copies of *Bleak House* Numbers I–V, with one part of each going to libraries. By the end of June, 38,500 copies of *Bleak House*, Number I had been printed. The press run for the second number, for April, was raised to 32,000, but even that proved insufficient, and two more printings, of 2,000 each, were done before July. Number III started at 34,000, and required another 1,500. Numbers IV and V began at 35,000 (216).

18. There were only twelve reprints of foreign works by Ticknor and Fields before 1850. Between 1840 and 1849, Ticknor focused on producing poetry, producing twenty-four new works. According to Michael Winship only three works of fiction were produced in the 1840s, putting 7,600 copies in circulation. However, from 1850 to 1859, there were 193 new works of fiction (Winship *American Literary Publishing* 64–65). That is, in the years 1850–59, the fiction output of Ticknor and Fields increased to sixty-two, or 22.6 percent of the company's catalog, with 173,581 copies in circulation (Winship 77).

19. Among British authors published by Ticknor and Fields, 1840 to 1859, were those of Walter Scott (94,134 copies), adventure novelist Mayne Reid (75,837), poet Alfred Lord Tennyson (69,894), Thomas DeQuincey (67,002), novelist Charles Reade (38,581), Charles Kingsley (27,376), Anna B. Jameson (20,096), Alexander Smith (18,670), Thomas Hughes's *School Days at Rugby* (19,122), Frederick W. Robertson (12,764), and George Coombe (11,080). Between 1840 and 1844, Ticknor placed

23,500 copies of twenty-four new works into publication. There were twenty-three different works reprinted and fifty-nine printings of these, putting 45,729 copies of reprinted works into circulation at a cost of $8,856. This number increased to 69,734 copies of fifty-nine new works between 1845 and 1849. There were thirty-five works reprinted in ninety-six different printings, producing 109,945 copies at a cost of $21,042. In the 1850s, Ticknor and Fields produced 274 new works and 335 other works were reprinted. The eighty-seven reprinted in 286 printings between 1850 and 1854 cost the company $87,155. Between 1855 and 1859 there were 148 works reprinted in 455 printings, producing 457,754 copies at a cost of $153,163. Ticknor and Fields produced a total of 187 reprints and 897 printings of these between 1840 and 1859, or 905,144 copies at a cost of $270,216 (Winship 59). The number of foreign works, primarily British, rose from two in 1840 to eighty in 1859. Dickens was distributed at this time by Ticknor and Fields from volumes produced by Chapman and Hall, or Bradbury and Evans. The Library Edition was launched in 1858, with an initial 3,500 volumes in the first half of 1858, with 2,000 more later in the year. In 1859, 500 copies of each volume were delivered (Patten 259). In 1860, 5,700 volumes arrived, although Ticknor and Fields "may not have retailed them at all" (283). The wholesale price per volume dropped in America in the late 1860s (284). There were in 1866, 2,400 copies in cloth of the Library Edition (177), The Library Edition was also sold by Lippincott, Scribners, Appleton, and Little Brown. It was followed after 1866 by Ticknor and Fields' "Diamond Edition" of Dickens.

4

Charles Dickens's First Visit to America, *American Notes*, and *Martin Chuzzlewit*

THE RECEPTION OF CHARLES DICKENS IN AMERICA WAS SHAPED, in part, within the seething cauldron of audience reaction to his *American Notes*, his record of his 1842 visit to America. As Americans looked to Dickens for an understanding of themselves, an image of the English enemy contested with popular adulation of the celebrated author of *Pickwick* and *Oliver Twist*. Dickens was "welcomed as a long-known and trusted friend," as Josiah Quincy said (Quincy in Wilkins 403), but was criticized for the same commercially self-centered motives he called American publishers to account for. The tensions involved in Dickens's American reception contributed to defining the American character.

Dickens wrote to John Forster on September 13, 1841, that he was "haunted by visions of America, night and day." Dickens was intrigued with America. In a letter, he wrote: "I have made up my mind to go to America—and to start as soon after Christmas as it will be safe to go" (*Pilgrim Edition Letters* 2: 386). In Philadelphia, the publishers Lea and Blanchard, hearing the news, prepared a reissue of all of Dickens's works in twenty parts. As Dickens's biographer Edgar Johnson says, "The Americans read him; the free, enlightened, independent Americans; and what more *would* he have? Here's reward enough for any man" (Johnson 1:421). Yet, within two years, Dickens's popular reputation would be assailed by an American media responding to Dickens's *American Notes* and to his advocacy of international copyright. Philip St. George Cooke, a Lieutenant Colonel before the Civil War, would suggest that when Dickens made his trip to America he had "crossed the Rubicon." This writer's lamentation begins in biblical tones:

Oh, Dickens! the Atlantic was thy Rubicon; on its broad waste thou didst ship-wreck much fame and honor. Wonderful indeed that thou shouldst, in a day, turn two millions of admirers, friends, into despisers! Whilst the arms of mil-lions were stretched to receive thee, and thou betrayest them, and sold them to a publisher! (Cooke 236)

The writer's comments point to a troubled period in the reception of Charles Dickens in America. For despite Dickens's considerable popularity and influence, his *American Notes* appears to have pleased hardly anyone in America. The text had a lingering presence in America's memory and experi-ence of an author whose fiction remained consistently popular. The tension in American reception of Dickens was a result of the contents of his book, the nationalistic setting in which it appeared, and the effectiveness of the press's campaign against his reputation. Dickens was perceived by some as having transgressed a boundary, and American nationalism was bound up with this. The casting of Dickens as a self-seeking foreigner had an impact upon how American readers approached *American Notes* and his later works.[1]

In 1842, Dickens was, by any measure, immensely popular. By the time of his American journey in that year, he had become a figure in the American imagination. When Dickens arrived in Boston on January 22, 1842, the spec-tator soon became spectacle, as Jerome Meckier points out. But who was the Dickens that Americans saw? How was he constructed by their reading and their encounter with his characters, or by his reputation? Meckier's thesis is that Dickens's experience, as an "innocent abroad" in America, led to his sharper satirical social realism: he became less idealistic and more conscious of the limits of any type of reform. Sidney Moss has claimed that Dickens engaged in a "quarrel with America."[2] In each case, the critic's focus is upon Dickens, the writer. However, what about his audience? Did Americans, in turn, become disillusioned with Dickens, or not?

American Notes, like Dickens's previous works, showed strong sales follow-ing its arrival in the United States. When copies of *American Notes* reached New York on Sunday, November 6, 1842, they were enthusiastically reprinted without compensation to Dickens by *Brother Jonathan* and the *New York World* and issued the next day. The *New York World* printed 24,000 copies in the first twenty-four hours. Harper and Brothers put out their copies on Tuesday, November 8. Philadelphia publishers Lea and Blanchard followed suit, as did the *New York Herald*, which sold 50,000 copies in two days. *Brother Jonathan* reported that by November 12, 60,000 copies had been sold (Patten 131). The sales of *American Notes*, however, were followed by a comparative slump in sales of Dickens's next novel, *Martin Chuzzlewit*. As both Patten and George Ford have observed, sales of Dickens's novels recovered. Yet, Ameri-cans' subsequent opinion of Dickens appears to be mixed.

It has been suggested that the power of the American press, responding to *American Notes,* may have had an impact upon Dickens's reputation among the American public. There was considerable backlash from American publishers following Dickens's 1842 remarks in favor of international copyright. The American press responded sharply to Dickens's portrayals of America and persisted in casting negative images of Dickens. The newspapers charged Dickens with "bad taste." James Gordon Bennett, publisher of the *New York Herald,* claimed that Dickens was "a scoundrel." He was a "contemptible Cockney," a "penny-a-line loafer." Colonel James Watson Webb of the New York *Courier and Enquirer* said Dickens had come to America for "pecuniary considerations" (Moss 40). The newspaper owners were incensed that Dickens should argue on behalf of international copyright, or payments to authors that would cut into their profits. Dickens' biographer Edgar Johnson has noted that "much of the anger was no doubt whipped up by the newspapers, who were themselves among the worst offenders against the rights of authors" (Johnson 1:376).

Comments from readers of Charles Dickens suggest that the American newspapers may have been moderately successful in their assault upon Dickens's reputation in America. The press opposition to Dickens evidently did have an adverse effect upon Dickens's reputation for a time. However, it did not diminish readership of his fiction or substantially affect sales of Dickens's fiction in the long run. *Martin Chuzzlewit* did not have strong sales in America, compared with Dickens's previous novels. However, this may be attributed, in part, to a downturn in the economy during the period of its first published edition. Subsequent Dickens novels continued to sell.

The newspaper editors, several of whom had interests in American publishing profits and were among the people pirating foreign novels, were angered by Dickens's comments on international copyright. They soon portrayed Dickens as an inconsiderate money-grabber, perhaps projecting their own approach to life and commerce upon Dickens. Dickens, in turn, satirized America in his *American Notes,* and more sharply in *Martin Chuzzlewit.* This pointed satire on the defects he saw in America served to color subsequent readings of *American Notes* and to modify Dickens's reception in America.[3]

However, Sidney Moss's term "quarrel" is not the right term to describe Dickens's relationship with America. Dickens was not quarrelsome; he was disenchanted. America proved to be no democratic dream or utopia, any more than was Britain. The new, open, democratic world of Jacksonian America disappointed; its ideal promise was, for Dickens, shadowed by deficiencies. American democracy now appeared to mean sameness, conformity, emptiness. "This is not the Republic I came to see," Dickens wrote. "This is not the Republic of my imagination" (Dickens *Pilgrim Letters* 3: 156).[4]

Often the criticisms that Dickens's audience brought to their reading of *American Notes* say more about their own concerns than much about Dickens, or the quality of his book. Mary Grey Lundie Duncan, in *America as I Found It* (1853), asserted that Dickens's text left out Christianity. She wrote:

> A passage in the conclusion of Dickens' "American Notes," one of the best in the book, is quoted verbatim as the best expression of my own sentiments, only adding to "cultivation and refinement" a more essential quality which he has omitted—I mean Christian principle. (24)

It wasn't what was left out of the text that irritated some Americans, however. It was what was put in by Dickens that irked them. Andrew Jackson Downing, a landscape designer who started the magazine *The Horticulturist*, wrote in 1847:

> Charles Dickens, in that unlucky visit to America, in which he was treated like a spoiled child, and left it in the humor that often follows too lavish a bestowal of sugar plums on spoiled children, made now and then a resale in his characteristic vein of subtle perceptions. Speaking of some of our wooden villages [...] he said it was quite impossible to believe them real, substantial habitations. (252)

Philip Hone, one-time mayor of New York, recorded mixed reactions in his journal. At first, he was supportive of Dickens's *American Notes*. However, after the publication of the satire in Dickens's next novel, *Martin Chuzzlewit*, Hone was quite displeased. In his diary on November 14, 1842, Hone wrote:

> [N]o notes have ever had a more prompt or rapid circulation, nor in my opinion has any writer been more unfairly treated by my countrymen. Lies were circulated in advance; sentiments were attributed to him which he never uttered. His name was forged in papers which he never saw [....] And all because a few hospitable people [...] made a little too much fuss about him on the occasion of his late visit, but more especially because Mr. Dickens saw with an unprejudiced eye the horrible licentiousness of the daily press in this country and uttered the language of truth in his denunciation of the stupendous evil [....] The truth is that (he) has written a very fair and impartial book about this country. (632)

Thus, Hone changed his tune. He asserted that America had been injured by a friend, much as Caesar had been betrayed by Brutus. He wrote in his diary:

> [H]e has written an exceedingly foolish libel upon us, from which he will not obtain credit as an author, nor as a man of wit, any more than as a man of good taste, or good manners. It is difficult to believe that such unmitigated trash should have flown from the same pen that drew the portrait of the immortal Pickwick[....] Et tu Brute! (ibid.)

Dickens's comments on "the American's practice of spitting tobacco juice and their universal disregard of the spittoon" (*American Notes* 144, 169) appear to have been most memorable for some readers. Dickens's descriptions of the habit lingered in the minds of some readers for many years afterward. In 1853, in an apparent defense of American behavior, an American editor and translator, M. Howitt, appears to interpolate an editorial opinion in the account of Frederika Bremer, a popular writer who had come to America from Sweden. "I saw none of Dickens' smoking and spitting gentlemen," Bremer is heard to say (18). However, then, we hear that in the hot and close atmosphere of a cabin "Just beside us sat two young men, one of whom smoked and spat incessantly just before Mrs. Downing and myself." "That gentleman needs a Dickens!" said I softly to Mr. Downing. "But then," replied Mr. Downing in the same undertone, "Dickens would have committed the mistake of supposing him to be a gentleman" (Bremer 37).

Others suggested that it was Dickens who needed to be more of a gentleman. Dr. Benjamin Stillman at Yale, reflected on his sense of Dickens's trip to America:

> Some of our people rendered themselves ridiculous by deifying Dickens and running mad after him, and he has repaid them with abuse, proving himself a man of low and vulgar mind. The attentions of Mr. and Mrs. [Charles] Lyell were, on the contrary, very proper, calm, respectful and kind, without adulation and folly. (204)

Philip St. George Cooke saw Dickens's 1842 trip as Dickens's downfall:

> And thou, the immortal creator of Little Nell! whose genius could make classical the name of Twist.
> Friend—He, too founded a new school of "serial" writers.

Here the writer makes his comment likening Dickens's trip to America to a crossing of the Rubicon. Friend responds:

> A dip into a good author, is often a mental shower-bath; it sets one's ideas in motion; is in some sort a substitute for the active emulation of the world! But that is essential to real progress. (Cooke 238)

With *American Notes*, the narrator's "Friend" says that he received a dose of Dickens quite different from what he had expectations of:

> Friend—I had a terrible disappointment yesterday! My daily allowance from the strata of newspapers, turned out I thought a prize, a number of Chuzzlewit; with

the accustomed anticipation of pleasure or amusement from his writing, I lay down to read it. Martin had just arrived in New York; never were my feelings so revolutionized; on the dull prairie I could have relished the novelty or wit at the expense of my very friends, or even moral poison, if it were tart; but, lo! it was dull and disgusting, I could scarce wade through it; as the essay of a nameless author it could never have paid the printing; it has proved the very Muzzlewit to Dickens! (Cooke 239–40)

The arrival of Martin in New York appears in Chapter 16 of most editions of the book. This is some 260 or so pages into the text, which eventually runs about 870 pages. There is no evidence that this reader continued beyond Chapter 16, which begins with a long sentence about a violent response of a mob to the election of an alderman: "Some trifling excitement prevailed upon the very brink and margin of the Land of Liberty; for an alderman had been elected the day before [...]" We hear that the newspapers are out in force and Dickens is quick to satirize the media. Martin sees the newspaper headlines from on board the ship, as it pulls into port:

"Here's the morning's New York Sewer!" cried one. "Here's this morning's New York Stabber! Here's the New York Family Spy! Here's the New York Private Listener! Here's the New York Peeper! Here's the New York Plunderer! Here's the New York Keyhole reporter! Here's the New York Rowdy Journal! Here's all the New York papers!"

Dickens is clearly critical of the kind of "news" that is based upon rumor and hearsay, or constructed by prying into people's business. Here he responds to personal attacks upon his *American Notes* by news media. He casts these news organizations as irresponsible with his typical wit and satire: "It is in such enlightened means," said a voice, almost in Martin's ear, "that the bubbling passions of my country find a vent" (267–68).

Here Martin is first asked, "how do you like my Country?" "I'm hardly prepared to answer that question yet," he answers, "seeing that I have not been ashore." Colonel Diver, the editor of the *New York Rowdy Journal*, with whom he is speaking, points to the ships docked in the wharves as "such signs of National Prosperity" (269). He claims that there is an aristocracy "of intelligence and virtue" and dollars.

Cooke, who has evidently been reading this section of Dickens's novel in serial form in the "newspapers," calls the chapter "dull and disgusting." It is unclear what "revolutionized" his feeling against the British Dickens. Was it Dickens's portrayal of the war correspondent Jefferson Brick of the *New York Rowdy*? He is described to Martin at a dinner as "one of the most remarkable men in our country, Sir!"(282). Brick speaks of how his newspaper can reveal the new nation's destiny. Martin challenges them about "forged letters," which appears as an oblique reference to the reprinting of non-copyrighted works from abroad. "Is smartness American for forgery?" asked Martin. The focus here is on the American newspapers. Dickens also has a character at the dinner offer the comment, "but some institutions develop human nature; others retard it." Cooke was clearly dismayed by this chapter and protested against Dickens and his book.

Other readers registered similar disappointment. Attracted by Dickens's stories but repelled by his account of America, they suggested that Dickens had substituted caricatures for facts, produced unjust "pictures," written superficially, and neglected to mention America's "better qualities" or "merits." They expressed these views in their essays and journals, perhaps overlooking that Dickens in *American Notes* had indeed pointed to many of America's positive qualities.[5]

Henry Copee (1821–1895), who later became the president of Lehigh University in Pennsylvania, wrote in 1873 on *American Notes* and *Martin Chuzzlewit:*

> The Notes might have been forgiven, but the novel excited a great and just anger in America. His statements were not true; his pictures were not just; his prejudice led him to malign a people who had received him with a foolish hospitality [....] In taking a few foibles for his caricature, he had left our merits untold, and had been guilty of the implication that we had none. (196)

Copee, however, goes on to mention eight Dickens novels and his Christmas stories and to point to Dickens's moral and social merits. In other writings, Copee expresses much enthusiasm for Dickens's fiction and to have not minded his caricatures, as long as they were not directed at Americans.

Henry Tuckerman (1813–1871), a popular essayist, also offers a mixed review of Dickens in 1864:

> Marryat and Dickens added nothing to their reputations as writers by their superficial and sneering disquisitions on America. Yet, however philosophically superficial and exaggerated in fastidiousness the great charm of Dickens as an author, his humanity, the most real and inspiring element in his nature, was as true, and therefore prophetic, in these "Notes," as in his delineations of human life. (221)

As Tuckerman distinguished what he viewed as Dickens's superficial impressions of America from the charm and humanity in Dickens, for Reverend James Pycroft (1813–1895), in 1854, Dickens appears to have served some Americans as an observer of democracy. However, Pycroft, best known as a writer on the English sport of cricket, also warned his readers about foreign writers who criticized America:

> On the United States, Basil Hall's "Travels" give us much information about the working of the democracy, and may be classed with the Journal of Mrs. Butler (once Fanny Kemble), the *American Notes* of Dickens, and the Sketch by Mrs. Trollope: but beware of mistaking caricature for fact, or lending yourself to those writers on American customs who are bent rather on holding up their peculiarities to ridicule, than their better qualities to imitation. (142)

Lydia Marie Child, a feminist writer and abolitionist, wished that Dickens had not applied so much caricature, because for her this made Dickens's narrative seem less realistic and reliable. In a letter from New York on November 15, 1842, to Ellis Gray Loring, the Massachusetts lawyer and abolitionist who started the first anti-slavery society in Boston, Child wrote about Dickens's *American Notes*:

> Dickens's book has, of course, brought down upon him all the wrath and patriotism of the penny press. They have already got out a caricature of him, dancing at Five Points, with a great, fat splay-footed "nigger." Witty, is it not? I am sorry that Dickens, in the funny parts, yielded so much to his irresistible propensity to caricature; for it casts a suspicion of exaggeration over the whole. John was in a great fever because he could not send you a copy on the road; I believe he would have chartered an express, if he had known where to find you. The hits at slavery almost tickled him out of his wits. As for Page, I didn't like him at all. He was vexed with Dickens for saying anything about slavery.

Thomas Nelson Page, one of the south's best-known writers, she goes on to say, found Dickens's "remarks were unseemly in a foreigner, who had so much despotism at home" (Child, *Letters* 142). Southern writers like Page rejected Dickens's anti-slavery comments. For example, Dickens had written on his trek through Virginia: "In this district, as in all others where slavery sits brooding [...] there is an air of ruin and decay abroad, which is inseparable from the system" (119).

Dickens's "irresistible propensity to caricature" in *American Notes* and *Martin Chuzzlewit* is obvious. However, as Child points out, his attacks upon slavery did agitate many southern writers like Thomas Nelson Page. Child recognizes the penny press response to Dickens, as well as the racial tone of the cartoons directed against him. She also recognizes "the funny parts," although she finds them exaggerated caricatures. Her abolitionist sympathies are clear and so too is her friend John's appreciation of Dickens's "hits" on slavery.

In 1842, Dickens spent far more time in the North of the United States than he did in the South. Traveling north, across New York state, Dickens visited the "vague immensity" of Niagara Falls, a sublime "Image of Beauty" that he says became "stamped upon" his heart. That morning, Samuel Manning Welch of Buffalo, New York, appears to have been enthusiastic about Dickens's visit to his town. However, Welch registers an ambivalent attitude toward Dickens in his autobiography. Early in his book, Welch notes that Dickens got off the train at Black Rock railroad near Pearl Street by the Western Hotel in Buffalo. (According to Dickens in *American Notes,* he arrived in Buffalo on a "chilly and raw" morning, between five and six a.m.) Welch recites a series of several of Dickens's characters "which were being read by all Americans, old and young." He then recalls:

> He was a great object of interest to my young eyes. *I was brimful of his creations and surrounded by his characters; whom I know as well as my friends and acquaintances, whom I know only in the flesh* [his italics]; so the reader may well imagine the fever of excitement with which I looked upon the man Dickens himself, right here in Buffalo, which was a long way from "Fleet Street" and "Seven Dials."

Welch may have been brimful with Dickens's fictional characters but he was apparently unhappy with *American Notes.* Welch writes:

> But alas! The ingratitude and base return he gave us for it was a stain on his character forever. No sooner had he returned within the sound of "Bow Bells" than he published his "American Notes" in which he scandalized, insulted, and maligned us. We condoned the offense, although we did not forget. He had not the generosity to ask our forgiveness nor apologize. We had our lesson. We continued to read his books, to laugh and grieve over the emanations of his brain, and always shall. He came again, twenty years later; we, all who could, went to hear him read and picture to us his ideas of the characters of those we all know. I enjoyed it much and felt grateful to him for giving us this pleasure; but we omitted to fete him, to play the sycophant to him, and outside the reading hall purposely forgot the man. He was the same self-conceited, surly, coxcomb as before, but intensified. We loved his books; we read them; we still read and love his books, and always will. (29)

Addressing his own American readers, Welch here affirms a collective "we," a national community. Other Americans like him continued, years later, to be enchanted by Dickens's fiction, yet to lash out at Dickens in their memoirs. As they write, they appear to be defending their homeland. Wharton Jackson Green (1831–1910), the grandson of a Tennessee senator, may have agreed with Dickens about Cairo, Illinois. For him, the place was "Such as a most uninviting village, as seen by me and the snob Dickens" (96). Jabez Lamar Monroe Curry, a Harvard-trained legal advocate of free universal education who was a member of the Confederate Congress, later president of Howard

College, and a U.S. diplomat to Spain (1885–1888) wrote in *The South in Olden Time* (1901) of "the descriptions of superficial observers like Dickens" (62). The New York lawyer George Templeton Strong was unforgiving, yet attracted by *A Christmas Carol*. At the time of Dickens's public readings in 1867, he wrote that Charles Dickens

> never uttered one word of sympathy with us or our national cause [....] (he) is a snob of genius, and that some considerable percentage of his fine feelings for the wrongs and sorrows of humanity is histrionic, but perhaps I do him an injustice [....] Anyhow, I should like to read the Christmas Carol: Scrooge and Marley's Ghost and Bob Crachit. (Strong *Diary*, IV, 173)

In contrast, there were some American readers who enjoyed *American Notes* and found them insightful. Traveling with the Mormon community in Nauvoo, Illinois, Charlotte Haven, a Mormon, wrote in 1846, "I seldom attend Mormon meetings." However, she did spend some of her time reading Dickens. Haven writes,

> We have been reading Dickens' notes on America, sent us by Mrs. D. of Quincy. We admire Dickens much, he has a keen sense of our national peculiarities which he paints in sparkling humor, yet he delineates the wild and beautiful scenery of _____ with graphic accuracy. You know H. and E. were on the boat with him down the Ohio and had several conversations with him. He certainly describes most faithfully travel on canals and our great Western rivers. (635)

More than 1,000 miles away, at home in Massachusetts, Ralph Waldo Emerson offered his own view on Dickens's *American Notes*. Emerson wrote in "Behavior,"

> Charles Dickens self-sacrificingly undertook the reformation of our American manners in unspeakable particularity. I think the lesson was not quite lost; that it held bad manners up, so that the churls could see the deformity. Unhappily, the book had its own deformities. It ought not to need to print in a reading room a caution to strangers not to speak loud. (1: 407)

George Francis Train, meanwhile, cited a *New York Tribune* writer who called American response to Dickens's remarks "thin-skinned." Train argued that Thomas Colley Grattan's book *Civilized America* (1859) was far worse and called it "outrageous, worse than Dickens, worse than Trollope" (6–7). Grattan, the former British consul in Boston, had written an assessment of America that Train insisted was "beyond the truth." "He wanted, like Boz, something that would sell," Train wrote (8). When Grattan called 'manifest destiny' "unscrupulous spoilation," Train asserted that "England has not a square mile of land on the face of the globe that she has not taken by the hand of violence" (11). After many pages attacking Grattan, he wrote:

> Dickens was the leader of the orchestra, then came fat Dickenses and lean Dickenses, round faced Dickenses and square toed Dickenses, little Dickens and great Dickens's—all of whom have entertained their readers with what would constitute an ocean of saliva. (32)[6]

Another reader who found worth in *American Notes* was Theodore Ledyard Cuyler, a Princeton ministry student, who wrote to his Aunt Charlotte Morrell Boyer:

> Where do you think she has been? To the Boz ball! & yesterday I received a full account of that splendid fete. She saw the lion & heard him say distinctly and audibly the words "beautiful, beautiful." (Cuyler, Letters, Box 1 [January 1842]; NYHS)

Cuyler launches into a description of Dickens, perhaps obtained through this third party. In it is a suggestion of the American press caricatures of Dickens as a devil:

> he is middling sized-gray eyes & long hair after the fashion of a "soap lock" & *has no horns* as was supposed by many [....] Mrs. C. (no doubt, their acquaintance) has the promise of his autograph for me & I shall make an attempt for it myself when he comes here next week. Don't you envy me the privilege of taking the hand that *created Little Nell?* (ibid.)

To his Aunt Charlotte, Cuyler wrote on March 11, 1842:

> I had hardly time to paste down my stray locks & pull up my collar, when the door opened, a jolly, laughing fellow caught me by the hand, bowed, said, "Mrs. Dickens, sir" & sat down, laughing like "Newman Noggs." There we were, nobody but Boz & I & "the old woman"! Only think of it. For a few moments, everything—the "Old Curiosity Shop" "Smike" "Tim Linkinwater" "Nell" and all the rest of them rushed thro my mind with such rapid confusion that I could not realize that I was in the presence of the greatest romancer of the time—he the handsome boy before me. (Cuyler Letters [March 11, 1842]; Box 1, NYHS)[7]

Cuyler emerges as a devoted fan of Dickens, one thrilled to have met him, much like the American author Bayard Taylor (1825–1878), who, while Dickens passed through Philadelphia, asked Dickens for his autograph and later received it by mail. In 1864, Taylor recalled musing on a cliff about his childhood reading, including Dickens:

> Two dollars of my seventeen had gone for a subscription to the Saturday Evening Post, an expense at which Uncle Amos had grumbled, until he found that Aunt Peggy took stealthy delight in perusing the paper. In its columns I found charming poetry [...] besides republications from contemporary literature, especially Dickens" (102).

Dickens's notes on America apparently did not bother either of these writers. Rather, Dickens appears to have inspired them both in their distinguished careers.

However, as later critics have observed, a far more pointed satire about American habits than *American Notes* came from Dickens's pen in his novel *Martin Chuzzlewit*. Dickens, writing this novel, perhaps was as Jerome Meckier sees him: disappointed in the new nation; an "innocent abroad," like Martin Chuzzlewit, who was "surprised" by America.

> "Pray, sir!" said Mrs. Hominy, "where do you hail from? where was you rose?"
> "Oh!" said Martin. "I was born in Kent,"
> "And how do you like our country, sir?" asked Mrs. Hominy.
> "Very much indeed," said Martin. "At least—that is—pretty well, ma'am."
> "Most strangers—and partick-lary Britishers—are much surprised by what they see in the United States." remarked Mrs. Hominy.
> "They have excellent reasons to be so, ma'am," said Martin. "I never was so much surprised in all my life."
> "Our institutions make our people smart much, Sir," Mrs. Hominy remarked.
> "The most short-sighted man could see that at a glance, with his naked eye," said Martin.

Here Mrs. Hominy, not the British travelers, is the critic. We hear that "Mrs. Hominy was a traveler [...] a writer of reviews and analytical disquisitions." In these she is the one who critiques her "fellow countrymen" for turning away from the principles upon which the nation was founded (MC 383–84). Dickens, of course, is the critic behind Mrs. Hominy: the critic of institutions that make Americans "smart much." Dickens's point about democracy devolving into a mob is not so very different from Alexis de Tocqueville's ideas of the 1830s. However, Dickens's satire is sharp and his portrayals are barbed. Tocqueville's mannered prose did not "get under the skin" of Americans. Dickens's satire did.

As Dickens's steam-boated past Cairo, Illinois on April 9, 1842, he found his satirical symbol for an incomplete American dream. As *Lloyd's Steamboat Directory* (1856) notes, the low banks of the Ohio River allowed for flooding and marshy soil contributed to outbreaks of fever (Meckier n.25, 245). When sitting down to write *Martin Chuzzlewit*, Dickens would offer the muddy, pestilential swamp around Cairo as "the new Eden" for a young architect and his dreams of making a fortune on land development. This inversion of a pre-lapsarian dream was a real estate scam; the duping of Martin Chuzzlewit served as an emblem for a story of Martin's own failings and those of the young America.

Dickens must have had a sure sense that Cairo, Illinois, would not become a metropolitan center when, in *Martin Chuzzlewit*, he satirically created his real estate paradise in that swampy, forsaken area near the Mississippi. Of Cairo, Thomas Wallace Knox in 1865 writes: "Sad, unfortunate, derided Cairo! Your visitors part with unpleasant memories [....] Dickens asserted your physical and moral foundations were insecurely laid" (149).[8]

In Cairo, Illinois, during the Civil War, London *Times* correspondent William Howard Russell was told by a passenger on board his boat of Dickens's *Martin Chuzzlewit*. His fellow traveler recalled a description from Dickens's novel that portrayed the town of Cairo. Russell writes:

> For two months I had seen only the rival stars and bars, with the exception of the rival banner floating from the ships and at the fort at Pickens. One of the passengers told me that the place was supposed to be described by Mr. Dickens in *Martin Chuzzlewit*, and as the steamer approached the desolate embankment, which seemed the only barrier between the low land on which the so-called city was built, and the waters of the great river rising above it, it certainly became impossible to believe that someone, even as speculators, could have fixed upon such a spot as the possible site of a great city—an emporium of trade and commerce. (330)

Although *American Notes* and *Martin Chuzzlewit* received bad press in the United States and there were reports of slow sales of the novel, in fact, sales of both books were strong in the long term. Patten has demonstrated, through publishing sales records, that the novel's sales rebounded in subsequent years, and Ford notes that it sold better when it appeared in book form (43). Some critics have said that the novel's slow sales in the 1840s were a result of economic recession and its impact upon the publishing industry. Ada Nisbet and Sidney Moss have argued that *American Notes* and *Martin Chuzzlewit* badly affected Dickens and profit on his novels. George Ford, recognizing the downturn in Dickens's sales, notes Dickens's "Chuzzlewit Disappointments." Jerome Meckier, in contrast, attributes slow sales of Dickens to overexposure: "*Martin Chuzzlewit* brought to six the number of novels Dickens had published in as many years" (58). However, it is clear that Dickens's fiction overall continued selling well throughout these recession years.

The novel appears to have gained greater approval among readers toward the end of the century. William Dean Howells wrote of it:

> I liked *Martin Chuzzlewit* too, and the other day I read a great part of it again, and found it roughly true in the passages that referred to America, though it was surcharged in the serious moods, and caricatured in the comic.

Howells claimed that Dickens had "caught the note of our self-satisfied, intolerant, and hypocritical provinciality, and this was not altogether lost in his mocking horseplay" (164).

Another prominent American who read *Martin Chuzzlewit* was Theodore Roosevelt, who wrote to his son Ted on May 20, 1906:

> Jefferson Brick and Elijah Pogram and Hannibal Chollop are all real personifications of certain bad tendencies in American life, and I am continually thinking of or alluding to some newspaper editor or Senator or Homicidal rowdy by one of these three names.

To his son Kermit, Roosevelt wrote on February 29, 1908, that

> Dickens was utterly incapable of seeing the high purpose and real greatness which (in spite of the presence also of much that was bad and vile) could have been visible all around him here in America to any man whose vision was both keen and lofty. [Even so, Dickens] was in his element in describing with bitter truthfulness Scadder and Jefferson Brick, and Elijah Pogram, and Hannibal Chollop, and Mrs. Hominy and the various other characters, great and small, that have always made me enjoy *Martin Chuzzlewit*. Most of the characters we still have with us. (*Dickensian* 82 [Summer 1986]: 118–20).

In a sense, with *Martin Chuzzlewit*, Dickens got his ironical revenge on publishers like Park Benjamin. This "first of Dickens's increasingly satirical novels," as one critic calls it (Meckier 56), also satirizes the newspaper publishers who, in turn, continued to be pushed by popular demand to reprint the very text that criticized them. Of course, whatever satisfaction Dickens may have found in this irony, he did not gain any money by this transaction. America appropriated the British author's fiction but seldom paid him for it. That *Martin Chuzzlewit* did not sell particularly well at first was a disappointment to Dickens and to his British publishers, Chapman and Hall, from whom Dickens soon departed.

In *Martin Chuzzlewit*, Dickens experimented with a tale of two nations. American readers initially asserted that their young nation had merits that the author had not clearly represented. A later generation appears to have recognized some accuracy in Dickens's critique of America and to have liked the book better. In his novel, Dickens "shifted his satire away from remote institutions such as the Yorkshire schools and directed it upon the Victorian sanctuary: the home and family," says Ford (48). Dickens himself called the novel "in a hundred points immeasurably the best of my stories" (Forster 1:331–32). Likewise, Forster did not believe that there was any "falling off" in Dickens's abilities, or in his reputation (Forster 1:327). Within four years, Dickens was back with another long novel, *Dombey and Son*, which Kathleen Tillotson and John Butt have viewed as the most well planned of Dickens's novels to that date. Perhaps the period between *Chuzzlewit* and *Dombey* ought to be "reinterpreted," as Meckier suggests, "as an attempt to ride out the slump in the publishing business and rekindle reader interest" affected by "publishing too many items in rapid succession (that is by Dickens's prolific-ness)" (61).

Notes

1. Several writers have claimed that anti-English sentiment and intense patriotism supported republican unity amid diversity. Through anti-English sentiment, Americans reaffirmed a sense of their cultural independence, even as they read English texts. Heideking says that "the enemy image helped to create and construct a separate national identity because it acted as a unifying force in the face of all the existing diversity and fragmentation in and between the states." Jurgen Heideking, "The Image of an English Enemy," in *Enemy Images in American History* (Providence: Berghan, 1997), 95.

2. See Jerome Meckier, *Innocent Abroad* (Lexington: University Press of Kentucky, 1990); Sidney Moss, *Dickens's Quarrel With America* (Troy: Whitston, 1984).

3. The American journey sections of *Martin Chuzzlewit* comprise about one-sixth of that novel. They develop the same themes that are present in the sections of the novel that are set in Britain. The selfishness that Dickens chose as one of his themes is present not only in America, it is in several of the British characters as well. Dickens's friend and biographer John Forster said that the American portions of *Martin Chuzzlewit* were not planned when Dickens started writing the novel. His claim is that Dickens sought to increase sales for the novel, which was not selling well in its serial installments. The American scenes do not appear to have helped the novel to sell any better.

4. Dickens, in his critique of America, was more direct than Alexis de Tocqueville had been in 1835. As late as 1862, an American editor, Francis Bowen, commenting in a note in a new edition of Tocqueville's *Democracy in America* interjects a criticism of Dickens: "This is a lively and faithful description of the system which Dickens taught us to stigmatize by the name of red tape," *Democracy in America* (New York, 1862), 114. Reader responses suggest it was Dickens's tone and his turn toward non-fiction that some American readers found objectionable. Some had expected a more quaint and familiar Dickens: that English humorist with his eccentric characters.

5. Dickens, for example, wrote in his "Concluding Remarks" in *American Notes* about Americans: "They are, by nature, frank, brave, cordial, hospitable, and affectionate" (*American Notes* 216). Dickens faced American antipathy for things British. Kim C. Sturgess accounts for sharp declamations against Britain in Fourth of July orations, anthems, and theater. Sturgess, *Shakespeare and the American Nation* (29–38).

6. This group described by Train may include public readers and actors who imitated and presented Dickens's works in public. George Francis Train, born in Boston on March 29, 1829, was the son of Enoch Train, the ship builder, and brother to Adeline Dutton Train Whitney, the author. Train quoted Mr. Ripley from *The New York Tribune*:

> Compared with Grattan, Dickens is the paragon of modesty, and the very flower of gentlemanly courtesy. Not that we complain of his severity of remark on American manners and institutions. We trust our countrymen are recovering from their thin-skinned sensitiveness to the cavils of foreign tourists and visitors [....] I took up the "American Notes" again, and I am surprised to find them overflowing with such good nature. Dickens has been abased. Sidney Smiths came so close upon Boz's footsteps that we have mixed the sentiment. Dickens is not so bad a man, after all. I retracted all I have written or said against him. Read "American Notes" again, then read "Civilized America." Dickens wrote for fun. Grattan for spite. (42)

7. Theodore Ledyard Cuyler's correspondence with his aunt includes several recommendations concerning books. (Cuyler Letters, Box 1, New York Historical Society Library).

8. Dickens wrote that to leave "the detestable morass called Cairo" and its Mississippi River location and to return to the Ohio River "was like the transition from pain to ease, or the awakening from a horrible vision to cheerful realities (*American Notes* 166).

5

Dickens and Library Reading

A LONG WITH THEIR WIDELY DISTRIBUTED SERIALIZATION IN PERIODICALS, the works of Charles Dickens reached his American readership in every region of the United States through their availability in a variety of libraries. Through the wide distribution of his stories, "Dickens democratized fiction," as Robert L. Patten has pointed out (224). Dickens's novels contributed to the making of a responsible democratic community because libraries, from mercantile, to subscription, to public, made them available to readers. Some general trends may be uncovered. For example:

- In library after library, records show that patrons confirmed cultural authorities' suspicions that if people were left to their own choices, the public would tend to choose fiction and novel reading. Lending records show that fiction was the main choice in most of these libraries, irrespective of age or class. Dickens's works were prominent within this fiction reading. Many cultural authorities appear to have disparaged dime novels. However, in contrast, Dickens's popular works made it into library collections and appear to have been considered reliable literature in most libraries. British works, like Dickens's novels, appear as popular among readers as America's emerging literature.
- Library records suggest that his books were shared by more than one reader in reading families. They suggest that reading Dickens was often a cooperative affair, because family names repeat on borrowing slips.

- There appears to be little or no difference in Dickens's appeal among readers with respect to gender or class. Library records show that both men and women read Charles Dickens's novels.
- Library records also make clear that Dickens was read by a variety of readers, including middle-class and working-class readers. Although Charles Dickens's works were recommended to children, his books were not read by children more than adults; in fact, Dickens was read by both young adults and older adults.

Dickens contributed to the American imagination because of this wide availability in nineteenth-century library collections that typically included sets of his books, as well as individual copies of his novels. There were, in most cases, at least two sets of Dickens, each obtained from a different publisher. These library collections generally included periodicals in which Dickens's stories were reprinted. Libraries were often able to purchase Dickens and other volumes at a discount from publishers, as a writer for the American Social Service Association reported:

All booksellers will allow a discount of at least 25, frequently 30 to 33½ percent on American books ordered for free libraries. English books imported for a free library are exempt from the 25 percent duty which is laid on books, except those published for more than twenty-five years. (*Public Libraries* 73)

The stocking of Dickens's fiction in libraries coincided with public library development in the United States. This was, at times, characterized in nationalistic and democratic terms, as when J.P. Quincy wrote:

When Thomas Hobbes declared that democracy was only another name for an aristocracy of orators, he never conceived of a democracy which should be molded by the daily journal and the free library. (*Public Libraries* 402)

Public libraries and journals would keep the public informed and responsible, not unduly persuaded by "the rhetorician and stump orator, with their distorted fancies and one-sided collection of facts" (ibid.). Rather, this reading, Quincy believed, would produce in and among Americans "that instructed common sense upon which the founders of our Government relied." The circulation of print would build a responsible democratic community.

Dickens's fiction was viewed as contributing to this. It was Josiah Quincy who wrote in 1842 that in America

In the empty schoolroom, the boy at his evening task has dropped his grammar, that he may roam with Oliver or Nell. The traveler has forgotten the fumes of the crowded steamboat, and is far off with our guest, among the green valleys and hoary hills of old England. The trapper beyond the rocky mountains has left his lonely tent, and is unroofing the houses in London with the more than Mephistopheles at my elbow. (Wilkins 32; McGill 112)

Records on both sides of the Atlantic indicate that Charles Dickens's fiction was popular library reading and that the imaginative energy of Dickens was made available to people across class, race, gender, ethnicity, and geography. For example, in an article in *Harper's* in May 1868, Austin Abbot reported that popular reading at a village library showed that "Next to Harper come Dickens novels." Quoting the librarian, Abbott added, "We have Scott's novels, but they are much less read than Dickens is" (Abbott 776).

If Americans developed "that instructed common sense" that J.P. Quincy spoke of through their library reading, they did so collectively as well as individually. Library records support the view that most people lived in nuclear or extended families and that they read together, or shared the same texts. In these borrowing records we can see that family members often show a run of reading the same authors during given time periods. At the New York Society Library, for example, the names of family members often appear as readers who brought Dickens books home. It appears likely that these people shared Dickens's stories with each other before returning them to the library. Family reading suggests that library use was, as Christine Pawley puts it, "a cooperative affair" (112).[1]

Library records show that Dickens was popular among both men and women. As Christine Pawley notes, "In the late nineteenth century, commercial publishers assumed that men and women liked different types of books and targeted publications toward these putative gendered needs" (112). However, the evidence of library records shows that reading by both males and females tended to move beyond the gender categories assigned by the publishers. Library records of Dickens's readers who were patrons of the New York Society Library, for example, support this observation. Of readers of Dickens between the years 1850 and 1854, when a women's reading room was established at the library, the records show that, proportionally, male reading of Dickens was equivalent with female charges of his books (*Public Libraries* 384).

Although libraries were key sources of a reader's access to the fiction of Charles Dickens, many readers did not have this access until after the public library movement began in the United States by mid-century. However, subscription libraries, the libraries of mechanics' institutes, mercantile libraries, and the collections of associations provided Dickens's fiction to their clienteles. Mechanics and apprentice libraries were created to support trades and for the self-improvement of workers.[2] Mercantile libraries were at times allied with business interests. Subscription library collections were ones shared by readers who paid a fee for borrowing privileges.

In the mid-nineteenth century the first public lending libraries appeared in America and in Britain. Charles Dickens, opening the Manchester public library, with a speech in 1852, the year of *Bleak House*, emphasized the value and power of books.[3] Dickens told his audience that he anticipated that one would soon hear from the working man

> the solid and nervous language which I have often heard such men give utterance to the feelings of their breasts, how he knows that the books stored here for his behoof will cheer him through many of the struggles and toils of his life, will raise him in his self-respect, will teach him that capital and labor are not opposed, but are mutually dependent and supporting will enable him to tread down blinding prejudice, correct misrepresentation, and everything but the truth, into the dust. (Dickens *Speeches* 152–54)

America's libraries were increasingly filled with patrons reading newspapers and readers interested in fiction. Several of these libraries began to stock their shelves with fiction more than any other type of publication. As Justin Winsor, Superintendent of the Boston Public Library, observed in 1876, students "find all the instructive reading they ought to have in their school books, and frequent the library for story books. These swell the issues of fiction" (*Public Libraries* 433). According to librarian's reports at mid-century, the novels of Charles Dickens, Walter Scott, and James Fenimore Cooper were among their most circulated works of fiction. William Jones Rhees, the Smithsonian Institution's chief clerk, noted of the Augusta, Georgia, YMCA, founded January 27, 1848, that it had 3,500 volumes in 1855. He wrote:

> During 1854, 484 books were taken out by 73 persons. The Reviews are more read than any other class of works, then fiction, travels, and biography. Sir Walter Scott and Charles Dickens are the favorite authors. (Rhees 28)[4]

Observing a trend toward placing popular material on the shelves, J.P. Quincy, in the 1876 United States Office of Education library report, the first major study of its kind, noted:

> No one has ever doubted that the great majority of books in a free library should be emphatically popular in their character. They should furnish reading interesting and intelligible to the average graduate of the schools [....] Can Milton's noble Ode on the Morning of Christ's Nativity reach the average ear like the lovely Christmas Carol of Charles Dickens? Few persons think it desirable to exclude all fiction from their town library. (*Public Libraries* 395)[5]

The presence in these libraries of Dickens's fiction and comments from librarians show that he was read by young people and by readers from working-class backgrounds. In 1857, at the Franklin Library Association in Hudson, New York, Dickens's works were often called for. During 1854, "6,240 volumes were lent to 120 persons," says the library's record. "Works of fiction were mostly called for—Uncle Tom's Cabin, The Lamplighter, Ruth Hall, Fern Leaves, Dickens Works, George W. Curtis's Works, Thackeray's Works, Melville's Works" (*Public Libraries* 489).[6] Similar selections are reflected in the 1854 reading of merchants, lawyers, doctors, and other professionals recorded at the New York Society Library. These records suggest that Dickens is one author all classes shared in common.

The report of the Apprentices and the Demilt Library speaks of the reading of apprentices in various trades. The school library, founded in 1820 by the General Society of Tradesmen of the City of New York, suggests an institution for boys that is kinder than the harsh atmosphere of the Yorkshire Schools and Dotheboys Hall of Dickens's novel *Nicholas Nickleby*. The 1855 catalog reports that there are 14,899 volumes.

> A large proportion of our readers are boys between the ages of 12 and 21 years who are employed in various occupations usually called mechanical. They generally come in the evening to the library to exchange their books, and numbers remain in the rooms until they are closed. The consequences of this is that they have little leisure to attend to anything but their wants, and we have not yet been able to devise any plan by which to keep a minute report of the various description of books taken; we have noticed, however, that the works most frequently called for, are the following, according to the order in which they are stated, viz: Cooper's novels, Simms, most of Scott, Marryat's, Dickens's, Levers', Mayne Reid, The Three Guardsmen, Twenty Years After, Bragalone, Monte Cristo, The Wandering Jew, The Arabian Nights, Robinson Crusoe, Shakespare's plays, some of James's works, some of Bulwer's works, some of Thackray's works, Uncle Tom's Cabin, Dred, Kane's Second Expedition and a few others. (*Public Libraries* 565)[7]

Musing upon what these boys might someday become, the librarian says: "and any time, these three years past, may have been seen by his fireside a man who ought to be a hero with schoolboys, for no one has ever felt so for them—Charles Dickens." Rhees calls the characters of Dickens the reader's "friends," who come not only from across the ocean "but across the darker and wider ocean of time" and "sit down at his table and discourse with him as long as he wishes to listen. The poet of the heart comes" (565–66).

While Dickens was not always the most frequently borrowed author in these libraries, he was one who had wide and lasting impact across all classes, ages, gender, and across several decades. The readers' friend was increasingly available at Young Men's Association libraries. For example, the Milwaukee

YMCA stocked *Harper's Weekly* in 1859–60 and in 1861. The library shelved 15,000 volumes by 1876. There were two copies each of Scott's *Heart of Midlothian* and *Guy Mannering*. There were also works by Irving, Disraeli, De Quincey, and a copy of Swedenborg's *Heaven and Hell*.

The library was plentifully stocked with periodicals, including Dickens's *All the Year Round, The Atlantic,* and *Harper's.* The YMCA library was particularly well-stocked with Dickens's novels, with two copies of each. The Milwaukee YMCA library catalog includes two copies each of *David Copperfield, Martin Chuzzlewit, Nicholas Nickleby, The Old Curiosity Shop, Pickwick Papers, Oliver Twist, Bleak House,* and *Great Expectations.* There is one copy of *Little Dorrit, A Tale of Two Cities, The Christmas Stories, Sketches by Boz, American Notes, Dombey and Son, Barnaby Rudge,* and *The Haunted House.* There is also a copy of the *Pic-Nic Papers.*

In comparison, the Middlesex Mechanics Association at Lowell, Massachusetts, accounted for 12,782 volumes. In 1854, Dickens's works appeared prominently among the books circulated. The librarian reports: "Works of fiction are most read, then voyages and travels and history. The favorite authors are Sir Walter Scott, Dickens, Cooper, James, Irving, Mrs. Stowe, Grace Aguilar" (Rhees 151).

However, Dickens's fiction was not always readily embraced by young readers. In an article in *The Atlantic Monthly* in January 1884, "What Children Read," Agnes Repplier points to a girl who "has probably never read a single masterpiece of our language."

> She has no idea, even, of what she has missed in the world of books. She tells you that she "don't care for Dickens" and "can't get interested in Scott" with a placidity that plainly shows she lays the blame for this state of affairs on the two great masters who have amused and charmed the world [...] yet, she may be found daily in the circulating library and is seldom visible on the street without a book or two under her arm. (27)

In 1894, poor immigrant children at the Andover House Library in Boston were able to take out books from 7:00 to 7:30 each evening, after having dinner. A single bookcase revolved and from it 200 children took out more than 2,500 books per year. The librarian observed that Dickens, Scott, and Cooper were read, but "with no degree of ardor." The children were mostly of Irish parentage and most frequently sought "fairy stories." In the librarian's view, without intervention these stories would represent "full fifty percent" of the children's reading. Of the 2,500 books, 353 were "of pure adventure" and there were 282 "books of travel." Illustrated books were favored. The librarian adds, "It is interesting to note that the girls read boy's books with avidity, while the boys will not knowingly touch girl's books." Peer influences, including the reading of "gang leaders" evidently influenced some of the book selections.

> The few boys that cannot read take out books as assiduously as the others. Another boy whom I had noticed gazing longingly at the top shelves, on which the works of Dickens, Thackeray, Tennyson, etc. were ranged, sidled up to me with abashed appeal that he be allowed to take out "a work." Plainly he looked on works as something too high and mighty for such as he [....] Calls for special books may often be traced to changes of program at the theaters. Thus, a temporary demand was created for *Oliver Twist, Rip Van Winkle, The Merchant of Venice, The Three Musketeers*, and even for Tennyson's *Becket*. (*North American Review* [September 1894]: 377–78)

Mercantile libraries were also a source of Dickens's fiction for some readers. The Mercantile Library of Philadelphia reported in 1867 that "More is done to satisfy the calls for new works on their first appearance, than is supposed by many. As illustrations of the practice in this matter: the Library is now furnished with twenty to forty of each of Dickens." The librarian was asked which books were the most read. The bound volumes of *Harpers*, he said. (Or so it was reported in *Harper's* itself.)

> We have Scott's novels, but they are much less read than Dickens is. We needed two sets. This was not strange, since the volumes contain half the works of Dickens, Thackeray, Reade and others, to say nothing of the original papers. (Abbot 776)

In the year of Dickens's *Pickwick Papers*, 1837, Edward Johnston introduced the New York Mercantile Library's *Systematic Catalogue* (New York: Harpers, 1837), which soon included both *Pickwick* and *Oliver Twist*. Records of the New York Mercantile Library Association in 1850 show that there were three copies of Dickens's *The Memoirs of Joseph Grimaldi* (1838) along with at least two copies of all of Dickens's novels. Conspicuously, mention of *American Notes* is not to be found in this library's catalog. The catalog refers to a copy of "Picnic Papers," edited by Charles Dickens, and the "Pickwick Club." While the latter may be an abbreviation of the Dickens' title, the former is obviously not Dickens's work. Rather, it is probably a re-packaged *Pickwick* by an anonymous American author or editor (*New York Mercantile Catalog*).

William Cullen Bryant stated that at the Mercantile Library the novels of James Fenimore Cooper were particularly popular. He said, "public libraries are obliged to provide themselves with an extraordinary number of copies of his works: the number in the Mercantile Library in the city, I am told, is forty" (Bryant Introduction, *Precaution* iv). Library records show that Cooper could be found alongside Dickens, Scott, and Bulwer and that America's emerging literature intersected with that of popular British writers. In 1871, R.G. Hassard reported in *Scribner's Monthly* that at the library "There is a steadily increasing call for Dickens, which of course was greatly augmented after his death; but the *Mystery of Edwin Drood* is not much in demand" (364).

New York Society Library charge records show the reading patterns of its library patrons: merchants and lawyers, clergymen or doctors who resided in New York City. The Annual Report of 1870 notes: "This is not a library to which the laboring classes readily have access. Its locality, its constitution, and its associates have tended to confine it to the wealthier portion of society" (Keep 492). Dickens, who signed the library's guest register in 1842, was well-known to these readers. Two members, A. Gordon Hamersley and Louis C. Hamersley, both lawyers, were "popularly known as Dombey and Son" (Keep 478). Library records show that patrons had runs of reading several books in a row of their favorite authors. Dickens, Scott, and Cooper appear prominently among these.

Borrowing records at the New York Society Library demonstrate the contest between English and American literature in the 1840s and 1850s. For example, Augustus F. Smith, a lawyer who lived near Fort Washington, in 1852, after reading Dickens's *Oliver Twist*, read Hawthorne's *Twice Told Tales* and *The Blithesdale Romance* and then read consecutively Melville's *Redburn*, *Omoo*, *Typee*, *Moby Dick*, and Cooper's *The Pilot* and *Deerslayer*. Joseph Shotwell read Dickens, then consecutively borrrowed Cooper's *The Last of the Mohicans*, *The Spy*, *Pioneers*, and *Deerslayer*. James Roosevelt, of New York's political Roosevelt family, in 1854 began *Waverley* on October 2 and consecutively borrowed Scott's *Guy Mannering*, *Abbot*, *Ivanhoe*, *Kenilworth*, and *Redgauntlet*. John D. Wolfe began April 1851 by reading *David Copperfield* and followed this with Melville's *Typee* and *Mardi*. He alternated between British and American authors, reading Thackeray's *Pendennis* and then Hawthorne's *The Scarlet Letter* and Emerson's *Representative Men*, before reading Browning's poetry, Disraeli, and *Vanity Fair* in August 1854. Wolfe's reading shows an interlacing of British and American works that typifies the reading patterns of most of the library's patrons.

Ten years later, in 1864, Wolfe, a lawyer, philanthropist, and one of seventy-two vice presidents of the New York Chamber of Commerce, donated $5,000 to create a house uptown for orphaned boys as part of a project called "The Sheltering Arms." We may wonder if Dickens's stories, like *Oliver Twist*, which he borrowed from the library, supported this benefactor's decision.

This intertwining of borrowing British and American literature continued at the library in the 1850s. Calls for Dickens, Bulwer, Carlyle, Thackeray, and Ruskin appear alongside calls for American authors. Cooper's novels were more popular with men. However, Cooper, like Dickens and Thackeray, had many female readers.

New York Society Library records show that female readers avidly borrowed adventure stories and travelogues as often as did male readers. For example, Mary H. Pennel, who read several works by Dickens in the 1850s, began 1855 with *Don Quixote* and then consecutively read Cooper's *Pathfinder, Redskins,* and *Prairie* before embarking upon voyages with four consecutive novels by Frederick Marryat. She then returned to Cooper's *Pathfinder* in December and followed it with *The Spy, Pioneers,* and *The Last of the Mohicans.* Ann Pierce also craved adventure and travel and followed Carlyle's *French Revolution* with *Polar Seas.* Pierce read *Barry Lyndon* and *Pelham* by Bulwer, Austen's *Mansfield Park,* and a great deal of popular fiction.[8]

Dickens's fiction is to be found in the midst of family borrowing records at the New York Society Library. These records suggest that family members influenced each other's reading. For example, Ellis Potter, an 1840 graduate of Columbia College, read Tennyson, Ruskin, and Browning and then four Cooper novels (*Prairie, Pioneers, Deerslayer, Pathfinder*) while his younger brother Edward Potter, also a Columbia graduate, likewise borrowed Cooper (*The Pilot*) and Tennyson's poems during the same period. However, there were also differences in family members' reading interests. Ferris Pell borrowed *David Copperfield* from May 27 to June 9, 1851 and *Pendennis,* August 5–12. In 1854, George W. Pell read three novels by Ainsworth and two by Cooper. In contrast, Clarence Pell's reading was more scientific (chemistry, *The Natural History of Vestiges of Creation*) and continental (Goethe, Schiller, Dumas).

Mary F. Wyeth, a merchant's daughter, borrowed *Household Words* early in May 1856, when she was about twenty-six years old, as Zboray has indicated (170). She followed this by borrowing *Martin Chuzzlewit* on May 12. Part 6 of *Little Dorrit* was also appearing at this time, but it is not clear from the library records whether Mary Wyeth read this Dickens novel. Her charges indicate that she was reading *Mayflower* by Harriet Beecher Stowe and *My Bondage* at the same time as *Martin Chuzzlewit,* which she had out for twelve days. She returned Cooper's *The Last of the Mohicans* to the library on the day she took out *Household Words.*

Society Library Records show that Leonard Wyeth charged out Margaret Fuller's *Woman in the Nineteenth Century.* Like his sister, he read Bayard Taylor's *Central Africa.* Zboray concludes from this that there was little evidence of gender differences in reading patterns. However, it should be noted that the readers he has examined are siblings. The "boundlessness in reading" Zboray speaks of is perhaps better exemplified by the reading patterns of other patrons of the library, like Mary Pennel and Ann Pierce, who read "male" adventure stories, or by male readers like Walton H. Peckham, who was drawn to the popular *Uncle Tom's Cabin* by Stowe and *Wide, Wide World* and *Queechy* by Susan Warner. That boundlessness is also evident in the borrowing of Dickens novels by both male and female readers.

Harriet Barker's reading, for example, included *Dombey and Son*, along with Dana's *Two Years Before the Mast*, Thackeray's *Vanity Fair*, and Hawthorne's *Mosses from an Old Manse*. Along with those novels, the single boarding house resident read books on mythology, Coleridge's poetry, various records of explorations and travel books, Sparks' *American Biography*, and works by Guizot and Fuseli, as Zboray has noted (172). Barker's borrowing suggests that reading interests went beyond contemporary definitions of male or female reading.

Dickens was read by both sexes. From 1840 on, *Oliver Twist* was one of the library's popular charges among both male and female readers. The novel was borrowed at least four times each year. The novel was charged in the early 1840s by patrons like William W. Diblee, who also read *Sketches by Boz*. It was charged at least four times or more by patrons consistently from 1847 to 1856, with some patrons, like George Pearce in 1851, borrowing it twice. The library shows charges of four times or more in 1847–49 and 1854–56, as Zboray has also pointed out (166). The novel was borrowed three to four times each year between 1850 and 1853.

Oliver Twist remained popular among both male and female readers in the 1850s. However, Dickens's 1850s novels in book form were read less often at this library than those of Thackeray, Scott, or Cooper. Thackeray's *Pendennis* was steadily popular with readers from 1851 to 1854. Walton H. Peckham, John D. Wolfe, Oliver H. Shepherd, George Pearce, and Reverend Henry B. Smith were among the many borrowers of the novel in 1851. Borrowing of *Pendennis* that year outpaced borrowing of *David Copperfield* four to one.

Dickens was not the most popular author of books borrowed at this library, although the reading of Mary Wyeth and others makes it clear that his works were read in serialized form in periodicals, as well as in books. From 1854 to 1856, New York Society Library patrons borrowed Walter Scott's *Waverley* novels thirty-eight times. (This includes patrons who borrowed the books more than once.) Cooper's *The Pilot, Deerslayer, Pathfinder,* and *The Last of the Mohicans* were also popular. Dickens's novels were borrowed on an average of about a half a dozen times for *Oliver Twist, David Copperfield, Old Curiosity Shop, Pickwick Papers,* and *Dombey and Son* (Borrowers Registers, New York Society Library Collection). However, Dickens's works, in book form, were consistently borrowed in the 1860s–70s and today sets of Dickens in the library's reading rooms attest to his longevity and popularity across several generations.

Dickens was equally popular among library readers in Boston. When the Boston Public Library, the first major venture in public library creation in a large American city, was dedicated on January 1, 1858, Robert Charles Winthrop (1809–1894) said: "Here the glowing pictures of fiction and fancy shall pass and repass before our vision, beneath the magic and of a Scott, a Dickens, or a Cooper" (Winthrop 388). For Winthrop, "Scott and Dickens" and "Bulwer and Thackeray" were "temptations." Winthrop said:

> How many persons present are there, of any age or either sex, who have resisted the temptations of Scott and Dickens, of Bulwer or Thackeray, of Blackwood and the Edinburgh and the Living Age, or even of the far less wholesome and less innocent literature—if, indeed, it deserves to be dignified by the name of literature—which solicits the prurient appetites of our young men and our young women at every shop window and at every railway station-, how many are there, I say, who have turned away from such temptations, to hold converse with these mighty master spirits of history, philosophy, and politics? (Winthrop 142)

The Boston Public Library, Upper Hall (1861) and the Index of Books in the Bates Hall (1866) lists the availability of the following periodicals: *All the Year Round*—vol. 1–7. London 1859–62. 7 vols.; *Household Words*, vol. 1–4, 8, 16, 17–19. London. 1850–59. A copy of *The Cricket on the Hearth* serialized in *Smith Weekly*, vol. 2. was also available. We are not able to get any decisive circulation records from the Boston Public Library. However, we do know that by 1869, about 9 percent of issues were for American history and literature. Boston readers still read more foreign history than American and Edward Edwards records 17 percent issues for English History and Literature. The library held a copy of theater versions of Dickens's *Cricket on the Hearth* by A. Smith and *Dombey and Son* by John Brougham, and a copy of the Wilkie Collins–Charles Dickens dramatic collaboration *No Thoroughfare*. According to the Public Libraries report of 1876: "In the Boston Public Library the reader will find Dickens's works in 53 volumes" (*Public Libraries* 827)

Beginning in 1870, Boston branch libraries spread out into the suburbs, and in them were Dickens's works. The Boston Public Library's Roxbury Branch in 1876 showed three copies of *American Notes* (New York 1842, Philadelphia 1874, Boston 1874) alongside copies of all of Dickens's novels. *Bleak House* was represented as "4 volumes in two." There were two copies of *No Thoroughfare.* James Fields' *Yesterdays with Authors* was on the shelves, along with John Forster's *Life of Dickens*, Douglas Jerrold's *The Best of All Company*, R.H. Stickly's *Anecdote Biography of Dickens*, and G.A. Pierce's *The Dickens Dictionary*. There were collections of Christmas stories, including ones by other authors bound with stories by Dickens.[9]

A.O. Archer, the librarian for the Blackington, Massachusetts, library reported that Dickens was among the authors read in that manufacturing town:

> The patrons of the library are mainly operators, who, after a day of toil, require reading of a light character, as a means of relaxation; hence a large part of our books are of the best class of fiction. The average factory girl takes amazingly to Mary J. Holmes, Marion Harland, and the like, while many of the men read Irving, Scott, Dickens, and Thackeray. Books of travel are favorites too, especially with the young folks. (Edwards 144)

Charles Ammi Cutter of the Harvard University Library in January 1868 noted "the marks of incessant use exhibited by the cards" of Dickens, Thackeray, Macaulay, and Shakespeare. Cutter referred to the popularity of Dickens among readers, as an example of the problem of library card misplacement.

> The titles of Dickens's works were so often taken out and misplaced, that the experiment of extending a wire over the cards from front to back was tried and proved successful. Being easily unfastened, it does not interfere. with the insertion of a new card. (99)

Another significant library in Boston that held circulating copies of Dickens's works was the Atheneum Library. In 1869, the Atheneum began issuing a bi-monthly listing of its recent acquisitions. These show that biographies of Dickens were purchased, along with sets of Dickens's novels. Thanks to Charles Ammi Cutter, the Boston Atheneum developed a dictionary catalog by 1874. This pioneering catalog, with entries for author, title, and subject, indicated that Dickens was well stocked at the library.

The library catalog shows a high percentage of German volumes purchased regularly from Leipzig, from Tauchnitz, and that a Philadelphia publisher, rather than a Boston or New York publisher, was the primary provider of Dickens books to the Boston Atheneum. The Index-Catalog also recorded parts of books and articles in periodicals. Some 105,000 books are recorded with an annual estimated circulation of 33,000. The library stocked periodical copies of Dickens novels serialized in *Bentley's Miscellany* (*Oliver Twist*) and *Harper's Magazine* (*Little Dorrit, Our Mutual Friend*) and in Dickens's own *All the Year Round* (*Great Expectations, A Tale of Two Cities, Uncommercial Traveler*). Dickens's periodical *Household Words* also appears to have been available, providing a copy, within its pages, of *A Child's History of England*.

South of Boston, in Rhode Island, librarians of the Providence Atheneum clearly tracked patron's calls for books in 1855 and 1857. There were 8,971 works of fiction called for in 1855 and 9,214 in 1857. Biography and history accounted for 2,158 charges in 1855 and 2,971 in 1857. The librarians noted:

> From an estimate by the delivery of their works, the following is the order in which the authors here mentioned are ranked by our reading community, or rather, we should say, by those who use the books in the Atheneum Library: First, Sir Walter Scott, next, Simms, Cooper, and Dickens, with not ten volumes difference between them; Irving stands next, then Mrs. Stowe, after her Prescott, the historian. (*Scientific American* [May 1858]: 393–408)

To the north, another means of access to Dickens's fiction was through circulating libraries in rural areas. Dickens's novels were popular in the circulating library of Keene, New Hampshire. Francis S. Fiske, writing in *New England Magazine,* looked back upon an earlier time in which enthusiasm for Carlyle, Prescott, Bulwer, Scott, and Cooper was strong, "while the contest for 'Pickwick' and the other new volumes of Dickens became almost a hand to hand encounter" (242).

Collections in New York and Boston may be considered alongside the equally large collection of the Library of Congress in Washington, D.C. The shelves of the Library of Congress in 1839 held copies of four titles from Dickens, representing all of his published works to that date. There were eighteen titles by Walter Scott, seven by Frederick Marryat, and six of Bulwer's novels in American editions (Ostrowski 124, 128). American novelists James Fenimore Cooper, Washington Irving, and John Pendleton Kennedy were also represented. The library in 1839, Carl Ostrowski points out, had seven titles by Catherine M. Sedgwick, and other romance writers, which would have appealed to women. There were more in the 1849 catalog (Ostrowski 136–37). In 1849 the Library of Congress catalog shows Dickens represented by fifteen titles, seven of which are American imprints. The works of Walter Scott appear with nineteen titles. As Ostrowski observes, these could not have been copyright deposits and must have been purchased by the Library Committee (195). By 1866, the library had forty-six volumes of Dickens on its shelves.

At the Library of the Interior in 1876, John Forster's *Life of Dickens* was checked out fourteen times, according to Reverend J.G. Ames, the librarian. *David Copperfield* was recorded as being checked out eleven times. *Little Dorrit* also was out eleven times. A *Dickens Dictionary* by G.A. Pierce was among the books most frequently taken out.

The growth of the eastern libraries stocking Dickens may be compared with Dickens's presence in libraries in cities farther west. In Cincinnati, the home of the early Western book trade, as Walter Sutton has described it, a public library was established in the months after Dickens's death. In 1876, the Cincinnati Public Library provides one marker of public reading of Dickens. The library held four copies of each major novel. Six copies of the last completed novel of Dickens, *Our Mutual Friend* (1865), were available.

The availability at the Cincinnati Public Library of Dickens's fiction existed despite a long-standing dispute regarding stocking fiction on its shelves. The circulation for novels for 1856 was recorded at 8,229. The next year, on October 2, 1857, Cincinnati's library board decided that "No novels should be given out to pupils of the high schools." However, the library's records show that two volumes of each of Charles Dickens's works were on its shelves in 1871. The catalog, created through the efforts of William Poole, indicates that uniform editions of Dickens's works were later added. Obviously, the Cincinnati library made a major purchase of Dickens's books shortly after 1868. The purchase from publishers in both Philadelphia and New York accounts for the collection listed in this catalog, with a few exceptions. Perhaps the most curious of these is the listing of *Master Humphrey's Clock* with *Barnaby Rudge* in three volumes from Tauchnitz in Leipzig in 1846. This suggests that the Cincinnati library had copies of Dickens earlier than 1868 that were not reported in this catalog. The Ticknor and Fields volume, *Dialogues from David Copperfield* (1870) was included in this library's listing under "Dickens." Other collected short stories by Dickens were also available.

By 1876, the library had added two additional copies of most of Dickens's books by purchasing sets of Dickens's novels during Poole's administration of the library. In the 1876 national library report, Venable recalled Vickers's restrictions on "light literature" and wrote that the persistent "conflict of opinion with respect to novel reading is curious to observe. It has come up again and again in Cincinnati" (*Public Libraries* 908). In 1872, Mr. Poole had said that "no public library can enjoy popular sympathy and proscribe prose fiction" (ibid. 911). Venable contrasts the public library's policies with those of the Young Men's Mercantile Library in Cincinnati. He writes:

> While the other public libraries of the city have until recently almost repudiated fiction, this one has always promptly met the demand of the novel reading public. Three-quarters of its circulation is of standard fiction. In the annual report of 1871, it is stated that twenty copies of Miss Alcott's *Little Women* and twelve copies of Mark Twain's *Innocents Abroad* did not half supply the demand for those pleasant books. (*Public Libraries* 904)

It should be remembered that Twain and Alcott were both avid readers of Dickens and that the Cincinnati Mercantile's readers of *Little Women* encountered the "Pickwick Club" within the pages of that novel.

Other libraries in the region were also well stocked with Dickens's works. The Indianapolis Public Library held two copies of every Dickens novel. In Indianapolis, patrons would call for books by shelf marks, not the titles. Slips were given on which patrons would copy these numbers. They were encouraged to indicate several, to try, in the words of librarian recommendations, "to increase the chances of finding one of them in" (xii). Records of Dickens, on pages 92–93 of the 1873 report, show that the library also housed copies of biographies on Charles Dickens by his friend John Forster (Philadelphia and London), R.S. Mackenzie (New York, 1870), F.B. Perkins (New York, 1870), T. Taylor (New York, 1870), and G.A. Pierce (Boston, 1872). Librarian Charles Evans reported in 1876 that the library, one of eleven in the city, held 17,000 volumes. Annual circulation figures were not recorded.

After the Civil War, the libraries of Milwaukee amply provided the novels of Dickens and works about the author. One of these libraries, at the National Home for Disabled Volunteer Soldiers, was created on March 3, 1865. In 1875, Dickens was represented there by two copies of each of his novels. The library also had biographies of Dickens by Forster, Mackenzie, and Pierce. Former soldiers could visit the library from 8 a.m. to 9 p.m. and could check out books from 8–11 a.m. or 7–8 p.m. They were only permitted to check out one book at a time, for a period of up to two weeks. The library remained under military supervision. The library's catalog lists "Dickens Works," "Coopers Works," "Darwin's Works," among others.

Dickens also reached the West Coast of the United States, carried there often by ship. In San Francisco, only one unauthorized Charles Dickens novel, *Hard Times*, was reprinted in the 1850s, according to Robert D. Harlan. Harlan states that final installments of *David Copperfield* published in England in November 1850 reached San Francisco by January 1851 (Harlan in Hackenberg 192). It was another fifteen years before San Francisco's libraries began to emerge, following the Civil War.

The Odd Fellows Library in May 1874 reported holdings of about 25,000 volumes, which grew to 27,000 by 1876. There were 230 bound newspapers and 1,850 periodicals. A circulation reported at "nearly 7,000 volumes a month, or about 80,000 a year" included a substantial circulation of fiction. The librarian (likely George A. Carnes) reported:

> In regard to popular tastes in reading [...] the results shown forth in the statistics of eastern libraries correspond, in the main, to our own. The eastern statistics find the demand for novels ranges from 70 to 75 percent. Our experience places the figures at 80 to 85 percent. With them, such writers as Dickens, Thackeray, George Eliot, Irving, and Hawthorne, acknowledged masters of fiction, take the lead. (*Public Libraries* 1003)

San Francisco was also home to What Cheer, a boardinghouse reading room begun by R.B. Woodward in 1852. Woodward consulted with Harper and Brothers and purchased 500 books from them. He then set up a restaurant with a library that eventually had 3,000 to 4,000 volumes by 1867. Irving, Thackeray, and Dickens are noted among favorite authors whose works were read there (Webb 603–06). J.M. Dent's copies of Dickens were amply distributed to California libraries after 1895. Illustrated volumes of Dickens and of Scott were among the popular works this company circulated, with Dickens editions printed in 1899, 1903, and 1907 (UCLA Special Collections, Online).

These findings show the broad distribution and availability of Dickens's works in libraries across the United States. Public libraries helped to democratize reading by making novels, essays, newspapers, scientific studies, and other documents widely available to a diverse public. Dickens democratized American reading because people of all classes and regions read Dickens and men and women who went to libraries read him in equal numbers. Reading Dickens was a social practice. The influence of peers promoted reading Dickens in apprentice libraries and YMCA libraries. Family members checked his books out of society libraries, or public libraries, and shared them with other family members. Libraries, which made Dickens's works widely available in periodical form, as well as in book form, contributed to the making of an America well-versed in Dickens's caricatures, sentiment, and spirit of reform.

Notes

1. Journals and letters that have been left by Dickens's readers also tell us that they approached Dickens independently, idiosyncratically. As Jonathan Rose has said, "These readers were not prisoners of the text, uncritically adopting a Dickensian frame of mind [....] when Dickens contradicted their own experience, they were not reluctant to say so" (113). While the reference here is to British common readers, there is evidence in library records to show that this is quite true of American readers as well. When Americans read journals or read in libraries, they were not controlled by reviewer preferences, or necessarily limited by public opinion. Nor do reviewers' readings necessarily represent the common reader's voice, as some critics have suggested. Rather, Dickens's American audience had their own readings of Dickens. This does not argue against the communal aspect of reading; it simply indicates that readers had their own minds and found what they each found in Dickens.

2. With respect to mechanics institutes and libraries, as Jonathan Rose notes, "mutual improvement provided invaluable training in forming and expressing opinions" (75). In America, as well as in Britain, autodidacts relied upon a network of friends for suggestions and guidance in their absorption with reading material. Through these networks, they developed their learning from books and periodicals. Peer influence upon reading habits is suggested in the sample of young apprentices presented here. As Rose points out, conscious co-operation with others in reading works available in the library was "an exercise in mutual education." Information and ideas contributed to a spirit of mutual education. Reading gained increasing acceptability as a collective activity (87).

3. Dickens's phrase about the mutuality of capital and labor was the comment, according to reports, which was most applauded. Martyn Lyons writes: "Charles Dickens, opening the Manchester Public Library in 1852, saw libraries as a guarantee of social harmony" (332). Lyons writes, "As Dickens himself was well aware, there was considerable reader resistance to the libraries' attempts to provide moral and edifying literature." See Martyn Lyons, "New Readers In the Nineteenth Century: Women, Children, Workers" in *A History of Reading in the West*, ed. Guglielmo Cavallo and Roger Chartier (Amherst: University of Massachusetts, 1999).

4. Rhees emphasized the importance of childhood reading. "A taste for reading useful books must, in like manner, be formed in youth, or it will rarely, if ever, be formed afterward." William Rhees, for one, believed that public libraries were as crucial as schools in the learning process. He wrote: "Good libraries are almost essential to the diffusion of useful knowledge, as good schools. Mere school studies do not reach every part and faculty of the mind. They do not discover and call out the latent powers which lie hid in our youth" (260).

5. F.B. Perkins of the Boston Library argued for placing fiction on the library's shelves. Providing what some people called "trash" could actually stimulate the reading habit the librarian said. "Readers improve, if so reading would not be particularly useful practice," he wrote. "The habit of reading is the first and indispensable step." He stated his belief that "those who begin with dime novels and story weeklies may be expected to grow into a liking for a better sort of stories" (Public Libraries [1876], 421–22).

6. Dickens is mentioned twice in Fanny Fern's *Ruth Hall* (182, 324) where we read "How the victimized man [...] like Dickens's young hero kept asking for "more" (182).

7. This librarian adds "There are, of course, many others called for quite frequently, but those named are much the more so, and several of them about equally." The librarian concludes that the boys read a lot of fiction because their minds and experiences of life are, at this point, most suited to this. Then underscoring the fondness of these boys for fiction, he adds a speculation of his own, revealing his own preference for "useful" non-fiction: "From this statement, it will appear that a large proportion of the books taken by our readers are works of fiction. This, we think, is to be attributed to their youth and limited education, and will, in many cases, be gradually changed for the better" (Rhees 261). Rhees writes, "He adds that this reading of fiction, however, has proved to be beneficial: we trust not a little good is accomplished even by this description of reading, as well as by its withdrawing them from idle and vicious associates" (262).

Most mechanics and apprentice libraries, however, were smaller than this one, ranging from about 3,000 at Newport and 3,500 in Philadelphia's Mechanics Institute at Southwark to 6,750 at the Association of Mechanics and Manufacturers in Providence.

8. The eclectic reading and similarity of titles read by both sexes is noted by Ronald J. Zboray, who claims that the doctrine of the women's sphere that argues for exclusivity in reading patterns does not appear in the New York Society Library 1852–54 records (164). It appears that women readers read male adventure novels. However, few

men read sentimental novels by female authors, aside from the most popular novels of the day, like Stowe's *Uncle Tom's Cabin*, or Warner's *Wide, Wide World* and *Queechy*. Ten percent of readers sought books in useful and fine arts, 9 percent read in theology and ethics, 7 percent in math and physics, and about 7 percent in periodicals.

9. Edward Edwards, in Free Town Libraries, estimated daily averages in Boston Library circulation at 250 in the first year, increasing to 588 by the library's sixth year, 628 in its ninth year, and 754 in the library's fourteenth year. In 1859, by Edwards' count, 149,468 books were borrowed. In 1862, 189,302 books were borrowed. In 1867, 208,963 volumes were borrowed. It was not specified how many of these books were Dickens volumes. Reading room statistics were "imperfectly kept," Edwards said. "Usually the number of readers is recorded, but not the number of volumes issued to them [....] Special record is made of the number of periodical publications, issued in the reading rooms, and also (during recent years) of the use made, within the building—in what is called Bates Hall—of books too valuable to be permitted to circulate" Edward Edwards, Free Town Libraries (New York: J. Wiley and Son, 1869), 289.

6

Learning from Fiction and Reality

CHARLES DICKENS'S FICTION HAD A SIGNIFICANT IMPACT upon the American imagination because his stories intersected with American life and his texts filled collective needs. Dickens's fiction served his American readers by providing markers of human experience: images, caricatures, manners with which they could identify. It gave them models by which to articulate their lives and stirred their imaginations, their sentiments, the social and theatrical construction of their lives where fiction crossed over into reality.

Post-colonial America took possession of Dickens. Reading the stories of Charles Dickens was a social activity, an exchange in which readers met and shared sympathy through their encounter with common texts. Dickens's American audience often interacted quite personally with his serialized texts, not only as a matter of imaginative escape, but as an act of imaginative re-creation. Dickens's stories encouraged this blending of fiction and reality by offering his audience what he called "the romantic side of familiar things" and characters who uncover the romance in the familiar by making discoveries or experiencing renewals. Dickens responded to the changes wrought by industrialization and unfolded his mysterious plots of inheritance to American readers who had inherited the potential of a vast continent. Dickens enabled Americans to see their world, to tell their own histories, and to enter the community of history, thought, and feeling that makes one's life immeasurably larger.

Reading Dickens could be described as a "democratic" activity: one that linked people across classes and regions. Walt Whitman, who worked as a printer for the *New World*, responded in 1842 to the *U.S. Democratic Review*'s claim that year that Dickens was anti-democratic, saying, "I consider Mr. Dickens to be a democratic writer [. . . .] I cannot lose the opportunity of saying how much I love and esteem him for what he has taught me through his writings and for the genial influence that these writings spread around them wherever they go" (Kaplan 99). Whitman saw that Dickens, much like the "Noiseless, Patient Spider" of one of his poems, was sending forth filaments and creating a web: a democratic space for his readers.

Besides being a source of laughter and merriment, Dickens's texts were for his American audience experiences in which their reality and his fictional figures met. Dickens was read in the midst of daily experience, both at home and in unlikely places, as in the case of George W. Bagby, who would one day become the editor of the *Southern Literary Messenger* in Richmond. Sailing on the James River on a boat through the Kunawha Canal, Bagby turned to his love for the novels of Charles Dickens. In 1869, he recalled that only the beauty of the scenery drew him away from his reading.

> As for me, I often went below, to devour Dickens's earlier novels, which were then appearing in rapid succession. But drawn by the charm of the scenery, I would often drop my book and go back on deck again. (42)

At the intersections of daily life and fictional experiences, readers like George Bagby took from Dickens what was useful to them. Dickens's characters entered the conversation of a variety of discourse communities and each group of readers reflected their specific concerns off his texts. Dickens helped some people to name their places in the world. As a model of writing, Dickens helped people to articulate their life stories, as Jonathan Rose has shown (111–15). Dickens was also a feature in the self-education of some readers like Amelia van Antwerp, who copied sections of *Dombey and Son* into her daybook (Antwerp Day Book, Sally Bingham Women's Center, Sm. Misc. Vols. Box 1). As people of different ethnicities used Dickens to help them to learn the English language, Dickens helped immigrants to become English-speaking Americans. For example, in the *Atlantic Monthly* in 1895 appeared an item about a German who came to America and enlisted in an army regiment of predominantly German immigrants. According to this report "in the leisure of camp life he undertook to learn English by himself by reading Dickens" (*Atlantic* [November 1895]: 718).

Likewise, Admiral C.H. Davis reported the story of an engineer who improved his English by reading Dickens:

> Mr. E. Schumann, an engineer, had been an assistant engineer in the service of Lloyd's Steamship Company, having been a long time on board the Saxonia. He was an excellent engineer and machinist. The manner in which he saved the Polaris from destruction [. . .] proved that he possessed great coolness and excel-

lent judgment. When he joined the Polaris, he could scarcely speak a word of English; before he returned to the United States he not only spoke the language well and fluently, but enjoyed reading the works of Dickens. (212–13)

Dickens became recommended reading. One reader, D.H.S., a 21-year-old Irish immigrant from Kerry, Ireland wrote to The Columbian Reading Union from St. Paul, Minnesota, asking for the editor's book recommendations. In his letter in *The Catholic World*, he wrote:

> To assist you, if possible, I will state what reading I enjoy. I love to read Dickens, not so much for his stories as for his sarcasm and the portrayals of all those odd characters of his. I have greatly enjoyed *Ben Hur, Fabiola, Vicar of Wakefield*, and a few of Bulwer's works. I have the complete works of Bulwer. Which, if any, of them would you recommend me to read? (*Catholic World* [July 1894]: 128)

No answer to D.H.S.'s query is recorded. However, many other nineteenth-century publications were quick to advise their readers on what they should read. Such reading advice appeared in manuals of conduct, or from ministers in religious tracts. This query to a newspaper reminds us that the texts of Charles Dickens attracted a variety of readers, for many different reasons.

Dickens's serialized texts offered an occasion for his audience to bring life-experience and imagination together.[1] Charles Dickens's novels, in the pages of American magazines, participated in the formulation of this personal and communal identity. For Dickens's readers, in recalling their own life-stories, were much like David Copperfield, wondering if they might become the heroes of their "favorite child," Dickens offered his readers a model of life-experience recorded. The novel, presented in the first-person narration of David, is a fictional autobiography. It offers a narrative form by which Dickens gave his readers a model by which to express themselves.[2]

Dickens's writing was used as a frame by which his American audience could interpret experience. As the language of Dickens's characters became part of American life, Dickens's fiction appears to have been quite close to reality for some. We have seen how Dickens's caricatures suggested to some readers people they had met in everyday life. For example, landscape architect Frederick Law Olmstead (1822–1903), the designer of New York's Central Park, referred to people he met in England as Dickens characters:

> As anybody who reads Dickens knows, this kind of rural package express is a common thing on the English roads, the carrier taking orders of country people for what they need from the towns, and bringing any parcels they should send for; taking live freight also when he is not otherwise filled up: David Copperfield, for instance. The representative of Mr. Barkis and Honest John Peerybingle was in the kitchen of the public house, and very glad to see us. (212)

This intersection of fact and fiction is found particularly in readers' encounters with a first-person narrative like *David Copperfield*. Some readers saw their own lives mirrored in Dickens's story. For example, Ida May Beard, writing her autobiography, mistook the first person narration of David Copperfield for Dickens's own autobiography. She writes of her marriage: "Our early married life reminded me of Charles Dickens and Dora, his first wife. You may remember what an awful time they had with their housekeeping"(14). This is an interesting comment, considering that Dora Spenlow is David Copperfield's "child-wife." Dickens's own wife was Kate. The Dickens's ninth child, Dora, named after the character in Dickens's novel, died in infancy. Even so, Ida May Beard sees her domestic life, or "housekeeping" reflected in Dickens's text, as if it were a factual account.

Perhaps this confusion of biography and fiction was not unusual, however. Certainly, *Robinson Crusoe* had been read by some as a true travel-account. John Bunyan's *Pilgrim's Progress* had also been taken by some for an actual journey, rather than an allegorical and metaphysical one.[3] Dickens signified something for these readers, who related scenes and phrases from his novels to their own lives. Mary Grey Lundie Duncan, writing in 1901 of her travels on a steamer across the English Channel, decided that her cabin was not to her liking. She cited Dickens as she wrote in her journal:

> The spacious saloon was hardly large enough to swing a cat in, and although like Mr. Dick in *David Copperfield*, I could say, "I don't want to swing a cat, I never do swing a cat; therefore, what does that signify to me!" Yet, I found it did signify, so I resigned my regret in the crowded cabin and very thoughtfully took a position on deck for the night. With a glorious full moon, and a sea without a ripple, the night passed most comfortably. (Duncan 24)

Fiction and reality appear to have come together in this woman's experience, as she alludes to her reading of Charles Dickens. Duncan assumes her reader's familiarity with Dickens's characters in *David Copperfield*. However, her associations are curious. Her particular focus on the chandler's shop bed has to do with her own voyage and her cabin accommodations. This has little to do with that "distress, want, starvation" that is greater for Mr. Dick. In Dickens's passage, in Chapter 35, Mr. Dick, despite the lack of "elbow room" is "perfectly charmed with his accommodations":

> Mrs. Crupp had indignantly assured him that there wasn't room to swing a cat there; but, as Mr. Dick justly observed to me, sitting down on the foot of the bed,

nursing his leg, "You know, Trotwood, I don't want to swing a cat. I never do swing a cat. Therefore, what does that signify to *me*?" (486)

Fiction writers, likewise, assumed their readers were familiar with Dickens. For example, in Adeline Dutton Train Whitney's novel *Patience Strong's Outings* (1869), her clearly resolute protagonist observes, "I can't help wondering, once in a while, if some people don't live all their lives in a climax." "I never heard of but one person who did," says another, "and that was Mr. Micawber [. . .] and you know how it was disposed of simply enough for him. If he is going to be continually arrested his friends have just got to be continually bailing him out" (117). Whitney, the well-traveled daughter of shipline owner Enoch Train, adds a note that she sensed the exaggeration of Dickens's creations: "Dickens put it in extreme, as his way is, but he puts the very doctrine of heaven into it, which is his way" (294).

In a story by Annie R. Blount of Augusta, Georgia, a poet, the narrator claims that *David Copperfield* has provided a kind of bibliotherapy, an education of feelings:

"What cured you?" "David Copperfield cured me, or, rather, that silly but loving little child wife of his. How wise of Dickens to remove her to a better world in her youth, and restore to the disappointed man the dreams of happiness that haunted his boyhood, by giving him that love which could alone satisfy an exacting soul like his. Fancy such a woman growing to mature womanhood, to old age, bah! and with such a husband! As it is, we can sympathize with, weep for, almost love the poor little butterfly, with its coaxing, winning ways. Its very foolishness is attractive because of youth, beauty, and an affectionate, clinging heart. But imagine her an old woman!" (446)

Here Dickens's story connects so deeply with one woman's empathy that she is "cured" by *David Copperfield*. She apparently sees her own life in Dora, who seems for her a perennial youth. Through Dora, Dickens provides this woman with an opportunity for sympathy with a young girl: one who may, in some ways, reflect herself as a younger woman. David Copperfield is viewed as a "disappointed man" to whom Dora restores "dreams of happiness." Blount, who was awarded the honorary title of Mistress of Arts at a Georgia college commencement and who dedicated her first poetry volume to Alexander H. Stephens, was interested in healing Confederate soldiers as a visitor to hospitals during the war. Dickens's characters, perhaps, served as a model for this empathy. Dora is for David Copperfield a romantic ideal, a hope, and sustenance. For Dickens, the "very doctrine of heaven which is his way" is placed into this character. We read David Copperfield's adulation of Dora in his narration:

> The more I pitied myself, or pitied others, the more I sought for consolation in the image of Dora. The greater the accumulation of deceit and trouble in the world, the brighter and purer shone the star of Dora high above the world... If I may so express it, I was steeped in Dora. I was not merely over head and ears in love with her, but I was saturated through and through. (460)

In Dickens's novel, we read: "Love was above all earthly considerations, and I loved Dora to idolatry, and Dora loved me" (537). Blount clearly regards Dora as a healing force within David Copperfield's life: the restoration of dreams of happiness.

This intersection of reality and fiction is underscored in an 1877 story by Mary Hart, in which a character Celine says: "There is David Copperfield, I liked so much because I saw it performed in the theatre, where everything is represented true to history." Celine, who represents a European immigrant to America, says that she reads "a great deal of English now." "I have been reading Dickens-Charles Dickens [. . . .] Are you acquainted with that author? I just think him splendid. What fine characters he thinks up!"

Celine may appreciate the author's fine characters, but Celine then places Miss Havisham (*Great Expectations*), Peggoty (*David Copperfield*), and Mrs. Bloss's servant Agnes (*Sketches by Boz*) in the wrong books. Perhaps this is because she got some of her Dickens through the theater, second-hand (Hart 430).

When young women, like Celine, read Dickens, the author apparently helped them to reflect upon their feelings. He also helped others to write. For example, Dickens's presence is obvious in the work of an anonymous writer of a story that appeared in 1872. While it is always difficult to tell whether a writer of fiction may have been drawing upon personal experience in developing an imaginative story, the following scene suggests that its writer was keenly aware of Dickens. Dickens's Lizzie Hexam has perhaps a shadow life in "Elinor's Trial," an unsigned story in *The Catholic World* in March 1872. "Lizzie" remarks on a mysterious copy of one of Dickens's novels that she has found in the household:

> "Why, Mr. Schuyle, the only copy of Dickens' *Barnaby Rudge* that I have at home is the New Riverside set papa gave me only lately—since—" She pauses a little confused "since I have seen Elly last. Besides, I don't make notes on the margins of my books, and I am quite sure Elly would not in mine. I think it could not have been my name you saw, "Elizabeth Lennox" and from your "brother Robert."

Then suddenly it dawns upon her: "Why, that's papa! And the name is his sister's! She is Elinor's mother." The mystery is solved. Dickens's *Barnaby Rudge* has made its rounds in the family (*Catholic World* [March 1872]: 790–802).

The story supports the view that individual copies of texts were exchanged among readers in families and households. The same Dickens novel might be read, at different times, by several different readers within the same family. These stories became a point of communal connection, a site in which a family's imagination and their experiences of the real merged.

Home was important to Dickens, even though his childhood home dissolved in poverty and the adult home of his marriage came apart after 1850. We can see the sense of hearth and home throughout many of his novels and some characters, like Nicholas Nickleby even offer a definition of home:

> "When I talk of homes," pursued Nicholas, "I talk of mine . . . If it were defined by any particular four walls and a roof, God knows I should be sufficiently puzzled to say whereabouts it lay; but that is not what I mean. When I speak of home, I speak of the place where, in default of a better, those I love are gathered together, and if that place were a gipsey's tent, or a barn, I should call it by the same good name notwithstanding." (NN, XXXV, 443).

In many accounts of home reading from this period, we hear of people reading aloud in their rooms. In Anita Dwyer Wither's diary in November 21, 1861, for example, she writes "The captain is reading *Oliver Twist* to me." (16) Elizabeth Missing Sewell (1815–1906), the British novelist and essayist, writes in 1858:

> A story read aloud is also a test of the characters of those who listen to it. More insight into children's dispositions may be gained in seasons of recreation, by the knowledge of their favorite heroes and heroines, and the criticisms passed upon their conduct, than by the most careful observation made during the hours of study. And it, besides—and this is very important—a band of sympathy between the reader and the listeners. There are comparatively few pleasures which the young and old can fully sympathize; and it is most important, therefore, to seize upon the enjoyment of reading, and to connect it with all that pleasant interchange of thought, and unity of feeling, which tends so strongly to bind human hearts together. (48)

When a Dickens story came into the home, it was read, or heard, by people of all ages. In this way, his works became like familiar friends, in effect bonding the family around common texts and sentiment. W.H. Venable underscores Dickens's sentimentality as he writes in March 1864:

> Dickens leads them through fiction's most enchanting fields [. . . .] Sam Weller said the art of writing a love letter is to make the recipients wish there was more

of it. This is the art of book making too! How we wish to continue some book! We do continue them in our own way, creating volumes and volumes of thought out of what has been suggested in the printed words. The authors feel a loathness to finish the best books. How fondly Dickens lingered on the last pages of Oliver Twist, weaving his words of parting into poetry! You would believe tears spotted those pages. (167)

Imaginative reading of this sort appears as a kind of promise for the readers of Charles Dickens. Readers encounter in his stories characters who, like themselves, read imaginatively. Esther Summerson reads to Mrs. Jellyby's children. In "Mugby Junction," a Christmas number for 1866 in *All the Year Round*, Phoebe, who is handicapped, teaches children to read. In "Doctor Marigold," the title character tries to teach an orphaned girl to read and helps her to attend a deaf and dumb school. In *Our Mutual Friend*, the newly financially endowed Noddy Boffin enlists Silas Wegg to teach him to read, so he can become cultured. Dickens suggests that it is good to be able to read with imagination. For Scrooge, who once read *Arabian Nights* and *Robinson Crusoe* with enthusiasm as a child, now only reads account ledgers. Dr. Alexandre Manette, the prisoner, can no longer read his aimless scratches on the Bastille wall. And pitiful is the life of Jo, the street sweeper, who is characterized by his lack of ability to read (*Bleak House*, i, XI, 177).

> Don't know that Jo is short for a longer name. Thinks it long enough for him. He don't find no fault with it. Spell it? No. He can't spell it. No father, no mother, no friends. Never been to school. What's home? Knows a broom's a broom and it's wicked to tell a lie.

As the narrator ponders the life of Jo, who sweeps the crossroads, Jo's lack of literacy becomes evident:

> It must be a strange state to be like Jo! To shuffle through the streets, unfamiliar with the shapes, and in utter darkness as to the meaning, of those mysterious symbols, so abundant over the shops, and at the corners of the streets, and on the doors, and in the windows! To see people read, and to see people write, and to see the postmen deliver letters, and not have the least idea of all that language-to be, to every scrap of it, stone blind and dumb! (i, XI, 198)

Readers of Dickens entered a tension between his fictional world and their own factual world. In his introduction to *Household Words*, Dickens himself gives us some idea of the emphasis he would place in his periodical on the imagination:

> No mere utilitarian spirit, no iron binding of the mind to grim realities, will give a harsh tone to our Household Words. In the bosom of the young and old, of the

well to do and of the poor, we would tenderly cherish that light of Fancy which is inherent in the human breast; which, according to its nurture, burns with an inspiring flame, or sinks into a sullen glare, but which (or woe betide that day!) can never be extinguished. To show to all, that in familiar things, even in those which are repellent on the surface, there is Romance enough, if we will find it out. (*Household Words* I.113–14)

The reader of a Dickens story encounters a fictional world in which a tension is established between the two poles of the romantic and the familiar. One senses a tension between the familiar and the strange. As Robert Newsom puts it: "Dickens fascination is for neither the romantic nor the familiar singly, but for both together" (9). Readers' responses to Dickens suggest this tension between the imaginative and the real. When they encounter the unusual or the strange alongside the familiar, they sometimes think of a Dickens story they have read.

It is in this connection, William Axton says, that G.H. Lewes's theory of the hallucinative character of Dickens's imagination "may tell us something about the peculiar nature of the novelist's relationship to his narrative on one hand and to his readers on the other" (Axton 142). Such hallucination creates atmosphere; in it he "appears to be as much a witness to events as the reader" (144). As Axton puts it:

He may have wanted, in short, to make this point of tangency between two orders of reality impinge on his reader with the same intensity it had for him. Moreover, a technique like this profoundly alters the relationship between reader and writer [. . .] for a personal contact has been created quite outside the framework of the narrative. (ibid.)

If this was Dickens's intention, comments from American readers suggest that his method was successful. For example, striking images in the ordinary circumstances of daily life remind Anna Alice Chapin (1880–1920) of Dickens. Chapin, who lived in Greenwich Village in New York, wrote a chapter in her autobiography called "The Magic Door," in which she describes a place that reminded her of the "stage sets" she recalled from Dickens's novels. One day, she came upon a place that looked to her like a warehouse. Then "it appeared to be a particularly desolate looking cellar [. . . .] an expanse of general dusty mystery, and in the dingy distance, a flight of ladder-like steps leading upwards to a faint light" (228).

"It's one of Dickens's impossible stage sets come true," I exclaimed. "It looks as though it might be a burglar's den or somebody's backyard, but anyway, it isn't a restaurant."
"It is too!" came back at me triumphantly. "Look at that sign."

By the faint rays of a streetlight in nearby Sixth Avenue, I saw the shabby little wooden sign, "The Samovar." This extraordinary place was a restaurant after all! (225–26)

The restaurant stairs in Anna Chapin's Greenwich Village strike her as being unusual, to her mind, Dickensian. This blurring of fiction and reality, or stage and world, appears in the reception of Dickens's works because Dickens himself encourages this through his texts. His sentiment and melodrama, his stage sets and hallucinative imagination compel readers to look with Louisa Gradgrind through the crack in the fence of reality at the circus that lies beyond it. In *Hard Times* (1854), with Louisa, the reader is invited to participate in the fire-gazing at the hearth that is an image of the imaginative life (25).

> "Have you gone to sleep, Loo?"
> "No, Tom. I am looking at the fire."
> "You seem to find more to look at in it than ever I could find."

Eventually, Louisa responds to her brother's inquiry:

> "I don't see anything in it, Tom, particularly. But since I have been looking at it, I have been wondering about you and me, grown up."
> "Wondering again!" said Tom.
> "I have such unmanageable thoughts," returned the sister, "that they *will* wonder." (Ch. VIII, 51–52)

As readers negotiated fact and fiction, Dickens's criticism of Gradgrindian "fact" appears to be what most American readers remembered about *Hard Times*.[4] The novel famously begins: "Now, what I want is, Facts. Teach these boys and girls nothing but Facts. Facts alone are wanted in life [. . . .]" In this novel, Dickens defends the imagination and the human need for "fancy," or unrepressed imagination. Wonder, play, imagination are positioned against the dehumanizing aspects of a utilitarian world of fact. American educational theorists, recognizing this, drew upon Dickens's themes in *Hard Times*. Hervy Backus Wilbur (1820–1883), a philanthropist who ran the state asylum for the mentally retarded at Syracuse, has *Hard Times* in mind when he claims, "the natural observation of childhood is so devitalized." He turns to *Hard Times* for an illustration of problems in education and writes of a system that is "so subverted from its ordained purpose of importing power and warmth and vigor to the whole spiritual nature, as to draw upon itself the scoring finger of the satirist" (23). While Hervy Backus Wilbur implicates English schools, he does not cite the same problem in American ones. However, one of America's most prominent educators, Henry Barnard, in 1876, points directly to Dickens to critique an American educational system based upon a British one: "No teacher before me who has read Dickens *Hard Times* will fail to recall the following scene." He quotes the scene in which Sissy Jupe is being asked what a horse is. Sissy's father is a horse trainer at the circus and for her the animals are beloved creatures. Grandgrind badgers her:

> "Give me your definition of a horse."
> (Sissy Jupe thrown into the greatest alarm by this demand.)
> "Girl number twenty unable to define a horse!" said Mr. Gradgrind for the general behoof of all the little pitchers. "Girl number twenty possessed of no facts, in reference to one of the commonest of animals!"

Barnard has read about how Gradgrind carries "a rule and a pair of scales, and the multiplication table always in his pocket" with which he is "ready to weigh and measure any parcel of human nature, and tell you exactly what it comes to." How this posture deprives humanity is evident in his treatment of Sissy Jupe, "Girl Number 20." Gradgrind's shaming is directed at a girl who loves horses and has a caring relationship to those that are featured in her father's circus: a world of entertainment representing imagination. Sissy, who also loves flowers, would wallpaper her room with flower designs. Gradgrind finds such representations intolerable and insists, "But you mustn't fancy [...] That's it! You are never to fancy." It is in such terms that Gradgrind dreams of the educational future: "We hope to have, before long, a board of fact, composed of commissioners of fact, who will force the people to be a people of fact, and nothing but fact."

After citing this, Barnard writes:

> The features of a school system thus graphically described are the features of the Home and Colonial society's system and I regret to say that what is known in this country as the Oswego System is its lineal descendant [. . . .] Is such endless repetition of obvious qualities a natural and nourishing food for the childish mind? Will it never tire of such a gruel of utilitarianism? (488)

In Dickens's famous scene in which the heart-filled Sissy Jupe is criticized for her inability to define a horse in pseudo-scientific classificatory terms, Dickens asserts the importance of feeling and imagination. Horses, as living creatures, cannot be defined in scientific terminology alone. Nor can human beings, like Sissy Jupe. These American educators recognize Dickens's suggestion that education combine fact and imagination.

John Swett, for his institute address in California in 1876, quoted the comments of Dickens's Gradgrind at length, reciting the entire beginning of *Hard Times*. He prefaced this with: "Charles Dickens deserves to be classed among English educational reformers, for his caricatures of English schoolmasters, in the character of Squeers." To this, Swett added Thomas Gradgrind (117). Like Swett, Wilbur and Barnard contrasted Dickens's dire images in *Hard Times* with what they regarded as the positive potentials of education. For Wilbur, this was "power," "warmth," and "vigor," for Barnard something "natural and nourishing." Each of them could see that throughout Dickens's novel, there are, as Paul Schlicke notes, "constant reminders of the inadequacy of Gradgrind's view of things" (143–44) and that there is renewal through Sissy Jupe, to whom Dickens calls attention at a point of crisis.[5]

A combination of fact and fancy is the ideal the novelist Justin McCarthy pointed to in his novel *Lady Judith* (1871):

> This school was equally strong on sentiment and statistics. If one could combine Gradgrind and Rousseau, he would thus have constructed an idealized symbol— *a beau ideal*—of Charles Escombe's Young England. (20)

Critics of Dickens's *Hard Times*, however, protested against what they viewed as Dickens's disparagement of facts. Bernard Henry Becker wrote:

> despite the denunciation of political economy, which is nothing if not statistical, as the "dismal science" and the unlovely portrait drawn of Mr. Gradgrind, the lover of facts—the errors into which the human intellect has been led by that great "parent of error a priori" have been in modern times abundantly exposed by the stern logic of facts. It would, indeed, be difficult to exaggerate the influence exercised by statistics at the present moment over every department of human thought. (278)

Writing on "Economic Science," Edward Livingston Youmans (1821–1887) registered his upset with Dickens:

> And here I cannot but express my deep regret that one to whom we all owe, and to whom we all pay, so much gratitude, and affection, and admiration, for all he has written and done in the cause of good, I mean Mr. Charles Dickens—should have lent his great genius and name to the discrediting of the subject whose claims I now advocate [. . . .] His descriptions are just as like to real Economic Science as "statistics" are to "stutterings," two words which he makes one of his characters not very naturally confound. He who misrepresents what he ridicules, does, in truth, not ridicule what he misrepresents. (283–84)

Could it be that Mr. Youmans did not grasp the satire, or that he did not read *Hard Times* as satire? Youmans, an American born scientist whose brother had studied with Thomas Henry Huxley, argues further against Dickens:

> Much as I am grieved, however, I am not much surprised, for men of purely literary culture, with keen and kindly sympathies which range them on what seems the side of the poor and weak against the rich and strong, and, on the other hand, with refined tastes, which are shocked by the insolence of success and the ostentation incident to newly acquired wealth, are ever most apt to fall into the

mistaken estimate of this subject which marks most that has yet appeared in his new tale *Hard Times*. Of wilful misrepresentation we know him to be incapable; not less is the misrepresentation to be deplored. (ibid.)

Dickens's biographers assert that he embraced facts and was not averse to the use of statistics. However, for Dickens, facts without fancy lead to a deadening of the imagination, which he regarded as a vital quality in life. And so he sought what he called "the romantic side of familiar things."[6]

> The English are, so far as I know, the hardest worked people on whom the sun shines. Be content if, in their wretched intervals of pleasure, they read for amusement and do no more. They are born at the oar, and they live and die at it. Good God, what would we have of them. (Letters N II, 548, Charles Knight, March 17, 1854)

Along with his concern for "the amusements of the people," Dickens regarded fancy as important to him personally. In a letter of June 1867, he wrote: "I think that my habit of easy self-abstraction and withdrawal into fancies, had always refreshed and strengthened me in short intervals wonderfully" (N, III 531, W.H. Wills, June 6, 1867).

To Miss Burdett-Coutts, he wrote in 1850: "It would be a great thing for all of us, if more who are powerfully concerned with Education, thought as you do, of the imaginative faculty" (Letters C, 175, September 6, 1850).

Some of Dickens's readers recalled their own experiences of school through the lens of Dickens's stories. Recalling Dickens's portrayal of Squeers, Mary Narcott Bryan (1841–1923) associated Dickens's *Nicholas Nickleby* with her memories of school in Greenbriar White Sulphur Spring in North Carolina. "My experience at this school was very sad indeed; the teacher became offended with me in some way and made my life miserable" (34).

Andrew Kennedy Hutchison Boyd's memories of school are laced with a fiery reform spirit as he recalls *Nicholas Nickleby*. He imagines, in 1866, that there are in the British schools more schoolmasters like Squeers, then writes:

> The bullying schoolmaster has now become an almost extinct animal, but it is not very long since the spirit of Mr. Squeers was to be found in its worst manifestation, far beyond the precincts of Dotheboys Hall. (Boyd, *Leisure Hours* 257)

The boys of Dotheboys Hall are kept under the strict command of Squeers. As Nicholas Nickleby first encounters them, on his first day as a tutor, the reader is introduced to this troubled group of students:

> Pale and haggard faces, lank and bony figures, boys of stunted growth, and others whose long and meager legs would hardly bear their stooping bodies. Faces

that told of young lives that from infancy had been one horrible endurance of cruelty and neglect. Little faces that should have been handsome, darkened with the scowl of sullen, dogged suffering. (NN VII)

Squeers is certainly demanding and abusive. Dickens's criticism is laced with a bit of satire, aimed at Squeers' ignorance:

> Obedient to this summons there ranged themselves in front of the schoolmaster's desk, half-a-dozen scarecrows, out at knees and elbows, one of whom placed a torn and filthy book under his learned eye.
>
> "This is the first class in English spelling and philosophy, Nickleby," said Squeers, beckoning Nicholas to stand beside him. "We'll get up a Latin one and hand that over to you. Now then, where's the first boy?"
>
> "Please sir, he's cleaning the back parlour window," said the temporary head of the philosophical class.
>
> "So he is, to be sure," rejoined Squeers. "We go upon the practical mode of teaching, Nickleby; the regular education system. C-l-e-a-n, clean, verb active, to make bright, to scour. W-i-n, win, d-e-r, der, winder, a casement. When the boy knows this out of the book, he goes and does it. It's just the same principle as the use of the globes. Where's the second boy?"
>
> "Please, sir, he's weeding the garden," replied a small voice.
>
> "To be sure," said Squeers, by no means disconcerted. "So he is. B-o-t, bot, t-i-n, tin, bottin, n-e-y, ney, bottiney, noun, substantive, a knowledge of plants. When he has learned that bottiney means a knowledge of plants, he goes and knows 'em. That's our system, Nickleby. What do you think of it?"
>
> "It's a very useful one, at any rate," answered Nicholas. (NN, VII, 90–91)

In Chapter 13, Boyd read:

> As they lay closely packed together, for warmth's sake, with their patched and ragged clothes, little could be distinguished from the sharp outlines of pale faces, over which the somber light shed the same dull heavy coulour; with here and there, a gaunt arm thrust forth: its thinness hidden by no covering, but fully exposed to view, in all its shrunken ugliness. (NN, XIII)

Squeers raps the staircase with his cane: an instrument of abuse. He greets the boys in his school derisively: "You lazy hounds!" His harsh intolerance is immediately captured. "Ah! You had better be down directly, or I'll be down upon some of you in less." Mrs. Squeers is equally abusive: "Do you want your head broke in a fresh place, Smike?" demanded his amiable lady in the same key. In Boyd's reading, Dotheby's Hall has many parallels with his own experience. He sounds a hopeful note, that bestial schoolmasters like Squeers are now "almost extinct."

American poet W.V. Thompson, in his poem "Savannah" in 1871, contrasts the "tyrant's rule" with the more beguiling experience of reading Dickens, a teacher of "great precepts":

> [. . .] To the boy at school
> Crushed 'neath the rigor of a tyrant's rule,
> When shadows born of ignorance give way
> To dawn of sober truth. We wept, we smiled
> A thousand times we laughed; we were beguiled
> Out for our very selves, we dwelt in air
> And far below us left each pining care
> When Boots appeared; when Weller cracked the joke
> Or Captain Cuttle, moralizing spoke . . .
> Our hearts like DICKENS never sage could teach
> Like him who gave us gladness without measure
> Great precepts hid in sweetness and pure pleasure. (407)

Mrs. Almira Hart Lincoln Phelps, an educator, insisted that the problems cited by Dickens were British ones. She wrote in 1876: "When Charles Dickens was recently in our country [. . . .] I had a strong desire to invite him here that he might see an American school, different from the miserable pictures which he had drawn of English schools" (114). Mrs. Phelps, in a nationalistic spirit, insisted that American schools were far different from these negative images of English schools that Dickens had presented. Phelps's language may contradict this at times, however. She refers to the "inmates of the establishment" she taught in "massive granite buildings overlooking the Patapsco River." Lessons were taught in buildings "giving to the indweller a sense of elevation and upliftedness" with deep recessed windows and massive walls with huge chimneys that Phelps says would "combine to give the impression of a Gothic castle of the middle age." She speaks of Dickens as she also discusses the work of Harriet Martineau: "we owe much to the genius of the former (Dickens), for his sketches of life in its various phases [. . .] but it is unfortunate when writers of fiction forget that there are such realities as truth and fact" (116).

William Bentley Fawle, who would become a teacher, thought differently. In 1867, he remembers an incident from school:

Once when I had done my two sums in Subtration [*sic*] and set them in my book, and been idle an hour, I ventured to go to the master's desk and be so good as to set me another sum. His amazement at my audacity was equal to that of the almshouse steward when the half-starved Oliver Twist asked for more. He looked at me, twitched my manuscript towards him and said, gutturally, "Eh! you gnarly wretch, you are never satisfied!" (53)

Others, like Taylor Root in 1869, found in Dickens a resource. Root saw in Dickens a means of developing interesting science lessons: "A scientific lecture can be made more interesting to children than a story," he wrote. "Whoever has read 'The Chemistry of a Candle' or 'The Chemistry of a Tea Kettle' in Dickens's *Household Words* will testify, I am sure, to the truth of this assertion" (180). In his section "On reading aloud," Root also emphasized the connection between education, Dickens, and an image of home:

> The good mother, ever busy in the service of her children and her husband, sits knitting on the opposite side of the hearth. The elder daughters are serving or crocheting, the children are half-busied with paints, or quiet toys, and all are listening to an elder son or brother, who is reading aloud some interesting book of travels, or one of Dickens's stories. He reads in no drawling, sing-song tone, but throws life and character into the language of the author. He delivers the remarks of "Cap'n Cuttle" in a rough, solemn, oracular voice, or imitates the hopeful tones of "Wal'r's" voice, or the "no-consequence" air of "Mr. Tots"—as if he were the traveller or the adventurer—so they'll want to stay awake to hear brother read [. . . .] Almost all children can be taught to read well. (89)

As Mrs. Phelps worked diligently on the formation of young women, several American writers were formulating an image of the successful commercial man. Not everyone saw Dickens in the shadow of American press criticisms of *American Notes* and *Martin Chuzzlewit*. For some, Dickens was an exemplary figure. Dickens was Americanized as a model of the success myth of the self-made man. Following Emerson's insistence on "Self-Reliance" (1841), through Samuel Smiles' *Self-Help* (1859), or the first novels announcing the American Horatio Alger myth (1867), the cult of self-help was strong in America. Several authors on the topic presented Charles Dickens as a representative figure and a point of reference for American exceptionality. Regarding Dickens as a celebrated maker, his readers could identify themselves with the heroic. The *American Whig Review* in September 1852 wrote: "The position attained by Mr. Dickens is eminent and remarkable. Were it not for the constant misuse of the term, we should style him as self-made man" (*American Whig Review* [September 1852]: 205).

In Charles C.B. Seymour's *Self-Made Men* (1858), Dickens is a central figure, mentioned eighty-four times. Likewise, William Matthews makes use of Dickens as a model of success in his self-help genre book. He refers to Dickens's character Mr. Micawber and to other Dickens characters for examples (Matthews 300). W.H. Barnes's "A Chapter on Self-Made Man" in *Ladies' Repository* (April 1855) makes much of Dickens's character. Mr. Bounderby of *Hard Times*. There are fourteen references to Bounderby, whose presumption to appear as a self-made man is deflated by Dickens in the course of that novel. Works by British authors printed in America also advanced the cause of self-improvement. In *Great Fortunes and How They Were Made* (1871), James Dabney McCabe (1842–1883) a British author of at least six books published in America, offers Dickens as one of his primary examples (116). Alexander Murdoch Gow, in 1873, notes a Dickens address in which Dickens attributed his success to "attention" (108).

Educator Henry Copee saw a different Dickens. Writing in 1873, he found historical value in Dickens's novels. Copee writes that "Dickens's delineations are eminently historic, and present a better notion for the period than the general history itself" (455). After mentioning several of Dickens's novels, Copee writes:

> Besides these splendid works, we must mention the delight he had given, and the good work he has done in expanding individual and public charity by his exquisite Christmas stories. (457)

Copee sees Dickens as a writer who touches the emotions:

> His tenderness is touching, and his pathos at once excites our sympathy. He does not tell us to feel or to weep, but he shows us scenes like those in the life of Smike, and in the sufferings and death of Little Nell, which so simply appeal to the heart that we are for the time forgetful of the world which conjures them before us [. . . .] Dickens is bold in the advocacy of truth and in denouncing error; he is the champion of honest poverty; he is the foe of class pretension and oppression; he is the friend of friendless children; the reformer of those whom society has made vagrants. (ibid.)

Beyond Dickens's appeal of sentiment, Copee values Dickens as a reformer. He suggests that readers of *Nicholas Nickleby* feel "wonder and applause" at the exposing of the harshness of the Yorkshire school of Dotheboys Hall.

> Many a school prison under that name was fearfully exposed and scourged. The people read with wonder and applause; these hints of cruelty were scrutinized, and some of them suppressed, and since Nicholas Nickleby appeared no such school can live, because Squeers and Smike are on every lip, and punishment awaits the tyrant. (455)

Copee points to Dickens's emotional appeal, to a sense of dramatic justice that he believes other readers like himself feel. For Copee, the contrast of Vincent Crummles' theater with Squeers' Yorkshire school in *Nicholas Nickleby* arouses "wonder and applause" in Dickens's audience.

Dickens's American readers entered the tension in his texts between the imaginative and the real, or the romantic and the familiar. Amid their actual journeys, they made imaginative ones. As they shared with each other Dickens's serialized fiction, fancy intersected with the ongoing facts of their lives. In this tension between the fictional and the real, some readers appear to have read Dickens's *David Copperfield* as if it were factual biography. Others recognized his texts as fictional, but used Dickens's characterizations to represent people in their own lives when they turned to writing their life stories. Dickens's texts became for them a source of learning. Several readers made use of Dickens's texts in their own efforts at self-improvement: Dickens's stories served as models by which they could write to begin to tell their own stories, or as a means for some to learn the English language. Situated in the midst of their daily realities, Dickens's audience participated in his stories as learners and discoverers engaged in an imaginative enterprise.

Notes

1. "How deliberately the Victorians turned commonplace activities into communal entertainments may be seen in their treatment of reading and writing," Anne C. Rose writes. "[. . . .] and they read to each other to build bonds of sentiment by savoring literature together" Anne C. Rose, *Victorian America and the Civil War* (Cambridge UP, 1992), 123. Patricia Okker points out that the communal reading experience of serialized fiction involved an awareness that others were reading the same "social stories." See Patricia Okker, *Social Stories* (Charlottesville: University of Virginia Press, 2003), 1–21.

2. For a discussion of how Dickens's readers modeled his writing as they wrote their autobiographies, see Jonathan Rose, *The Intellectual Life of the British Working Classes* (Yale UP, 2001), 111–15.

3. Readers like Ida May Beard may have confused fact and fiction, or the author with his narrator. An interesting discussion of readers participation with texts can be found in Jonathan Rose, "The Difference Between Fact and Fiction" in *The Intellectual Life of the British Working Classes* (Yale UP 2001), 92–115.

4. Dickens wrote: "[. . .] to teach the hardest workers at this whirling wheel of toil, that their lot is not necessarily a moody, brutal fact, excluded from the sympathies and graces of imagination; to bring the greater and the lesser in degree, together, upon that wide field and mutually dispose them to a better acquaintance and a kinder understanding is one main object of our Household Words" (*The Speeches of Charles Dickens*, Kenneth Fielding, ed., Oxford UP; MP I.113–14). G.H. Lewes spoke of Dickens's "hallucinatory" qualities: "Of him it may be said with less exaggeration than of most poets that he was of 'imagination all compact'; if the other higher faculties were singularly definite in him, this faculty was imperial. He was a seer of visions; and his visions were of objects at once familiar and potent [. . . .] So definite and insistent was the image, that even while knowing it was false we could not help, for a moment, being affected, as it were, by his hallucination" (G.H. Lewes, "Dickens in Relation to Criti-

cism" *Fortnightly Review*, 17 (February 1872), reprinted in Stephen Wall, ed. *Charles Dickens: A Critical Anthology* (Harmonsworth: Penguin, 1970), 191–202.

5. Dickens, in *American Notes*, observed the rote responses of girls in a Cincinnati classroom who performed their lessons for him. For him, these sincere, passive repetitions were probably not unlike those of Bitzer in *Hard Times*. Reading from "a dry compilation, infinitely above their powers," Dickens says that they "blundered through" and says that he "should have been much better pleased and satisfied if I had heard them exercised in simpler lessons, which they understood." Cincinnati was "a beautiful city," he said. But of the city's "means of education, which are extended, upon an average, to four thousand pupils annually," it is clear that Dickens would have preferred more imagination and understanding (*American Notes* 144–46).

6. Dickens's phrase appears in his opening address to his readers as he begins his periodical *Household Words*. A discussion of the relation of this to Dickens's approach to his fiction appears in the work of Robert Newsom, *Dickens and the Romantic Side of Familiar Things* (New York: Columbia UP, 1975).

7

Dickens in a House Divided

DICKENS'S STORIES OF SOCIAL CRITICISM of the 1850s were a pervasive and influential part of the public conversation among diverse American readers, north and south. These stories had social influence because Dickens's audience was engaged in the common ceremony of reading them in serial installments as the nation splintered politically, economically, and regionally. Dickens's texts were a common denominator among a variety of constituencies throughout America, contributing to the conversation of democracy, even amid division. Some readers disputed Dickens's claims when he touched upon issues personally relevant to them, such as southerners, when the topic of slavery arose. But all of America—white, black, north, south, male, female, in all classes and occupations, read him.

Dickens's serialized novels specifically participated in the American public's self-discovery of their common identity as human beings, despite regional, class, and racial differences. They were common texts shared at a time when home, community, or nation was put to the test by regionally situated politics and when political needs appearing in print divided that imagined community. Readers were engaged in acts of interpretation affected by each reader's identity and specific cultural situation. Dickens's stories, while usually set in Britain, express the tension of these times in America, the pressure that change and modernity placed upon home and community. Reading Dickens had an impact on the reader's sense of self. Indeed, Dickens's stories were read differently by readers from different regional and socioeconomic backgrounds. However, the point is that they were read widely.

Regionally situated American readers brought their concerns to their reading of Dickens's texts. Despite class and gender differences among them, as well as considerable ethnic, religious, and occupational variation, sharing similar texts, like those of Dickens, helped them to reflect upon the problems of their time. Dickens's texts were referred to in the public sphere where debate over these issues was occurring. His texts suggested a convergence of home-space and public-space, the mediation of which presented a challenge for his readers.

The American appropriation of Dickens brought the author's ideas into contact with the audiences of southerners like William Gilmore Simms, the popular author who edited the *Southern Quarterly Review*, who defended the institution of slavery, and abolitionists like Frederick Douglass, editor of *The North Star*, who opposed it. Dickens continued to be the British opponent with whom American authors like Simms or Melville contested and the popular friend whom many readers embraced. In this way, Dickens continued to intersect with American issues and with America's efforts to create a literature of its own.

American hopes and sorrows were mirrored in the struggle that Dickens portrayed within a London environment. Luther Giddings, a soldier in California, in 1853 reflected upon the issue of entangled justice in *Bleak House* and compared it with American courts:

> Hence there was at least, none of that tedious, heart-breaking and mind destroying litigation against which Dickens has recently turned his powerful pen. Certes, but our court at Monterey would have decided even the tough case of "Jarndyce and Jarndyce" at a single sitting. (47)

Although set in an English context, *Bleak House* suggested the troubling political, social, and regional dimensions that were causing a breach between Americans. Like Giddings, Frederick Douglass, Harriet Beecher Stowe, abolitionist minister Samuel May, and others saw that Dickens's *Bleak House* pointed to social divisions that stemmed from systemic causes, while revealing unexpected human connections (Samuel J. May, Diary, 1868; Cornell University Library). In *Bleak House*, as David Paroissien has asserted, by linking ideals of reform with a compassionate vision of life, Dickens fulfilled the purpose of promoting his audience's self-reformation (31).

Dickens's socially charged novels of the 1850s had influence in America because they provided a language for critiquing human behavior, institutions, and political or educational systems amid powerful political and economic circumstances. Read in the atmosphere of home, or in other communal settings, Dickens provided an imaginary space in which people could deal with these public issues.[1] Ministers like Andrew Kennedy Kutchison Boyd (1825–1899) of Massachusetts found inspiration for sermons:

Your returning good for evil must be a real thing. It must be done heartily and without reservation in your own mind, or it is nothing at all. Uriah Heep, in Mr. Dickens's beautiful story, forgave David Copperfield for striking him a blow. (Boyd, *Autumn Holidays* 207)

Later readers like Robert Q. Mallard of Virginia, a Presbyterian minister who wished to write about public issues, admired Dickens and viewed him as a model:

I wish I had the genius of a Dickens, so skillful in portraying life among the lowly, that I might do justice to the odd creature whose name heads this letter. (64)

For these readers, the issues of ethics, justice, and charity were foregrounded by Dickens's fiction. Meanwhile, collective reading of Charles Dickens's fiction supported communal contact. Despite a growing regional divide, north and south, Americans read Dickens aloud together, sharing the sentimental drama of his fiction at home. The reading of *Bleak House*, a text featuring division, was a socially unifying practice. This ongoing fictional experience shared by families and friends brought together groups of people in social acts of reading. Dickens's serialized fiction, circulated widely in America as a common text, provided for affective ties, helping to connect people who shared his stories.

Through his appeal to sympathy and sentiment, Dickens created reading companions, or friends, and supported sympathetic connection. Dickens was the American readers' literary companion, even as social, political, and economic forces divided them. In numerous reviews and commentaries, he was recognized as the reader's friend. For James Nack (1809–1879), who had lost his hearing at a young age and worked at City Hall in New York, Dickens was a "friend." His poem "To Charles Dickens" addresses Dickens's ability to open the heart and points to the sympathy and sentiment aroused in Dickens's American audience by the childhood deaths of Paul Dombey and Little Nell:

> Friend of my heart! friend of the human race!
> Though I may never gaze upon thy face
> Nor clasp the hand that has such wonders penned
> by thy prevailing spell
> I watch the ebbing life of gentle Paul
> Or, looking up, as at an angel's call
> Pursue the heavenward flight of "Little Nell"
> Heart leaps to heart, and I embrace my Friend (72)

Viewed by some as a friend and by others as an English enemy, Dickens and his novels intertwined with American writing and reading. *Bleak House,* representing an overturning of home, could be read alongside Hawthorne's *House of the Seven Gables* and Stowe's *Uncle Tom's Cabin,* which appeared at about the same time. Mutual influence among these writers is apparent here, as Weisbuch and others have indicated. Dickens's novel also stimulated resistance and response from Herman Melville in "Bartleby the Scrivener." As Weisbuch points out, Dickens was not only America's favorite novelist at this time, but also could be viewed as the primary English novelist: "Thus, it is not merely Poe and Hawthorne whom Melville is defending. Melville against Dickens is, for Melville, a representative case: the New World against Britannia" (Weisbuch 51–52).

In the light of Dickens, some readers like Melville defended the prospects of the American nation against English culture. Others put Dickens to political uses, such as defending the causes of abolition or reform. Many southern readers, who otherwise enjoyed Dickens's fiction, argued against his depictions of slavery. The author's social critiques did not appeal to all American readers, however. Some American readers preferred the comical Dickens and wanted him to go back to the lighter style of *Pickwick,* as Ford has pointed out (100). They persisted in their view of Dickens as a comic writer, even when Dickens increasingly showed a darker side of his social criticism. For example, Dickens the humorist was clearly preferred by physician John Brown (1810–1882), who wrote in 1865:

> Thackeray and Dickens, the first especially, are, in the deepest and highest sense, essentially humorists, the best, nay, indeed the almost only good thing in the latter being his broad and wild fun; Swiveller, and the Dodger and Sam Weller, and Miggs, are more impressive far to my taste than the melo-dramatic, utterly unreal Dombey, or his strumous and hysterical son, or all the later dreary trash of *Bleak House.* (12–13)

Rather than returning to his lighter style, Dickens increasingly couched his humor in satire and proceeded to draw out the ambiguity in characters like Dick Swiveller and to portray alienated urban environments in which displaced children like the Artful Dodger dwelled. Dickens's *Bleak House,* like many of his novels, is a story of the loss of home, as in *Oliver Twist,* or *The Old Curiosity Shop,* and the search to discover deeper connections, or reconstructions. Reading Dickens aloud was one way in which families or communities of readers could restore these connections.

The reform impulse in Dickens influenced its literary counterpart in America. Dickens affected the sentimental and reform-minded efforts of Harriet Beecher Stowe, whose *Uncle Tom's Cabin* was the best selling novel of this time. Stowe was an avid reader of Dickens. Despite some early reservations about Dickens's religious outlook, she admired the spirit of reform in Dickens. Her sentimental scenes of Little Eva in *Uncle Tom's Cabin* owed much to Dickens's Little Nell and, as in much of Dickens's work, home appears often as a central figure in her novels. According to Stephen Railton, *Uncle Tom's Cabin* was "the most Dickensian of all Victorian American novels" (87). Railton says, "One lesson that Stowe learned from Charles Dickens was that the mass audience could be made to feel an injustice more readily than it could be logically convinced of one" (78).

Dickens exerted an impact upon America through Stowe, who created characters in her own fiction who read Dickens. We meet readers of Dickens in the second paragraph of her story *The Coral Ring* (1855), as we read: "'You insulting fellow!' replied a tall, brilliant looking creature who was lounging on an ottoman hard by, over one of Dickens's last works" (Stowe, *Coral Ring* 375). Judge Ferguson, a character in Stowe's story *Pink and White Tyranny*, is another reader who is deeply affected by Dickens: "He confessed toleration of Scott's novels, and had been detected by his children both laughing and crying over the stories of Charles Dickens" (Stowe, *Pink and White Tyranny* 188).

For Frederick Douglass, Dickens's *Bleak House* and Harriet Beecher Stowe's popular *Uncle Tom's Cabin* were akin in spirit: both challenged injustice. Douglass attempted to construct a readership around Dickens's *Bleak House* by reprinting in the Rochester based *Frederick Douglass Paper* the story for his readers, many of whom were African Americans. For Douglass, the repression of the slavery issue in America mirrored the repressive legal machinations of Chancery in Dickens's novel.

Because a discussion of Stowe's novel occurred alongside the serialization of Dickens's novel in the *Frederick Douglass' Paper* in 1852, it is important to consider the possible interaction of these two novels in the minds of Douglass' readers. It is clear that his readers brought their concerns about slavery to their reading. Unfortunately, with respect to the reading of Dickens's serialized story in the *Frederick Douglass' Paper*, the record is sparse. As Elizabeth McHenry points out, Douglass' readers were more inclined to carry on a dialogue about Stowe's anti-slavery novel (124–26). Dickens was hardly mentioned. One is left to conjecture about how the intertextuality might have brought themes of justice, anti-slavery, and reform to bear upon any further reading of a Dickens story by African American readers. We may ask if the readers of the *Frederick Douglass Paper* saw the thematic connection between *Bleak House* and the Stowe novel they repeatedly discussed, or if the editorial positioning of *Bleak House* on the fourth and final page of the paper made it an afterthought for these readers.[2]

While it is difficult to pinpoint the responses of the African American readership of the *Frederick Douglass Paper* to *Bleak House*, it can be ascertained that there were several such readers. That some African American readers were familiar with both Dickens and Stowe at this time is suggested by the dialogue in a novel, *Megda*, by African American writer Emma Dunham Kelly. Meg, the primary character of *Megda*, is described as an enthusiastic Dickens reader:

> "Wonder where they are," observed Meg absently. She had just made up her mind to begin *Martin Chuzzlewit*; it was so thick she would not be able to finish it before the next week if she didn't. Meg was an ardent admirer of Dickens. (36)

This is a household of readers, in which Lill is also reading a book by Harriet Beecher Stowe:

> "Tuesday night, isn't it?" asked May.
> "Of course, goose," laughed Lill, looking up from "*Pink and White Tyranny.*"
> (Emma Dunham Kelly, Schomberg Collection, New York Public Library)

Dickens's fiction also inspired New Orleans poet and dancer Adah Isaacs Menken (1835–1868), who dedicated her first and only book of poetry, *Infelicia*, to him (Philadelphia: Lippincott 1873). The *Cincinnati Commercial* referred to her as "the very queen of melodrama, Protean farces, and comedy." The *Cincinnati Daily Times* wrote questioningly: "As Pip, in her own dramatization of Dickens' *Great Expectations*, she is the embodiment of the author's ideal—a pure and innocent character?"[3]

African American poet Mary E. Tucker's sentimental poem of the 1880s, "Did You Call Me, Father?" was suggested by lines in Dickens's *Our Mutual Friend*. Tucker begins her poem with a caption from that novel: "She opened the door, and said in an alarmed tone: Father, was that you calling me?" The poem indicates that there was no response (18).

Willie Parker, in *The Freedman's Story* (1866), was hopeful that perhaps someday a writer would emerge to vividly tell the story of African American life. He wrote, "It is reserved for a black Shakespeare or Dickens to lay open the wonderful humor, pathos, poetry, and power which slumbers in the Negro's soul" (152). Dickens was a model for David Fulton, a Pullman Palace Car Company employee in Brooklyn who often wrote to the *Brooklyn Eagle* under the pen name John Thorne about the difficulties of southern blacks. He looked to Dickens as a writer who expressed "the human viewpoint" that was needed from any writer approaching these difficulties. Thorne asserted in 1895 that Hamlin Abbott, a writer in *The Outlook* on "the Negro problem," was wrong to see racial relations as "a problem that a white man must settle."

Instead, Thorne, observing that "[t]he disposition to kick the underdog is as old as the human race" thought of images from Dickens:

> I often think of Charles Dickens's story of that wretched boy, Oliver Twist, chased by a wild mob through the streets of London, headed by the real thief. (27)

Anna J. Cooper suggested in the 1890s that "the average English man takes no exception to the humorous caricatures of Dickens" (175). Cooper asked whether there had been an American literature when America was "a mere English colony" and claimed that copying English texts "cuts the nerve of originality." Cooper admired Dickens's work, but said "twas not till the pen of our writers dipped in the life blood of their own nation and pictured out its own peculiar heart throbs and agonies that the world cared to listen" (ibid.). Drawing upon Dickens and thinking of his British readers, Cooper sharply criticized the history of American slaveholders. Such men, she suggested, were hardly the model of morality. Dickens, likewise, in writing of the British had to provide a reliable assessment of human character:

> But were Dickens to introduce an average scion of his countrymen to a whole congregation of Quilps at the same time informing him that these represented the best there was of English life and morals, I strongly suspect the charming author would belifted out of the toe of said average Englishman's boot, in case there shouldn't happen to be a good horsewhip handy. (124)

Charles Dickens's reach among African American readers like these was something unknown to John Stevens Abbot (1805–1877), who in *South and North* (1860) refers to those "debased negroes" and claims: "Their souls were not stirred by the [. . .] silvery toned and polished periods of Edward Everett, or by the irresistible humor of Irving or Dickens"(106). Obviously, Ada Isaacs Menken, Mary Tucker, Willie Parker, and John Thorne were not only stirred by Dickens but also sought to stir other people with their writing.

Dickens appears to have been familiar both among freemen and among literate slaves and their children. Curiously, one child of a slave in Jacksonville, Florida, was named "Charles Dickens." According to Cyrus Augustus Bartol, in a letter to James Fields of January 29,1869, he had met "a black man Boz." Would it not please Mr. Dickens, Bartol wrote, "to know his influence, so long ago, penetrated into the barbarism of that very slavery among us he hated, with such a flavor of the humor which is the organ & outlet of his own humanity as to give him this double name-sake" (Fields, Letter 242). Did a slave, who had read Charles Dickens, name his or her child after the author? Or did a slave holder, who read Dickens, name the boy that Bartol met in Florida?

Dickens was well known to a literate southern audience that did not agree with his position on slavery. Yet, they read Dickens and southern periodicals reviewed his novels. The *Southern Literary Messenger*, for example, regularly carried news or reviews of them. One of its writers asserted the beauty and integrity of southern homes by pointing to Dickens's England for contrast. In describing a Spring day in the Virginia mountains in 1857, the writer proclaims: "Even a Gradgrind or a Bounderby, if he possesses a differential of a soul, must rejoice" (*Southern Literary Messenger* [June 1857] : 332–36). Likewise, writing in 1860, Samuel Mordecai says that in Richmond, Virginia "Dickens eyes might be relieved from the glare of new houses by moss covered old houses"(27). Mordecai's pointing to moss covered houses may be his way of asserting Virginia's venerable traditions, while thinking of Dickens's descriptions in *American Notes* of the fledgling nation's apparently insecure new habitations.

David Brown (1786–1875) took up the issue of slavery in 1853, referring to Dickens's *Bleak House* in a narrative that wandered between personal commentary and fiction. He wrote:

> When I read the graphic accounts of D'Israeli and Dickens, of the miserable state of the London poor, and reflected gratefully, that in our far more favored country such things could never be. Alas, what a delusion! (183)

Brown quoted Dickens's *Bleak House* (1852) and said:

> I dare say Mr. Skimpole Dickens, you know very little about it (slavery). I dare say that English writers who meddle with our affairs in this way, would often appear less ridiculous and dangerous in their own country, less, if they would try honestly to know more and write less about what they are shamefully and it seems blissfully ignorant. They have much knowledge of our geography as they ought to have of the geography of the moon. (274–75)

Lurking behind Brown's text is a long memory of Dickens's final chapter of *American Notes*, in which Dickens sharply criticized slavery. Brown asserts that Dickens is ignorant of slavery and southern "geography." Indeed, Dickens never travelled south of Virginia. Yet, this "geography" is also a metaphor for a social institution, an economic practice, and an agrarian way of life central to southern commerce and the southern lifestyle.

In a venture into fiction, Brown created southern characters, one of whom remarks on the slaves that "They are rarely exposed to great dangers of any kind." The writer's images of England are from Dickens: A man who addresses English ladies claims that there are British women "in the charitable work of subverting the institution of southern slavery or at least to begin with to interfere with it as to prevent its frightful results."

Sister: "What frightful result? Are the Negroes starving to death, like the poor people of Ireland and Scotland?"

"Ladies, unless your celebrated Mr. Dickens be as reckless a romancer as our Mrs. Stowe, your own institutions of jurisprudence alone, disrupt and ruin, in person and estate, many more families than do our institutions of slavery. *But the fancies of romance aside,* the authenticated facts communicated by your Parliamentary investigations of the working of your poor laws, and even your poor house reports, tell of such cruelties as are utterly unknown to our system of slavery, and in such numbers as to make any heart but one of stone bleed, if not to break!" (47–48)

This text asserts a benevolent system of slavery that contrasts with *Bleak House's* Chancery, or Stowe's Simon Legree. The character this writer invents, a fictional voice, posits a perceived reality against "the fancies of romance." Dickens's *American Notes*, with respect to slavery, are viewed as fictional. Likewise, an earlier writer in *The Southern Quarterly Review* places evidence from southern newspapers against Dickens's alleged comments of reports of physical violence against slaves. Citing the authority of a gentleman, "a respectable medical friend" who has looked through reading rooms, this writer puts forth his or her own view that the system of slavery is not as harsh as Dickens portrays it to be. Noting Dickens's examples, the writer asserts that "these are not every day occurrences" (*Southern Quarterly Review* [June 1843]: 308).

In case after case, most southern autobiographers call Dickens's brief accounts of southern slavery in *American Notes* the views of an outsider. Many southern readers, who held firmly to the importance of slavery for the southern way of life, sharply rejected Dickens's anti-slavery comments. Lucien Bonaparte Chase (1817–1864) of South Carolina wrote, in *English Serfdom and American Slavery* (1854), of his opposition to Dickens's comments, which he quoted from *Household Words* (173, 179, 202–4). Letitia M. Burwell states in her memoirs, *A Girl's Life in Virginia Before the War* (1895), that Charles Dickens had no business criticizing the southern institution of slavery because he had no first-hand experience of it:

Mr. Thackeray was once a guest in one of these places, but Dickens never visited them. Could he have passed a month at any one of the homes I have described, he would, I am sure, have written something more flattering of Americans and American life than is found in *Martin Chuzzlewit* and *American Notes*. However, with these we should not quarrel, as some of the sketches, especially the one on "tobacco chewers," we can recognize. (131)

Ms. Burwell proceeds to make Dickens' writings on America a nationalistic matter and the exemplar of English public opinion. She writes:

Every nation has a right to its prejudices—certainly the English people have such a right as regards America, this country appearing to the English eye like a huge mushroom, the growth of a night, and unsubstantial [. . . .] No one has a right, without thorough examination and acquaintance with the subject, to publish as facts the exaggerated accounts of another nation, put forth by its enemies. The world in this way receives very erroneous impressions. (132–33)

Burwell makes some attempt to excuse Dickens, whom she sees as essentially a comic writer, while holding her ground in support of America and southern institutions. "But sorrow and oppression, we suppose, may be found in some form in every clime [. . .] Even Dickens, whose mind naturally sought and fed upon the comic, saw wrong and oppression in the 'humane institutions' of his own land!" (134).

We have previously seen that Mary Narcott Bryan (1841–1923) associated Dickens's *Nicholas Nickleby* with her memories of going to school in the south at Greenbriar White Sulphur Spring in North Carolina. "My experience at this school was very sad indeed; the teacher became offended with me in some way and made my life miserable" (Bryan 48). Bryan, in her autobiography, also defended the benevolent slave-holding she had seen on her family's plantation. She writes:

When I heard Mr. Dickens read scenes from *Nicholas Nickleby* the tone of voice in which he personated Smike sent a chill through me, for I had never before heard a human voice express such hopeless despair. Can there be in England, thought I, human beings afraid of the sound of their own voices? (28)

In Bryan's statement, the mistreatment of Smike is seen as something foreign and distant from Bryan's own experience, or perceptions, of slavery. Instead, Bryan talks about her inclination as a young girl to teach and to nurture the slaves on the family plantation. For her they were "the smiling indispensibles." She responded to their music and dance, the "music of the banjo, quilting parties, opossum hunting." Some of these slaves were literate, she says. "Many could read and in almost every cabin was a Bible. In one was a prayer book, kept by one of the men, a preacher" (49)

Bryan claims that she and her sister taught some of the slaves how to read:

As soon as my sister and myself had learned to read and cipher, we were inspired with a desire to teach the negroes who were about the house and kitchen; and my father promised to reward my sister with a handsome guitar if she would teach two boys, designed for mechanics, arithmetic, and the guitar was awarded. All who tried learned to read, and from that day we have never ceased to teach all who desired to learn. (48–50)

Given Bryan's familiarity with Dickens's *Nicholas Nickleby*, we may wonder if she read any Dickens with the slaves on her family's plantation.

Dickens's merits were a subject of debate among some southerners. In a letter to the *Southern Literary Messenger* "L.L." defends Dickens against the comments of one of the magazine's writers, who prefers Thackeray:

> I refer to his estimate of Mr. Dickens. His paragraph referring to this great writer seems to me unjust in the highest degree, and I think very few of your readers, with the exception of those who swear by Major Pendennis and Becky Sharpe, will be likely to agree with the author of the article.

At this point, "L.L." says that he/she will now discuss "what elevates Mr. Dickens as a novelist above his distinguished rival." For this reader, Dickens's quality turns upon what he/she sees as the author's charity and philanthropy and what the reader views as Dickens's capacity to remain cheery and to laugh.

> Mr. Dickens loves and pities while he derides. I am not quite sure that Thackeray is wrong in his philosophy of human life, but I know that Dickens has a purer philosophy whether it be truer or not [. . . .] Mr. Thackeray desponds and doubts about this humanity which we wear [. . .] while Mr. Dickens finds in human life and character far more of sunshine, even when temporary clouds obscure it. Where the author of 'Esmond' sighs, the author of 'David Copperfield' only laughs. (*Southern Literary Messenger* [March 1853]: 490)

Dickens's *Bleak House,* appearing in America at the time of this letter, was widely circulated throughout the south. In Virginia, the parents of E.S. Nadal read *Bleak House* and dubbed their son "Mr. Guppy," after the clerk in the story who proposes to Esther Summerson and then investigates her identity. Years later, Nadal recalled being bewildered by the new identity his parents had given him:

> *Bleak House* was then coming out in *Harper's Magazine* and my father and mother were in the habit of speaking of me as "Mr. Guppy," because I was thought to look like Mr. Guppy in the illustrations of that novel. I didn't know who Mr. Guppy was, but I believed him to be the author of Mc Guffrey's "Second Reader." (4)

What is obvious from these examples is the widespread popularity of Dickens's fiction among southern readers. Dickens's characters have a memorable place in their lives. It is clear that Southerners continued to read Dickens's work and felt a connection with them, even though they may have disagreed with the man's stance on slavery. Regional politics may have affected *how* they read but it did not slow down *that* they read.

By the mid-fifties it was clear that Charles Dickens was writing a darker, social criticism into his novels. *Bleak House* was followed by *Hard Times* (1854), with

its critique of divorce laws, labor strikes, and industrialized education and its affirmation of fancy and imagination. American poet Thomas Williams Parsons
saw the social critic in Dickens. In the year that *Hard Times* appeared, he wrote:

> Yes, Nestor, pause! quit not your home for this
> Imperfect picture of an author's bliss:
> Let Dickens tell you how this age of steam
> Reduces poesy to weight and ream
> Retails cheap genius, brings the Muses down
> And turns Parnassus to a trading town
> Yes, the fine flashes of instinctive thought
> In silver lines and golden periods wrought
> In some blest mood of happy Fancy Struck
> From flinty labor, by a touch of Luck
> Little shall there be whispered or be thought
> About the last new book, and what it brought;
> Little of copyright and Yankee thieves
> Or any wrong that Dickens' bosom grieves. (36)

For the poet, industrial fact has reduced poetry to measurement and has
turned a holy place, America's promise, into "a trading town." Parsons appears to hope that with "a touch of Luck" some "fine flashes of instinctive
thought" and fancy might be thought. Reformers and politicians may have
found this inspiration in Dickens's novels. Lydia Marie Child observed the
impact of Dickens's characterizations on human feeling. To her friend Sarah
Shaw she wrote on March 23, 1856:

> I have admired several of Bulwer's heroines, but I never loved one of them and
> hugged them to my heart as I do Little Nell, and Esther, and Little Dorrit. Dick-
> ens is the great Apostle of Humanity. God bless him. (96)

Child compared Dickens's talent for characterization with Harriet Beecher
Stowe's skill. Discussing Stowe's *Dred* in a letter to Lucy and Mary Osgood,
she wrote:

> Dickens has transfigured humanity in the same way in several characters placed
> amid the meanest surroundings. Witness dear Little Dorrit. How miserably trashy,
> in comparison, seems N.P. Willis's twaddle about "the porcelain clay of human-
> ity," meaning those who dance with dukes, and speak in the 'subdued tone indica-
> tive of social refinement.' Bah! Ugly old Tiff is worth a hundred such. *His* tones are
> modulated by inward feeling. He wears the star of God's order of nobility. (119)

Dickens's sentimental appeals for moral justice through Oliver Twist,
Smike, Little Nell, Tiny Tim, or Jo the crossing sweeper in *Bleak House*, made

an impact among American readers like Child who were well prepared for Dickens's stories of reform.[4] As Raymond Williams observes, many stories in magazines during this time embodied reform themes, and writers at this time developed improvement tracts; "the tales belong, however simply, to an older tradition of moral fable or parable" (78).

America's legislators responded to *Bleak House* (1852), *Hard Times* (1854), and *Little Dorrit* (1856). In the halls of government in Washington, the oratory of William Seward in his "Hail Columbia" speech drew upon Dickens. The *National Review* noted that Seward "is reported to have used expressions that seem to have been borrowed straight from the notebook of the immortal Pogrom" in Dickens's *Martin Chuzzlewit* (*National Review* [July 1861]: 22).

Henry Clay, long involved in the international copyright debate in Congress, referred to Dickens in a Senate discussion toward the end of his illustrious career. Clay apparently was expressing his discontent with political circumlocution when he said:

> *Redgauntlet* has been cited as an authority in this body, but I think I might cite another of the same class which would be more in point. It is *Bleak House* by Charles Dickens, in which the circumlocution office is so graphically described. It would be decidedly more appropriate to our present action. (Chittenden 320)

Clay effectively made his point, although he had referred to the wrong book: Dickens's Circumlocution Office appears in *Little Dorrit*, the novel that followed *Bleak House*. At least one government official must have recognized the inaccuracy. According to James Fields, Charles Dickens once said that Abraham Lincoln's Secretary of State, Edwin Stanton, had "a most extraordinary knowledge of his books and a power of taking the text up at any point."

> It gave him (Dickens) natural pleasure when he heard quotations from his own books introduced without effort into conversation [. . . .] He did not always remember, when his own words were quoted, that he was himself the author of them, and appeared astounded at the memory of others in this regard. (241)

Charles Sumner, who had been Dickens's guide around Boston during Dickens's first visit to America in 1842, shared letters about Dickens with the poet Henry Wadsworth Longfellow. In the U.S. Senate, Sumner referred to "the disparaging pictures by Dickens of the Pennsylvania System" (514).

Dickens's Smike was held up as an illustration of slavery by William Darrah Kelley (1814–1890) in the election debates of 1864. While speaking in the House on Andrew Jackson and Stephen A. Douglas, Kelley was heard to say:

> Mrs. Nickleby said that Smike was 'the most biddable creature in the world' and after the Democratic Party yielded to the dictation of Southern slave drivers, it

became just about as biddable a creature as Smike; it did whatever the Southern Nicklebys told it to do. And thus it has taken to denouncing all the doctrines held by the great leaders and founders of our party. (96)

Political figures in the public eye themselves were at times compared with Dickens's caricatures. For example, political writer Maunsell Bradhurst Field compared former president Franklin Pierce to Dickens's Horace Skimpole and Mr. Micawber:

He was no more to be relied upon than Horace Skimpole or Micawber. He had no fixed will of his own, and all through his administration he was battledored and shuttlecocked about by Jefferson Davis and William L. Marcy, the masterminds of his very able cabinet. (162)

Another Washingtonian, Mary Clemmer Ames (1839–1884), drew upon Dickens to critique the politicians she saw around her in the capital city. She wrote:

The Gradgrind politicians of today have voted to dump down a railroad depot in its very center, because Mr. Thomas Scott wants it and because they have fine railroad passes, and a few other prerequisites in their pockets. (155)

These examples of the wide reading of Dickens among American politicians suggest not only his popularity but that his novels had an impact upon their thinking about public issues. It is not clear that Dickens's fiction had any political impact in the United States but it can be suggested that Dickens's fiction did enter the conversation about social reform. Politicians, northern abolitionists, and southern readers were all acquainted with these texts. So too were female readers. Many women found in Dickens's novels models of womanhood. Esther Summerson, in *Bleak House*, represents a young woman venturing into the social world. She becomes a governess, the would-be keeper of a house, later the keeper of an impoverished neighborhood. Her self-denying activity, which appears terribly self-effacing to some contemporary feminist critics, was viewed by some readers as an exemplary model of charity.

For example, Ella Farman creates a character who wishes to be like Esther:

I have pored over Muriel's *Bleak House*, lingering about that sweetest Esther Summerson, wishing I might be like her in my household, but that day I looked long into my bedroom mirror to see if it really was a face to comfort and rest anyone. (219–22)

In Constance Fenimore Woolson's story "The Ancient City" in 1875, Sara tells Martha:

I am like Esther in *Bleak House*, when after that unwished for and unpleasant offer of marriage, she nevertheless found herself weeping as she had not done since the days when she buried the dear old doll in the garden. (292)

While Esther Summerson was a favorite angel for her female readers, others read Mrs. Jellyby not as the satirized proponent of telescopic philanthropy but as the "new woman." Whereas, *Scientific American*, in September 1864, saw Mrs. Jellyby in *Bleak House* as part of "the mission of machinery," she was viewed as a modern woman by a female character in "A Woman's Luncheon," a play by an anonymous writer published in *The Atlantic* in August 1895. In the play, several women, who are intended to represent actual Dickens readers, discuss Mrs. Jellyby. Indeed, here fiction meets fiction, but the playwright's characters might be said to represent types of response to Dickens's character.

> Mrs. Walton: When Dickens wrote *Bleak House*, Mrs. Jellyby was considered an amusing caricature, just the type of woman to be avoided. It seems rather odd that she is at last being brought to the front as the typical modern woman.
> Teresa: I cannot admit it. We neglect no home duties.
> Mrs. Coxe: I'm sure I do. I neglect everything.
> Mrs. Ogden Smith: And so do I.
> Miss Walton: Mrs. Jellyby was in advance of her day. Nowadays civilization has caught up with women's expanding energies . . .
> Teresa: I cannot admit that Mrs. Jellyby [. . . .]
> Miss Synott: Oh, yes, Dickens possessed "the prophetical soul of the wide world dreaming on things to come" and actually invented the modern woman.

This play, like the diaries of readers, show nineteenth-century female readers to be accepting of Dickens's women, rather than resistant. The wife of David Brown in 1853 wondered what reading was like in Charles Dickens's own home. "I wonder if Mrs. Charles Dickens has read *Oliver Twist* and *Bleak House*," she asks (Brown 44). Mrs. Jane Tandy Cross, in 1870, thought that Dickens portrayed females very well and admired the talent of Charles Dickens for portraying women and reflecting the female psyche. She wrote:

> Dickens knows more of her than most women know of themselves. How often does he, in depicting her, startle you into tears! I once spoke to a gentleman of a passage in one of Dickens's books, in which he represents a poor woman as devoured by anxiety all the while she is absent from home, lest her child should suck the steam from the spout of the tea-kettle. The gentleman saw nothing in it, and thought it silly. I said to him: that is because you are not a woman. Dickens saw deeper, and knew that these very absurdities and impossibilities are what seize upon her apprehensive heart. He understands how she is a self-torturer.

How he has painted her fidelity in the character of Nancy in *Oliver Twist*! As you read her sad story of her life, you say: That has all happened. And in *Little Dorrit*, what touching glimpses does he give us of the not violent, but lifelong desolate wretchedness of poor Pet, who married the unworthy artist! In a single page, in describing the death of Mrs. Dombey, he lays before you such years of dreariness that the heart grows sick and faint over it. Even in the flimsy and selfish character of Little Dorrit's sister is it all woman.

The writer emphasizes the pathos in Dickens's writing. Cross appears to consider Dickens's recognition of emotion and sentiment a "deeper" insight into a woman's heart. She believes that there is a psychological realism in Dickens's portraits of his female characters.

The prototype of that foolish, passionate girl is found everywhere. In a single page describing the death of Mrs. Dombey he lays before you such years of dreariness that the heart grows sick and faint over it. I need not remind you of how many fathers have written from the backwoods of America saying they saw revived some darling child which had been lost. Old Betsy Trotwood is every inch a woman, striding through life, holding the hand of her mythic niece, David Copperfield's sister Betsy [. . . .] But it is useless to enumerate the women that one finds in those charming books of Dickens—women that grow up under his hand as they do in nature, living, breathing creatures, full of thought and feeling. (153–55)

Mrs. Cross's story points to the models of womanhood that she saw in Dickens's female characters. These were women, like Betsy Trotwood, "every inch a woman," or the self-torturing Nancy and the dying Mrs. Dombey. In Mrs. Cross's view, they are women of "fidelity," women anxious for their children, who hold to their "mythic" hands. In Little Nell, these female readers saw the suffering child, whose hand they wished to hold. The sentimental underpins their responses. Like Annie R. Blount in 1860, perhaps others felt "healed" by the image of Dora Spenlow in *David Copperfield*. Such female readers were obviously drawn to Dickens's women and sensed a correspondence between his fictional worlds and their own lives.

Meanwhile, American women were gradually working in the new factories, like those at Lowell, joining reform activities through churches, or assisting in emerging professions like nursing and teaching. An independent figure such as this appears in Louisa May Alcott's novel *Work: A Story of Experience* (1873). The protagonist, a girl named Christie, becomes an actress who becomes very familiar with the works of Charles Dickens. The novel begins with Christie's shocking affirmation of her independence:

"Aunt Betsey, there's going to be a new Declaration of Independence."
"Blessed and save us, what do you mean, child?"

"I mean that, being of age, I'm going to take care of myself and not be a burden any longer." (2)

The image reflects that of Nicholas Nickleby, who goes off to support his family by teaching at Dotheboy's School and then in Mr. Crummles' acting troupe. The narrator says that

> toward the end of that second season several of Dickens's dramatized novels were played, and Christie earned fresh laurels. She loved those books, and seemed by instinct to understand and personate the humor and pathos of many of those grotesque creations. (47)[5]

Alcott suggests that work is necessary for a young woman's well-being. We can see the theme in the novel's first pages, as Christie says to her aunt: "if I had been a boy, I should have been told to do it long ago. I hate to be dependent, and now there's no need of it, I can't bear it any longer" (ibid.).

Women like Christie, in Louisa May Alcott's tale, or like Esther Summerson in Dickens's *Bleak House,* point to the emergence of women working within the public sphere.

When Dorothy Richardson, an Iowa woman, went to work at a box factory in New York, she encountered two women, Mrs. Smith and Phoebe, who were unfamiliar with Dickens's novels:

> They had never heard of *David Copperfield.* They stared at me in amazement when I rattled off "goody goody writers for goody goody girls"; their only response being that their titles didn't sound interesting. (84)

She writes in 1906 of Mrs. Smith, stirring a paste pot as she comments on "story books" like Jean Libbey's *Little Rosebud Lovers* (1886), a melodramatic and sentimental romance. Phoebe, the other worker, chimes in with titles that Richardson refers to as "trashy fiction." Richardson mentions to the women that she has read Alcott's *Little Women* four times and says, "Their curiosity was aroused over the unheard thing of anybody ever wanting to read a book more than once" (84–85). Richardson's account shows that Dickens had not reached these women, although other fiction had. However, library records and sales of Dickens in America strongly suggest that working class women were among his readers.

Other female Dickens readers remained focused in their traditional domestic role. One of these was Mrs. Starrs, who compiled a scrapbook that was kept by her son. Beyond Willie Starrs' inscription, "My mother's old scrapbook revised and amplified" are clippings from Mrs. Starrs' reading, including notes on history, social topics, the Methodist Book Concern, and "Dickens's

Picture of the True Woman." Mrs. Starrs kept pieces titled "Female Education," "An Angel in Every House," "A Word to the Wife" (Starrs 8–10). In a
study of Civil War period reading, Ellen Gruber Garvey points out that "many
people, North and South, male and female, compiled newspaper writing into
scrapbooks" (171). Meanwhile, the exchange of newspapers, or of fiction like
the novels of Dickens, reassured people on the battlefield that they were in
contact with those at home. Dickens's stories served as resources for what
Garvey has called "the work of feeling" (175).

Dickens's fiction participated in this "work of feeling" in women's lives
as some young women took their influence out of the home, through their
churches, into charitable works in their neighborhoods. The spirit of reform
in Dickens had caught their imaginations. For the character Muriel in William Douglas O'Connor's story, *Harrington, A Story of True Love* (1860), it is
Dickens who provides the model of charity:

> "Where are you going?" asked Emily.
> "First and foremost, I am on a pardiggle excursion among two or three fami-
> lies of my parish," replied Muriel.
> The narrator then says:
> Dickens' *Bleak House* was coming out in serials at that period, and Muriel,
> with the rest of the town, was full of it, and was particularly delighted with Mrs.
> Pardiggle, to whom she jestingly likened herself when she made visits of charity.
> "The Pardiggle path will first lead me to poor Mrs. Roux," continued Muriel.
> "Mrs. Roux, in Southern Street, the wife of a colored man who was here the
> other day to wash the studio. She had another child a couple of months ago, did
> I tell you? And we must take care of the black babies as well as the white ones,
> you know." (130)

While fictional, Muriel may be representative of women of the author's
acquaintance who were engaged in such activities. These actions of charitable
service appear as an image of binding inter-racial community in a novel produced at a time when race was a significant issue in American public life. Maternal concern for a baby brings Muriel out of the home, into a black woman's
home, where she is Mrs. Pardiggle, the philanthropic associate of Mrs. Jellyby
in *Bleak House*. There is no satirical reading of Mrs. Pardiggle here; rather, she
is a model of goodness.

Dickens's novels of the 1850s became part of the conversation of his American audience. As *Putnam's* editor writes: "But, whenever Dickens tells a story,
the world listens, and as fast as his tale is told it becomes a part of the world's
daily life and conversation" (*Putnam's* [August 1857]: 46). These novels,
which suggest domestic settings unsettled by public events and legal, educational, or political systems, were distributed across race, class, and region to

northern and southern readers in the years before the Civil War. Democratizing reading, Dickens's stories intersected with the social concerns of American readers. The novels presented female readers with characters they viewed as significant models of female conduct. Dickens's social criticism and spirit of reform stimulated reformers with sentimental appeals for moral justice. As the American nation divided regionally over economic racial, political, and social issues, Dickens's novels were read in common and heightened the sentimental spirit that connected people in causes of mutual concern.

Notes

1. In *Social Stories*, Patricia Okker points out that "reading magazine novels provided individuals with an opportunity to connect with a community of disparate members and, at the same time, to reshape the community itself." Okker states that the ability of serial form to address social issues was both tested and enriched by the political crises of the 1850s. She writes, "Like the nation, which was itself deeply divided among regional borders, the magazine industry became increasingly specialized, and authors responded with political novels intended for specific rather than generalized audiences" (159). Okker tells us that serialized novels like those of Dickens "inspire not just private experiences, but also the same kind of bonds scholars have long associated with periodicals, particularly newspapers." Noting that the "mass ceremony" of newspaper reading creates what Anderson has called imagined community, she asserts that serial fiction in newspapers participated most significantly in this experience (16). See Patricia Okker, *Social Stories* (Charlottesville: University of Virginia Press, 2003).

2. Charles Dickens's *Bleak House* (1852) immediately followed and intersected with the readership of *Uncle Tom's Cabin*, the best-selling novel of its time. *Uncle Tom's Cabin*, the writing of which was instigated by the Fugitive Slave Law of 1850, became a significant cultural text, a book with political implications that went beyond Stowe's politics.

3. Dickens wrote of Menken: "there has been much puffing at great cost of a certain Miss Adah Isaacs Menkin [*sic*] who is to be seen bound on a horse in 'Mazeppa.' Now who do you think this lady is? If you don't already know, ask that question of the brightest Irish mountains that look eternal and they'll never tell you—Mrs. Heenan!" (Menken 138) Some biographers allege that Menken had taken Dickens to her boudoir. See Ada Isaacs Menken (New York, 1974), 143.

4. According to Raymond Williams, Dickens had several things in common with the reformers: 1. Impatience with conservative idealization of the past; 2. Insistence on legal reform; 3. Contempt for aristocratic social pretensions (148). Williams contends that, like many reformers, Dickens was, at least for a time, an optimist, although the optimistic Dickens of *Oliver Twist* and *Nicholas Nickleby* may have changed into a less hopeful writer by mid-century. As Williams observes, with a reformer's sense of

obligation and social stewardship and a sense of the interdependency of human life, his darker tales and the essays of *Household Words* of the 1850s suggest a rather serious Dickens writing in the cause of social improvement. Dickens's social analysis grew sharper and American reformers seized upon his texts.

5. Dickens's Edith Dombey, Louisa Gradgrind, Bella Wilfer, and Estella are "schooled by an acquisitive society for a certain kind of marriage, and for a certain kind of culture" writes Barbara Hardy. In Hardy's view, "The daughters show the corruption of love, marriage and maternity" (Hardy, *Moral Art*, 58–59). Dickens's women, in this view, tend to become passive domestics. Such a woman did not have to be involved in public life, for at home, in her domestic circumstances, she had "influence" (Douglas 45). Nineteenth-century women who read Dickens, typically, would not have read Dickens's female characters in the manner in which Barbara Hardy has approached them. Rather, they emotionally participated in his stories and identified with his female characters, as we can see in reader's comments. Dickens's contemporary female readers often saw his female characters as role models.

8

Civil War Reading

I N A TIME OF STRUGGLE AND NEED, when America was divided by war, the sharing of Charles Dickens's fiction enabled friends and family to maintain
their emotional connections. Despite the division, Dickens's stories circulated
popularly in both the North and the South among families and entertained
soldiers, helping them to endure periods of waiting, in camp, in hospitals, or
in prison. Dickens's stories were a source of shared sentiments and contributed to the sentimental style of letter writing which was prevalent at the time.
Dickens's serialized stories were, for his American audience, a place to rest
temporarily amid the unfolding process of their own lives in which they were
creating a home and living in history.

When the imagined community of the United States fell apart in the Civil
War, Dickens remained a significant source of entertainment in all regions of
the country. His continuing popularity across all regions attests to a universal-
ity in his writing that allowed his work to be appreciated by people with different social agendas. For despite the regional divide, letters and journals suggest
that Northern and Southern reading experiences of Dickens during the war
were not substantially different from each other. Indeed, Dickens's stories
were appropriated to fit into readers' world-views. For example, in the South
most readers rejected Dickens's position on slavery in *American Notes*, yet
they embraced his fiction widely. In the North, Dickens's stories serialized in
Harper's were set within a context of war and heroism. Differences in reader
response simply suggest human individuality and the indeterminacy of the
text: in any community of readers, those readers will read differently. However, it appears that all readers recognized the spirit of charity, the quality of

humor, the entertaining energy, and the warm human sympathy in Dickens's
fiction. Divided politically and regionally, they found their common humanity underscored by Dickens's stories.

Appearing in America just prior to the Civil War, a serial like Dickens's *A
Tale of Two Cities* (1859) might have reflected a tale of one nation divided
into two regions at war. *A Tale of Two Cities* has about it the clatter and rush
of stagecoaches and people in motion. As Hughes and Lund have pointed
out, the serial form of Dickens's art is akin to history itself; it is a model of
development that says that life is organized by a series of stages and suggests
movement in time. Dickens's novel is underscored by restless travel, a kind
that reflects societies in motion (36). Dickens's American readers were drawn
into a long story that was "creating a home" for them. In "the gap between
installments" readers could be "discussing with others the more memorable
scenes and making predictions about the future" (ibid.). The literary form of
the serial suggested to readers that they were engaged with progress, change,
and development. It was "an articulation of the values of the age," as Bill Bell
has pointed out (Bell 125–44). Serials created an imagined community of
readers who followed the ongoing activities of Dickens's characters and participated in the sentiment of his stories.[1]

Dickens's *A Tale of Two Cities* was brought home by readers, who shared
it with their families or friends. On January 21, 1860, southerner Ellen Mordecai, who was an avid reader of Charles Dickens, wrote to her aunt Ellen
Mordecai: "If you want to read an interesting story get '*A Tale of Two Cities.*'
Dickens you know. I have just read it." Caroline Mordecai Plunkett, however,
says that her blind brother who had listened to the story did not care for the
book. She writes to another of her brothers: "Today when I had finished the
letter Solomon said, "What book is it that Ellen asks me if I liked? "T of Two
Cts" Tell her I do not like it very much, particularly the conclusion which I
tho't quite unworthy of Dickens" (Jacob Mordecai Papers, Duke University,
Southern Historical Collection). The resolution of Dickens's novel, including
the theme of self-sacrifice may not have appealed to this reader. However, he
gives no indication why he disliked the conclusion of the novel.

Family letters like those between Caroline and Ellen maintained affective
bonds. Dickens was part of the conversation. For example, in the years before
he became a widely read author, Samuel Clemens (Mark Twain) shared his
observations of Dickens with his family. He reports to his brother Orion from
St. Louis on November 20, 1860 that "Pamela has got a baby" and goes on
to write:

> And her nurse is almost the counterpart of Mrs. Gamp in *Martin Chuzzlewit*,
> who used to say "No-no," which them is the very words I have said more nor
> once to Mrs. Harris. (Twain *Letters* III, 104)

As he describes his experience of a relationship with "Miss Laura" (Laura M. Wright 1844–1932), he refers to himself as "like one Dickens' characters," alluding to the lovelorn Augustus Noodle in *Martin Chuzzlewit* (112). At the age of twenty-five, in a letter of February 6, 1861, to his brother Orion Clemens and his wife Mollie Clemens in Cairo, Illinois, he alludes to Captain Cuttle in Dickens's *Dombey and Son*. In January 1862, from Carson City, Nevada, he writes to his mother that he had "the necessaries of life" and some luxuries:

> Ten pounds of Killinick, two decks of cards, "Dombey and Son," a cribbage board, one small keg of lager beer and the "carmina sacrae." (Twain *Letters* II, January 16, 1862)

Captain Cuttle and the Dombey family are mentioned again in a letter of February 28, 1862. Clemens, writing from Aurora, Colorado, on April 18, 1862, speaks of Dickens to another family member, William H. Clagett. He writes about Mark Tapley in *Martin Chuzzlewit*: "My love to Dad and the boys—and tell Dad not to be discouraged, but 'come out strong' like Mark Tapley.—Sam L.C." (Twain *Letters* II, April 18, 1862). Again, in each case, the Dickens references link family ties. As Samuel Clemens writes his letters, the fictional family of Dickens and his own actual family are on his mind. Indeed they appear to intertwine. This supports the observation that letter writing maintained affective bonds during the Civil War period, as Ronald Zboray and Alice Fahs have pointed out.

The affective connections supported by family reading are evident in another author's childhood. Mary Terhune, better known as Marion Harland, noted that her family was "a reading family." She writes, "We had all the new books that he (our father) adjudged to be worth buying and reading, watching eagerly for anything from Dickens, Marryat, and Cooper" (88). Some of Dickens's characters reminded family members of people that they knew. "*Martin Chuzzlewit* was not written until a score of years later. When it was read aloud in our family circle, there was not a dissenting voice when my mother uttered, in a voice smothered by inward mirth, 'Mr. Carus!' as Mr. Pecksniff appeared upon the stage." Ms. Harland's mother had recognized the image of a relative in Dickens's portrayal of Pecksniff. "The portrait was absurdly striking," Harland writes. "The Yankee Pecksniff was good-looking after his kind, which was the dark-eyed, well-featured, serenely sanctimonious type" (54).

Harland's mother was at the center of an apparently inexhaustible supply of periodicals and newspapers. At home, the family read from *Godey's Lady Book* and *Graham's Magazine*. "Cousin Mary [. . .] took *Graham's Magazine*, *Godey's* only rival," Harland recalls. "She likewise subscribed for the *Saturday Evening Courier*, and exchanged it regularly with my mother for the *Saturday Evening Post*, all published in Philadelphia. *The New York Mirror* [. . .] was another welcome guest. For Sunday reading we had the *New York Observer,* *The Watchman and Observer, The Presbyterian* [. . . .] We children had *Parley's* *Magazine* sent to us, as long as I can recollect, by our grandmother" (84). Dickens found an honored place amid this reading.

Harland's family of readers often read in "the chamber," a big room on the first floor. In this room was her mother's heirloom bureau. They sat in rocking chairs, and "thick curtains, matching the bed hangings, shut out wintry gusts, and a great wood fire leaped and laughed upon the pipe-clayed hearth." Harland's father was at the center of this family reading circle, bringing home books for them to read, including many volumes of Dickens (85).

Among the periodicals that Harland read was Dickens's *All the Year Round.* Dickens's emphasis on the transatlantic distribution of his new journal *All the Year Round* suggests his growing awareness of his American audience. As John M. L. Drew observes, "Concessions to a new transatlantic readership are perhaps only detectable in such slight touches as Dickens's adding geographical markers unnecessary for British readers into his self-introduction as the 'Uncommercial Traveller'" (149). Dickens's awareness of his American public is also underscored by the deal he made with the Harpers, who paid him 1250 pounds for advance sheets of *Great Expectations*, which ran in *Harper's Weekly.*

When the storms of war emerged in 1861 and North and South divided, shared reading of Dickens served as one link between family members or friends whom the war set at a distance from each other. The exchange of letters, newspapers, and fiction among soldiers and their families helped them to maintain affective ties (Zboray 113). The recently released *Great Expectations* and its precursor, *David Copperfield* (1849–50) were popular among soldiers. Jane Stuart Woolsey, a field nurse, writes:

> Soldiers were omnivorous readers, but many wanted a better order of books than novels and magazines. One of the frowsiest of the "inv'lids" was a devourer of everything Mr. Sumner wrote. Files of the "Scientific American" were in demand. The personage of Cicero and the store-room of Shakespeare went about the wards. Dickens was very popular. I think *David Copperfield* was the favorite story. (59)

Dickens was read by both officers and enlisted men, and he was read not only in silence but aloud: "General George H. Gordon liked to read Dickens's *Pickwick Papers* aloud by the hour," recalled one soldier (Gray 26). Another soldier recalled: "Especially when the army was in winter quarters and books were in short supply, a good reader with a copy of Bulwer-Lytton, Scott or Dickens could be assured that his hut would be filled with listeners. The standard rule about extinguishing lights at taps was seldom enforced under such conditions" (Williams in Kaser 47).

Dickens was read both North and South, evidently in equal measure. The chaplain of the 8th Connecticut Volunteers wrote home: "Dickens has a great run. The tales of Miss Edgeworth and T.S. Arthur are very popular" (Koch 4). Charles Appleton Longfellow, the poet's son, wrote to his sister Alice of reading Dickens in camp in Virginia: "It has been raining all day, so that I have finished the 'Tale of Two Cities,' it is first rate, isn't it?" (Longfellow *Letters* 1: 94).

For soldiers of both armies, a campfire served as a makeshift memory of the family hearth. George Freeman Noyes recalled, "Around each pyramid of flame sat the men, engaged in various avocations; some, of course, cooking, for no camp fire was ever without a soldier making coffee, no matter what the hour; some reading or playing cards" (223). Noyes said he regretted the boredom of do-nothingism in camp during the war. He recommended reading the books of Charles Dickens and others as a healthy remedy.

> If you wish to demoralize a man, to dilute his manliness, corrode his patriotism, steal away his cheerfulness, destroy his enthusiasm, and impair his health, pen him up in an isolated camp with little to do, no books to read, no resources against idleness; if you wish to demoralize an army, march it off from a severely contested battle-field into the woods, and condemn it to a month or two of listless do-nothingism. At such a time the men need, as never so much before, books of a cheerful and moderately exciting character, strong, bracing stories like those of Charles Kingsley, quiet pictures of homelife like that fascinating sketch of "John Halifax, Gentleman," military tales like those of Lever, the wonderful character pieces of Charles Dickens, and choice productions of our American authors. (224)

For Noyes, books were a substitute for action, a guard against idleness and boredom. Dickens's books, described as "wonderful character pieces," conveyed something more: a means of inspiration.

> In these latter days, the novel has risen to its true position; it has become, in our own country, and in England, almost the rival of the pulpits as the medium of patriotic impulse, elevated sentiment, moral and religious culture; and thus, the good novelist becomes to the soldier not only his physician to animate and invigorate him, but his preacher to elevate and inspire him. (ibid.)

Charles Dickens, Walter Scott, and James Fenimore Cooper, or Thackeray and Bulwer-Lytton may have served some of those functions. So did cheap fiction, for often when the soldiers read they read nickel and dime novels. There are no regional politics expressed by these readers. Rather, they continually refer to the entertainment value of Dickens's stories and to memories of home. Dickens animated and invigorated the spirits of soldiers; he elevated and inspired them.

George Cary Eggleston of Virginia was one of the many soldiers who obtained reading material, such as newspapers, by mail. Eggleston read copies of *The Examiner* and "the *Whig, Dispatch, Enquirer,* or *Sentinel,* for half that sum" (84). However, in his view, books were scarce commodities for soldiers in the south. "The one thing which we were left almost wholly without, during the war, was literature," he wrote in 1875. "A Mobile firm reprinted a few of the more popular books of the time, *Les Miserables, Great Expectations,* etc." (103). The cost of books was another of his concerns:

> Singularly enough, I bought at the same time a set of Dickens's novels, well-printed and bound in black cloth, for four dollars a volume. In looking through a file of the *Richmond Examiner* extending over most of the year 1864, I find but one book of any sort advertised [. . .] and the price of that was five dollars. (104)

Eggleston found Dickens-like humor in some scenes in military life. Drills reminded him of Bob Sawyer's bachelor's party in the *Pickwick Papers*:

> The drilling, of which there was literally no end, was simply funny [. . . .] Every amateur officer had his own pet system of tactics, and the effect of the incongruous teachings, when brought out in battalion drill, closely resembled the music at Mr. Bob Sawyer's party, where each guest sang the chorus to the tune he knew best. (20)

Home for Christmas, Confederate soldier Samuel Andrew Agnew wrote in his diary, December 25, 1863, that his father, who had been complaining of colic two days earlier, was now reading Dickens. Agnew had been awakened that morning by the sound of "the little negroes in the yard running." Curiously, this was several months after Lincoln's Emancipation Proclamation. Agnew wrote:

> We have the prospect of a wet night. Pa is reading The Message from the Sea tonight. It is a Christmas story by Dickens. (132)

Soldiers in motion like Eggleston and Agnew, marching and camping many miles away from home, stayed in communication with their families and friends through letters and by exchanging newspapers. Dickens offered them a model for this letter writing. Shared texts and the rhetorical conventions taught in schools combined in a sentimental style of letter writing in which emotions poured forth. These effusive letters developed personal stories that attempted to wring the heart in the manner of *Wide, Wide World* and *Uncle Tom's Cabin* (Zboray 115). Or, one might add, Little Nell's story in *The Old Curiosity Shop.* Dickens served these letter writers well.

Most of the stories that soldiers read were in newspapers. Northern journals like *Harper's*, in which Dickens was serialized, reached men in the field like Captain Richard Burt, from Newark, Ohio. "We pass away the time reading the news in the latest northern papers, or perusing old magazines sent to us by kind and loyal friends up north," he writes from Vicksburg on June 10, 1863. A week later, on June 21, 1863, he urges a news editor: "Advise your readers to send the soldiers plenty of newspapers" (42). In *Harper's*, July 1864, Editor's Drawer, one anonymous soldier writes, "Having received from the United States Christian Commission some reading matter among which were old Harper's Monthlies and being much pleased with the Drawer, I wish to become a contributor" (*Harper's* [July 1864]: 269).

Soldiers read while convalescing after battle injuries. In Epes Sargent's novel *Peculiar, a Tale of the Great Transition* (1864) his protagonist, Vance, quits the hospital after paying the surgeon and recommends some reading to his love at home. In his room at St. Charles he writes:

> To Perdita: I shall not be able to see you again today. Content yourself as well as you can in the company of Mozart and Beethoven, Bellini and Donizetti, Irving and Dickens, Tennyson and Longfellow. The company is not large but you will find it select. (60)

One source of soldiers' reading material was the regimental library. Alonzo Hall Quint, a Union soldier who kept the volumes within one of these pointed to Dickens's popularity. According to Quint, among the most read of the books were those of Dickens:

> Among devices for this vacation period we have a small regimental library [. . . .] I owe public thanks for this especially to Mr. MH Sargent, who interested himself most generously and heartily in obtaining and forwarding the books . . . the nest egg of which was a kind donation from Mr. Tolman's church at Wilmington . . . If the donors could see the eagerness with which the books are read, they would feel still happier in doing good [. . . .] Among the most read (I take from the book where I charge volumes, to show the taste) are Deacon Safford, Winthrop's John Brent, Dickens's Christmas Stories, Abbot's Practical Christianity, Dexter's Street Thoughts, the Lives of Washington, Jackson, Fremont, Franklin, and Boone. (94)

Walter Scott appears among soldier's letters and journals as Dickens's closest British competitor. It has been suggested that Scott's medievalism, chivalry, and Scottish clans, appealed primarily to southern readers. Mark Twain commented: "The South has not yet recovered from the debilitating influence of his books" (Twain, *Life on the Mississippi* 416). However, Dickens and Scott appear to have been equally popular in both north and south. James

A. Connelly of the 7th Illinois Infantry, for example, read Dickens's *A Tale of Two Cities* and Scott's *Marmion* in camp (Kaser 9). He wrote of the other soldiers: "Some are perusing old Waverlys, and others amusing themselves with Harper's cuts, one has a volume of Shakespeare" (15). Virginia attorney Jason Niles (1814–94) recorded a conversation with his friend Joseph Gallo-way in his diary on May 28, 1863, that a mutual friend, a Confederate soldier, was reading Scott in camp: "Galloway's remark about Jim George's reading Scott's novels in camp" (Niles Diary [June 8, 1864]: 96; *Documenting American South*). John Sergeant Wise (1846–1913) says of his older brother Richard that "he put me to reading Walter Scott" (93). Wise, a Confederate lieutenant and Congressional representative from Virginia, read both Scott and Dickens. He asserted in 1899 that Virginians during the Civil War were well-read and that their private libraries destroyed in the war "would have filled every public library in the north to overflowing" (64). He pointed to a legal colleague, John B. Young, who "in the forefront of his profession still found time to read Dickens until he was a walking encyclopedia of Dickens's wit" (70).

Familiarity with Dickens among soldiers was widespread. Soldiers who would never meet shared the experience of Dickens's fiction. From across the Atlantic, one naval serviceman referred to Dickens's circumlocution office in *Little Dorrit* as comparable to Spanish "red tape." Raphael Semmes wrote:

> Charles Dickens has given us an amusing account of an English Circumlocution Office, but English red tape dwindles into insignificance by the side of Spanish red tape. Getting into the hands of the Spanish officials was like getting into a Chancery suit. (299)

Soldiers from the invading Union army saw Dickens's novels on the shelves in southern homes. August Joseph Hickey Duganne wrote in 1866 of seeing books while he was part of an northern occupying force during the war:

> Meanwhile, here we sit, hostile strangers from the North, amidst the dusty lumber of a southern home. The family portraits rest against the wall, backs turned upon us. I handle many a duplicate of favorite authors in my home library. Here stand, in line, battalia of books, which show the classic taste of their collector. The British Poets muster, rank on rank, some ninety strong; the British Essayists beneath, and here are Dickens, Irving, Cooper, Bulwer, Thackeray; with hundreds, rank and file, of literary yeomen, and brave historians. (56)

In *Camps and Prisons*, Duganne added that

> Our Yankee foragers allow no smuggling [. . . .] But we counted "Artful Dodgers" in our motley midst, who would have joyed the heart out of the venerable Fagin! (378)

Reading was also practiced by the prisoner of war. Confederate Captain Robert E. Park of the 12th Alabama Regiment wrote on February 8, 1865 from a Baltimore prison:

> Some read novels and histories, others study ancient and modern languages and mathematics, and these divert for the time, their minds from the painful, desperate, hopeless surroundings. (46)

Henry Kyd Douglas of Hagerstown, Maryland, wrote that he had plentiful reading material to help him pass the time:

> In August 1865, I was a prisoner in Fort Delaware, sent there by the sentence of a military commission. My imprisonment was not a hard one, and what with the courtesy of the commanding officer, and free access to a well-filled library and the liberty of the island, my time passed easily if not rapidly. (Douglas in Harrison 240)

Confederate soldier Anthony M. Keiley alluded to Dickens as he assessed conditions at the prison at Elmira, New York. "I speak by the card respecting these matters, having kept the morning return of deaths for the last month and a half of my life at Elmira, and transferred the figures to my diary, which lies before me." Looking at the statistics before him, Keiley stated that mortality at Elmira was 4 percent to the notorious southern prison Andersonville's less than 3 percent. Then he wrote:

> Now, the proportion of North Carolinians was nothing even approximately what might have been expected from this record. *I commit the fact to Mr. Gradgrind.* (144)

Camps, prisons, or hospitals, were temporary resting places in the process of life where Dickens was read. Keiley saw *Hard Times* in the prison. Duganne saw Artful Dodgers in Union foragers. Semmes saw Chancery "red tape" in foreign officials. The Dickens story, held in memory, was at the intersection of the public and the private. For Americans involved in the historic process of a war, gathering around a Dickens novel, or sharing a card game in camp, provided a social connection, recalling hearth and home.

In Southern homes, away from the battlefields, children were reading Dickens. Thomas Hughes, born in 1850, the same year that *David Copperfield* appeared in book form, learned of Dickens from his father, a newspaper editor in Richmond. In 1900, Hughes recalled: "His roommate [*sic*] was absent. Before entering he handed me a copy of *David Copperfield* and this was my first introduction to the delights of Dickens's works" (24). Mrs. Burton Harrison (1843–1920), whose father also worked for a newspaper, recalled in 1911 comparisons of her neighbor with Miss Havisham in Satis House. "Those of her kindred who went through the forsaken house collecting their scattered belongings described a scene like a page from Dickens's *Great Expectations*" (83). J.D. Cameron (1820–1897) in his *A Sketch of Tobacco* (1870) lists his childhood reading as "Cottage Home," "Waverly," "Ruby," "Little Town Brick Factory," "Gold Dust," and "Oliver Twist" (61). James Battle Averitt (1837–1912) commenting on his childhood in *The Old Plantation: How We Lived* (1901) recalls reading aloud Dickens, Bulwer, Shakespeare, and Scott, all British writers. Averitt, speaking of his tutor, the Reverend James Melsey Sprunt, says:

> Before this volume is finished we hope to see him of a winter's night and with kindling eyes and the sweetest of voices reads aloud Shakespeare, the Waverly novels, Dickens, Bulwer, and other authors of world wide fame. (42)

Dickens generated enthusiasm and sentiment among some young southern readers. Belle Kearney of Vernon, Mississippi, recalled in 1900 that she made a bargain with her younger brothers, enticing them to house work in return for reading aloud to them from Dickens or Scott.

> "Well," I answered, "suppose we make a bargain? If you will cook every time mother gets sick, I will tell you one of Dickens's stories or one of Walter Scott's novels as regularly as the nights roll around." "All right! I'll do it!" was the ready assent; and the compact was sealed. It was never broken. (25)

Dickens's stories affected these children, prompting uproarious laughter at times and tears on other occasions. Belle Kearney observes the delighted responses of her brothers. For them, Dickens's characters are welcome guests. The hearth provides a center of maternal warmth, as Kearney herself substitutes for the ill mother by providing these domestic readings "around the hearth in mother's room." Kearney elaborates on the stories, "going into the smallest details." Dickens's novels suggest to her that she should be "dwelling on the peculiarities of characters" and "waxing humorous or pathetic according to the situation" (ibid.).

Dickens's stories were available in Northern homes as well as Southern ones. Evidently, in some cases, the younger children just looked at the pictures. While Dickens's *Our Mutual Friend* was being serialized in *Harper's* in 1864, one reader wrote about the fondness of her children for the visual content of the magazine: "The appearance of *Harper's Magazine* at our house is an event of great importance with my children. The illustrations in it are the chief cause of this." She says that her little boy ran out of bed to get the magazine and pointed to a page, saying "The Indians didn't catch Kenton yet!"

(820). On the page opposite this appears an illustration of winged children as "Angels of the Household" (821). All the children are mischievous: One raids a cookie jar as her sister looks on and reaches up for it; three children slide down a bannister; one pulls at a cat's tail; another breaks a mirror; a little girl with wings holds up torn pages in her hand and stomps over shattered shards on the floor as her parents look on (*Harper's* [May 1864]: 28).

The sharing of *Harper's Monthly* by this family, including by children intrigued by the pictures and the serialization of a story, suggests that Dickens's tales, and the serialized works of other authors, were social stories which were part of the ongoing life of many families like this. It also underscores the importance of caricatures, or visual illustrations, for some of Dickens's American audience.

In *A Southern Girl in '61*, Louise Wigfall Wright (1846–1915), a Confederate senator's daughter, remembered turning to Dickens:

> I recall one night particularly when I had been beguiled into reading until a late hour the charming pages of Dickens's A Tale of Two Cities. (114)

Other southern women, when recalling the war years, turned to Dickens's writings to describe people and places from their childhoods. For example, Frances Butler Leigh (1838–1910) recalled a place in her childhood in Georgia:

> The site has a fine frontage of marsh and reeds, and very much resembles Charles Dickens's "Eden" to which poor Martin and Tapley were allured [. . . .]

Another Georgia woman, Rebecca Latimer Felton, emphasized how deprived she'd found one child she'd known in her youth. The child was

> kept [. . .] nearly all her lifetime in the harrassments of the courts and the facts are surprising beyond anything Dickens ever wrote of the Wards in Chancery. (44)

Leigh recalls a place and associates it with the specious "Eden" of *Martin Chuzzlewit*, without any criticism. Felton, with a concern for child welfare, recalls *Bleak House* for comparison, to make her point. These women's recollections of Dickens's stories are devoid of politics. Dickens's fiction is a familiar reference point for them as they write their memoirs.

Dickens is also to be found in southern diaries of the Civil War period. For example, Sarah Morgan Dawson, in her notable Civil War diary, refers to Dickens to help her to describe a man:

> This one is very handsome, quite, and what Dickens calls "in a high-shouldered state of deportment." He looks like a moss covered stone wall. (160)

In what has become the most famous diary of the war, *A Diary from Dixie*, Mary Chesnut frequently speaks of her avid reading of Dickens. Chesnut makes many allusions to *Old Curiosity Shop, Nicholas Nickleby, Little Dorrit* and other Dickens novels. For example, on August 17, 1861, she wrote in her diary: "Read Oliver Twist again. <<Had forgotten how good it is>>" (141). In conversation during that same month she refers to *Old Curiosity Shop*:

> "Do you think two married people ever lived together without finding each other out? I mean knowing exactly how good or how shabby, how weak or how strong—above all, how selfish each was?"
> "Yes—unless they are dolts—they know to a tittle. But you see—if they have common sense, they make believe and get on—so, so—like the marchioness's orange peel wine—in Old Curiosity Shop, you know. (173)

When war erupted at Fort Sumter and Charleston, Mary Chesnut, whose marriage placed her close to the Confederate command, lamented that the war had interrupted her reading of northern and British periodicals, thus cutting her off from part of the world. On November 20, 1861, she wrote:

> Read Dickens *Pictures from Italy*. Pleasant company in my airy retreat. Last January I sent for all the English reviews: Blackwood &c &c Atlantic, Harper's, Cornhill &c. Threw away my subscription money. Everything stopped with Fort Sumter. How I miss that way of looking out into the world. The war has cost me that. How much more? (496)

While *Harper's* circulation in the South was disrupted by the war, Chesnut was well-off enough to have copies of Dickens's novels and she appears to have read them often. Chesnut asserted her steadfastness to the Confederacy with a reference to Dickens. "Poor old Confederacy of my heart, desert her, never. See Micawber," she wrote. Chesnut's allusion is to the steadfast wife of Mr. Micawber. For in *David Copperfield*, Emma Micawber repeats that she will never leave her husband, no matter what the crisis. Mary Chesnut, likewise, was firmly wedded to the southern cause (614).

The war did not interfere with her reading, or re-reading, Dickens's novels. Her diary suggests that she and her correspondents knew Dickens's works so well that she could make passing references to them, including a variety of allusions. For example, while discussing the English and weddings or love affairs, Chesnut writes: "Splendid plan, though. Like the waiter, in Dickens's book. Her on suiting—and she suits" (523). She refers to *Nicholas Nickleby*, writing: "As grateful as Mrs. Squeers was to innocence of grammar." Referring to Colonel Chesnut, she uses Wemmick's term of endearment for his father in *Great Expectations*, "my aged P." Considering what to call "Mrs. K's new baby," Chesnut refers to Marleena Kennigs in *Nicholas Nickleby*.

When she was not naming babies, Mary Chestnut agreed with Colonel Goodwyn to call a sleepy Richmond detective "Inspector Bucket," after the character in *Bleak House*. She writes that "A man slept through everything [. . . .] Colonel Goodwyn wrote on a blank page of my book (one of the De Quinceys, the note is there now) that the sleeper was a Richmond detective. We called him, in memory of Bleak House, Mr. Bucket" (460). She records that there is in Richmond a man who calls himself Jeems, after the Dickens character "and will wear a dress coat to breakfast" (170).

Writing of Ellen, a woman from a Sumter district planting family talking to Ransom Spann, Chesnut records their conversation. One of them makes use of a Dickens character's often repeated phrase in *Great Expectations*: "What's the matter? Why don't you two make it up and marry?" "Ask her. Barkis is willing" (471).

Chesnut states that she will re-read a Dickens volume given to her by Mrs. Hager. "She lent me *Martin Chuzzlewit*. Now that we separate ourselves in thought from the Yankees Dickens laughs at, it will bear a second reading. He would not come south because of slavery. So he does not know we spit as much as the Yankees" (548). Mrs. Hager was obviously involved in Chesnut's reading of Dickens, for she is thought of again just before Chesnut writes about her loaning of a Dickens story to someone else. "Lent General Preston 'Mrs. Lirriper's Lodgings,' our latest Dickens. He says he holds me responsible for his reading, as Judge Withers did" (573). On February 21, 1862, she writes: "A crowd collected here last night and there was a serenade. I am like Mr. Nickleby, who never saw a horse coming full speed but he thought the Cheeryble brothers had sent posthaste to take Nicholas with copartnership. So I got up and dressed, late as it was. I felt sure Nicholas with copartnership. I felt sure England sought an alliance at last. And we would make a Yorktown before long" (293). Rather than resisting English culture, Chesnut cherished Dickens and appears to have held the hope that the English might become allies in the southern cause.

In 1862, as the war entered its second year, Dickens was again present in Mary Chesnut's thoughts, as she measured human character and social issues. In March 1862, she refers in her diary to Sally Brass, a scheming spinster who starves and poorly treats her servant in *Old Curiosity Shop*, and says that she asked someone, "Did you ever read Dickens? We are no worse than other people. Sally Brass, now. Do you fancy, there are many Sally Brasses in this world?" (311). In June 1862, she refers to Dickens and to Shakespeare as she reflects upon Stowe's *Uncle Tom's Cabin*: "After all this, tried to read Uncle Tom. Could not. Too sickening. A man send his little son to beat a human tied to a tree? It is bad as Squeers beating Smike in the hack. Flesh and blood revolt. You must skip that—it is too bad—or the pulling out of eyeballs in Lear" (381).

Dickens is no less present in Chesnut's thoughts two or three years later. In January 1864, she refers to Dickens's character Dick Swiveller in the *Old Curiosity Shop*: "Took the Carys to rehearse at Mrs. Randolph's. Found there Captain Tucker, Mr. Denegre, and an Englishman, Vizetely by name who, as Dick Swiveller, smoked, played cards, and put his feet on the table. He was admirable. He was as free as air, air in free America" (533). On January 12, 1864, she writes that "at the Cary's all in confusion and the rehearsal in full blast. John Saunders makes a perfect Smike" (536).

In troubled times, Chesnut thinks of Dickens. While in North Carolina, February 1865, she writes:

Here I am brokenhearted—an exile. Such a place. Bare floors [. . . .] At the door—before I was well out of the hack, the woman of the house packed Laurence back, neck and heels. She would not have him at any price. She treated him as Mr. F's aunt did Clennam in Little Dorrit. (717)

Dickens's stories were familiar to the household. On March 15, 1865, a month before the war's conclusion, *Little Dorrit* is again mentioned:

Isabella made a list of the things sent me in my time of need [. . . .] Ellen supplemented in haste: "Oh, Miss Isabel, don't forget the two picked chickens fat as pigs Miss McDaniel just this minute send." "Heavy chicking," as the small morsel of a child in the hospital sighed you know, in Little Dorrit. Don't let us forget moonshine and stickies. (762)

The novel *Nicholas Nickleby*, often mentioned, appears to have been one of her favorites. On November 28, 1864, she writes:

Harlott Green, too, raises one's spirits. A male Mrs. Nickleby—he expected every minute to see a man on horse back gallop up—not to announce the Cheeryble Bros have taken Nicholas into copartnership but that by the help of, or in spite of, Old Nick, every Yankee in the land is killed. At least he says: "Take my word for it. Good news—wonderful news is coming." (678)

There was little good news for the Confederacy at the end of 1864, or in 1865. Emma Le Conte, who lived near Columbia, South Carolina, read Dickens distractedly on February 23, 1865:

I tried to read a volume of Mad. de Stael, 'De la Literature.' It was impossible. I tried something lighter—one of Dickens. I soon found that I did not know what I was reading [. . . .] I suppose it is the reaction from the frightful strain and nervous tension. (45)

The march of William Tecumseh Sherman's troops through Georgia and the sacking of Columbia, South Carolina upset Le Conte, an ambitious, self-educating reader, who had become a "school maam" to a girl named Sallie, teaching her "arithmetic, Latin, spelling, and elementary Natural Philosophy, besides reading and composition" (48).

Dickens's fiction is a companion for Chesnut and for Le Conte. Each of these women reflects on her experiences and turns to Dickens for solace. These women hope that Dickens may provide affective connections—a sense of human sympathy, or the possibility for entertaining distraction—in the midst of "frightful strain and nervous tension."

The context of war reported in the pages of *Harper's* interacted with the serial publication of *Our Mutual Friend*. The story ran in *All the Year Round* in twenty monthly numbers from May 1864 to November 1865. In June 1864, *Harper's* began serializing Dickens's story in its pages. In the Editor's Drawer, which always cited comments and stories from readers and presented a tone of inclusiveness, George William Curtis said: "It is no more necessary to invite our friends to read Dickens's new story than to exhort them to eat fresh strawberries" (*Harper's Monthly* [June 1864]: 96). Dickens was positioned in this edition as a competitor with Thackeray, whose *Denis Duval* was also being serialized. These British texts appear with the American writing in *Harper's*, but frequently are grouped together with British topics and set off from American ones.

Did *Our Mutual Friend* create mutual friends, readers who read the story at the same time, while a war was raging beyond their windows? As Jennifer Hayward points out, "serials appear literally side by side with other texts; even when issued in independent parts, novels would be absorbed concurrently with the month's magazines and newspapers" (44). There is in *Harper's Monthly* a mingling of fiction and fact, British texts and American ones. The edition in which *Our Mutual Friend* first appeared opens on "A Chapter on the Coolie Trade," citing concerns about slavery: "Gigantic outrages have been enacted." While pointing to foreign slavery, there is the implication of domestic slavery in the South. Before *Our Mutual Friend* appears comes "Your Humble Servant," about British housekeepers or domestic servants. One can also read on "Wine Making in California," or read "The Small House at Allington," which is also being serialized. Or, one can read a selection from Tennyson's *Morte d'Arthur*. Dickens's story begins on page sixty-seven and concludes on page eighty-four. There it is followed by "Only Twelve Left," a poem, and by "The Letter G," a story.

"The Letter G," while evidently fiction, insists upon being factual. It begins: "Madge, you are an angel." "Oh, Peter!" exclaimed the angel. The narrator then says, "How can I help it if my hero's name is Peter? I don't invent like other storytellers; and this is owre [sic] true talk" (85). Such "reality" is set beside Dickens's fiction. This is followed by a female writer's slice of reality. "Why I Wrote It" concerns an article that *Harper's* rejected. The writer, who tells of her efforts to get it published so that she could get feed and clothe her baby, emphasizes the importance of hearth and home: "Our homes and our firesides! Nothing will rouse and fire a people like that cry. The watchword of our flag and the Union are fireless in comparison" (*Harper's* [June 1864]: 100). Dickens's story installment concludes immediately before this story and overlaps with its sentiment.

Two months later, the *Harper's* editor writes:

> The fertility of Dickens's power is amazing [. . . .] We hope that no reader omits the new novel of Dickens, "Our Mutual Friend," in the vain expectation of reading it when it is finished and published collectively. If he does, he loses a great deal of pleasure each month, and declines to probing his delight [. . . .] The sale of the first number, separately, in London, was forty thousand copies within the first few days [. . . .] Never forget that every number of the tale has a certain completeness, and that serial reading in these days is a most desirable and economical habit. (*Harpers* [August 1864]: 407)

Serial reading was desirable, in part, because, it provided the opportunity for experiencing drama and human connection in an ongoing fashion. It provided a point of rest amid the restless activity of the war that divided the nation. *Our Mutual Friend* is a text that plays upon images of division: John Harmon and John Rokesmith are one person divided, feigning death. Yet, readers often experienced the story together, in communal settings.

Together the readers of *Harper's Monthly* encountered Dickens's story in which drowned bodies float in a polluted Thames. In January 1865, *Harper's* editors placed an installment of Dickens's novel next to a poem "After the Storm," which is apparently a metaphor for the war. The poem is illustrated with a water-drenched woman looking out across a rough ocean to where, in the lines of the poem, "Alas! where far the dark sea-line / The sky from the ocean doth divide." The poem is preceded by the regular column "Heroic Deeds of Heroic Men" and a piece on the "Siege of Vicksburg" (150–160). Dickens's installment is thus surrounded by images of war and drowning and heroism, including the article which follows it: one on the *Defense of New Orleans* in the War of 1812, a war that was fought against Britain (*Harper's*, [January 1865]:160). Elsewhere Dickens's story, filled with Thames River drownings, follows an article on "Treatment of the Apparently Drowned."

Throughout the run of Dickens's story in *Harper's*, we can see that often the text of Dickens's story is grouped with other texts that refer to Britain. In November 1864, *Harper's* "Easy Chair" quotes Thackeray on his American lectures. "These good people," he said one day, "it is astonishing how patiently they listen to us. However, my boy, some day we shall be found out" (*Harper's* [November 1864]: 812). In December 1864, *Our Mutual Friend* follows Wilkie Collins's *Armadale*. When, in January, *Armadale* continues, it is followed by "An American War Correspondent in England" (229–235), which leads into the Dickens story. Again, there is a grouping of British material and reference. Within the war correspondent's article is a rejection slip he received from Dickens. He describes it as a "lithograph facsimile of the handwriting of Mr. Dickens" (235). "Mr. Charles Dickens begs to thank the writer of the paper entitled 'A Battle Sunday' for having done him the favor to offer it as a contribution to these pages. He much regrets, however [. . . .]" (235). As the third book of *Our Mutual Friend*, begins, Dickens's story follows "Recollections of Sherman" (*Harper's* [April 1865]). In May, *Armadale* is followed by an article on the University of Oxford. Then comes Dickens's story. In each case, the American Civil War is very present in the pages of *Harper's*. Dickens's tale is ever so slightly set apart amid other British subjects from reports of war and the "Heroic Deeds of Heroic Men." The format may suggest America's increasing separation from British influence and its emergence, through many trials, as a nation.

The contents of *Harper's* shows that Dickens's stories were appropriated for an American cause, as well as for profit. Dickens's *Our Mutual Friend* and the surrounding material in *Harper's* suggests heroism in the midst of a storm and apparent drownings. Like Dickens's novel, the periodical may suggest a baptismal resurrection from war. Dickens's fiction is set within the pages of *Harper's* to provide a diversion for Americans beset by war, while also offering them drama and urging participation as subscribers.

Charles Dickens's serialized fiction brought sentiment and contact with friends and family closer for readers in an America ravaged by war. From *A Tale of Two Cities* (1859) and *Great Expectations* (1861) to *Our Mutual Friend* (1864), his fiction circulated among communities of readers north and south, including civilian readers, public officials, and soldiers in camp or in hospitals or prisons. The exchange of his texts supported affective ties, while the "imagined community" of nation splintered into two rival factions. In Dickens's fiction readers could see nations torn by conflict as sites for heroic sacrifice (*A Tale of Two Cities*). Soldiers could read of bleak winter evenings and empty churchyards on the marshes, where traumatized boys are tossed into new discoveries, given new roles, and drawn to see the value of their relationships (*Great Expectations*). Families could read of characters who go through deathlike experiences to discover meaningful lives: the mysterious John Harmon and the noble Eugene Wrayburn, whom the angelic Lizzie saves from drowning (*Our Mutual Friend*). These plots, serialized, entwined with their daily lives. For soldiers in camp or prisoners of war, these entertainments helped them to endure periods of hardship or waiting.

As Dickens' stories continued to be shared by communities of readers, they arrived side by side with other texts, which included war news and cultural concerns. Fiction met reality, as Dickens's stories were read in connection with American issues. Dickens was adopted by America. His fictions were drafted into the cause of maintaining hope and he was welcomed into camp and home, much like a brother in arms.

Note

1. Dickens himself arranged with American publishers for sale of "foreign rights" to *All the Year Round* through Thomas C. Evans, who contracted with Emerson and Company of New York. Dickens contracted with Harper's for thirty-one installments of *A Tale of Two Cities*, appearing in *Harper's* one week after they appeared in *All the Year Round*.

9

Theatricality

C HARLES DICKENS INFLUENCED AMERICA through his theatricality: his effective use of theatrical devices, his appeal to sentiment, and the wide unauthorized recasting of his stories as dramas on the American stage. Dickens's American audience was keenly attuned to melodrama and sentimentality, and nineteenth-century America can be likened to a stage on which sentiment was enacted. As Shakespearian actor Henry Irving wrote: "The number of theatres in America and the influence they exercise constitute important elements in the national life" (Irving 197). As Edgar Johnson points out: "The middle class audience which crowded into the vast Victorian theaters was the same public that eagerly awaited the numbers of *Nicholas Nickleby* and *The Old Curiosity Shop*; and the problems of communication across the footlights or by the printed word were in many respects the same" (Johnson 1: 91).

Dickens observed the American theater, often staged with English actors, appropriating his novels and contesting with British culture. In May 1849, this nationalistic tension produced a deadly riot outside the Astor Theater in New York, in resistance to a performance by Dickens's friend, the Shakespearian actor William Macready. The incident was indicative of class tensions and nationalistic tensions. It began as a confrontation between supporters of Edwin Forrest, America's star actor, and those of William Macready, Britain's most significant actor of this period. Macready was supposed to appear in *Macbeth* at the Astor Place Opera House. Forrest was scheduled to perform *Macbeth* a few blocks away at the Broadway Theater.

Today, one may wonder why this would set off a riot that left as many as 25 people dead and 125 injured. The theater was a public gathering place where class tensions and political concerns were enacted by the public. Shakespeare was popular entertainment and Forrest and Macready were its star actors. The actors were popular figures who represented Britain and America. Forrest's background lay in the American working class, who called his vigorous acting style "American." He had a loyal following. The tension in Anglo-American relations and a struggle between New York working class and the more Anglophile upper class was complicated by the hostility between nativist and immigrant groups. Partisanship fueled this hostility.

On May 7, supporters of Forrest bought many tickets to the upstairs gallery of the Astor Place Theater. A few nights later, bent on causing trouble, they brought items to throw. The May 10 riot raged until the National Guard was brought in to quell the dispute.

The *New York Tribune* wrote:

> As one window after another cracked, the pieces of bricks and paving stones rattled in on the terraces and lobbies, the confusion increased, till the Opera House resembled a fortress besieged by an invading army rather than a place meant for the peaceful amusement of civilized community.

Clearly, this event gave Charles Dickens some pause about making a second trip to America. Following the rough treatment his *American Notes* and *Martin Chuzzlewit* had received, even a decade later, he was somewhat hesitant at first to extend his reading tour across the Atlantic. This violent acting out of American nationalism and reminders of the threat of Fenian Irish nationalism in New York entered Dickens's calculations for his American reading tour. Further, as early as his first tour of America in 1842, Dickens had begun to recognize that he himself had become a dramatized character. He had encountered dramatic displays of resistance in the American press, following *American Notes*, and America's patriotic rejection of English culture was theatrically stated in Fourth of July orations, as Sturgess has pointed out (32).

Yet, the theatrical Dickens held sway over his American audience as one of the most popular authors of the time. *Oliver Twist* was produced repeatedly on American stages and Dickens's Pickwick was a caricature so popular that he entered the mainstream of American life and manners.[1] Henry Wadsworth Longfellow viewed *Pickwick* as if it were a staged opera:

> Pickwick—It contains all Dickens in embryo, as an overture does an opera: themes and motives just touched upon, which are more elaborately developed in later works. (Longfellow *Journal*, March 28, 1861)

Peter Ackroyd suggests that Dickens' self-conscious theatrical self may have made his audience also self-consciously theatrical:

So strong was Dickens imaginative hold upon his readers, in fact, that it is also entirely probable that people began to behave in a Dickensian fashion when they were in his presence; in other words, they unconsciously exaggerated their own mannerisms and behavior in order to conform to the types which he had already created. (260)

The behavior of Dickens's characters appears as a model copied by youths who wished to appear "fashionable." Donald Grant Mitchell, who became a chief editor of *Harper's Monthly*, wrote in 1851:

He usually walks Broadway, at this stage of incipiency, arm in arm with a companion, for he has seen cuts of this mode of procedure, in the high-life illustrations of Dickens' works. (28)

As *The Pickwick Papers* begins, we read of the dapper quality of Mr. Pickwick and his Association:

The eloquent Pickwick, with one hand gracefully concealed behind his coat tails, and the other moving in air, to assist his glowing declamation; his elevated position revealing those tights and gaiters, which, had they clothed an ordinary man, might have passed without observation, but which, when Pickwick clothed them—if we may use the expression—inspired voluntary awe and respect; surrounded by the men who had volunteered to share the peril of his travels, and who were destined to participate in the glories of his discoveries.

Reverend Noah Porter in 1871, likewise, claimed Dickens's novels had great influence:

Indeed we may go further, and say that the devoted reader of a favorite novelist often becomes for the time an unconscious imitator or a passive reflex of his author. Like the chameleon, he takes the color of the bough and leaf from which he feeds. He is more likely to absorb and reproduce his defects than his excellences. The admiring and passionate devotee of Dickens is in danger of copying his broad caricature, his not very elevated slang, and the free and easy swing of the society in which Mr. Dickens delights. (230)

One may picture Dickens as an actor who spent most of his life reaching across the garish glow of gaslamps and footlights toward an audience. As Elizabeth S. Martin in "Melopomene" in the *Ladies Repository* observed in 1866:

It is impossible to read the works of Charles Dickens, himself an amateur performer in private theatricals, without our eyes filling with tears, and our hearts in sorrow over the lost ones who belong to the stage. (Martin 42)

Dickens's narrative gifts and his theatricality enabled him to suggest to his American readers the face to face encounters he later actualized in his public readings, projecting a direct personal contact with readers while writing for a mass audience. This connection between reader and writer underscores the idea of a community of readers and was expressed by William Makepeace Thackeray, when he wrote:

> in his constant communication with the reader the writer is forced into a frankness of expression, and to speak out his own mind and feelings as they urge him [. . . .] It is a sort of confidential talk between writer and reader. (33)

In fashioning this connection, Dickens's novels and public readings were based in a contemporary sense of theatricality that involved melodrama and sentiment. American actor Stephen Massett says that upon Charles Dickens's entrance to one of his readings "he was greeted with a storm of applause" and that "laughter and sobbings alternately rewarded his efforts" (Massett 349–50). "His command over the laughter and tears of an audience was absolute," Douglas Jerrold wrote of Dickens's public readings in Britain (25). Proposing a toast to Thackeray at a banquet of the Royal General Theatrical Fund, Dickens said that "every writer of fiction, though he may not adopt the dramatic form, writes in effect for the stage" (Dickens, *Speeches* 262).

The theatrical presence of Dickens, often remarked upon by critics from William Axton to Robert Garis, can be seen in the interplay between sentimentality and melodrama in his novels. It appears in his use of theatrical devices and in his attention to patterns and registers of speech in his characters. The fog-draped opening of *Bleak House*, for example, is much like an operatic overture, in which the imagery resembles the then new-stage devices of transparent gauze curtains, gas lighting, and fog effects made by stretching the gauze across the arch of the proscenium. Thus, *Bleak House* is London reality, but it is also theater.

> Fog everywhere. Fog up the river, where it flows among green alts and meadows; fog down the river, where it rolls defiled among the tiers of shipping, and the waterside pollutions of a great (and dirty) city. Fog on the Essex marshes, fog on the Kentish heights. Fog creeping into the cabooses of collier brigs; fog lying out on the yards, and hovering in the rigging of great ships; fog drooping on the gunwales of barges and small boats. Fog in the eyes and throats of ancient Greenwich pensioners, wheezing by the firesides of their wards; fog in the stem and bowl of the afternoon pipe of the wrathful skipper, down in his close cabin; fog cruelly pinching the toes and fingers of his shivering little 'prentice boy on deck. Chance people on the bridges peeping over the parapets into the nether sky of fog, with fog all round them, as if they were up in a balloon, and hanging in the misty clouds.

Many of Dickens's characters are theatrical and reproduce the features of melodrama: they are sentimental heroes and sharply defined villains, characters introduced by the alternating tones of narrative, caught in dramas of good and evil, spilling forth emotion, and distinguished by voice or habits in speech. Drawing upon melodrama, Dickens used the same wide array of stylized characters, as well as sharp contrasts and variations of humorous play and pathos. As Edgar Johnson observes, "he appropriated from the stage a vast repertory of artifices to create expectation of what was to come and to facilitate the retention of what had already taken place" (1: 92–93). Louis James adds: "*A Christmas Carol* owed a considerable debt to effects popular in the early Victorian playhouse" (81).

Some of Dickens's American readers associated him with the theater. Actress Anna Cora Ogden Mowatt Ritchie (1819–1870), the great-granddaughter of Francis Lewis, a signer of the Declaration of Independence, recalled an incident backstage in Baltimore, during her play *Honey Moon*. To make a quick costume change, she darted back across the stage and ran into a man reclined on a couch:

> A sofa had carelessly been left in one of the passages. Some tired carpenter was stretched upon it in an attitude which Dickens would have described as peculiarly American. His feet protruded over one arm of the sofa in a somewhat more elevated position than his head. My flight brought me suddenly in contact with a pair of heavy boots. (253–54)

This suggests that Mowatt had read or heard of Dickens's comments in *American Notes*. While Mowatt implies that Dickens had described Americans as lazy (which he had not), that she thinks of Dickens in relation to backstage activity, or inactivity, is suggestive (254). Adelaide Dutton Train Whitney observed Dickens's tendency to melodrama in the exaggeratedness of some of his character portrayals: "Dickens put it in extreme, as his way is, but he puts the very doctrine of heaven into it, which is his way" (48).

Readers navigated turbulent and uncertain plots before they reached Dickens's sentimental or coincidental resolutions. Little Nell and Tiny Tim were introduced to American readers in a context that included heart-wrenching incident, romance, tears, and ecstatic melodrama. Dickens's friend W.C. Macready cried upon the death of Little Nell and described Dickens's melodramatic reading of "Sikes and Nancy" from *Oliver Twist,* as a tangle between "two Macbeths." Some historians have viewed the sentimentalism surrounding Little Nell or Tiny Tim, or the melodrama surrounding characters like Sikes and Nancy, as an escape from the hard facts of the industrial age. However, sentimentalism provided Americans in the nineteenth century with a way of seeking understanding, not just escape. Sentimentalism defined conduct, as Karen Haltunnen has noted (60). Or, as Richard L. Bushman points out, sentimental plots helped meet the cultural needs of the period, reconciling, for people trying to live genteel lives, the allure of fashion and the refinements of modesty (302).

Sentimentality and melodrama appear at the end of many Dickens novels, when, following a melodramatic crisis, he brings his characters together. This reveals what Karen Haltunnen has called "the ties of confidence that bound men together in society. These ties, they believed, were fundamentally sentimental: affection, not coercion, linked man to man, heart to heart, in the American republic" (57). That affections connect people is among Dickens's primary themes and plot resolutions.

Dickens's theatricality invited his audience to participate emotionally in the winding emotional journeys that led to these conclusions. Such melodrama stirred the sentimentalism and democratic populism that was shaping middle-class public life in America between 1830 and 1850. For Dickens appealed widely, across class, race, and gender, and melodrama like his both entertained and brought emotional insecurities under control, as James L. Smith points out. "In the ideal world of melodrama, life is once more simple and uncomplicated, character and motive are reduced to blackest black or whitest white, coincidence and chance are tamed, unlucky accidents are overcome, and virtue after many thrilling and precipitous reversals is guaranteed to triumph over vice and end up with a choice assortment of material rewards" (viii).

Dickens's novels were a focal point for his readers, a home-space in which the outside world could be mediated through a story. The domestic sphere, often cast in sentimental terms, was set in contrast to the commercial world. The parlor, or front room, was a meeting ground between home and world, the place where visitors were greeted. It was also a place where books were read, often by families and guests together. It was as if their pages were welcomed companions mediating self and society, the home and the world. The Dickens text, read in a home-space like this, provided images and models of public behavior and attempted to reconcile these with homelike sincerity. The novel read at home became homelike: a place for the theatrical expression of feeling. As stories were read aloud and people were entertained by a social drama, Dickens's readers could return to this center of hearth and home and communal values, touched by the sympathy and benevolence that critics repeatedly found in Dickens's fiction. There they met the Cratchitts, or Florence Dombey, whose "patience and compassion, often operating over great distances, become models for Dickens's audience outside the fiction," as Hughes and Lund tell us (31).

Belle Kearney read Dickens aloud at home to her younger siblings, who responded to this reading as if it were a stage drama:

Every night after our lessons were learned for the next day, we gathered around the hearth in mother's room and I told the boys the promised stories; going into the smallest details; dwelling on peculiarities of characters, painting minutely their environment, waxing humorous or pathetic according to the situation; all the while watching closely the faces of my auditors. There they would sit for hours, my little brothers, listening intently to every word that was uttered; at time clapping their chubby hands with intense enjoyment, or doubling up their bodies with convulsive laughter, or holding their lips together with fore-finger and thumb to prevent too boisterous an explosion of hilarity, at other times allowing the great tears to roll down their cheeks, or with bowed heads sobbing aloud. My precious little comrades! They constituted my first audience and it was the most sympathetic and inspiring that has ever greeted me in all the after years. (25)

Dickens brought theater into the home. American families became theatrical, reading Dickens's stories aloud, integrating them into private theatricals. There was a "new acceptance of the theatricality of middle-class social life [. . . .] a product in part of the surge of economic self-confidence," Haltunnen tells us (186). As she points out, after 1850, private theatricals in the home became a popular form of entertainment in America. Guides to private theatrical making emphasized stylized melodrama. Much like Dickens, his audience poked fun at characters in public life and satirized public displays with charades and original plays in their home theaters. Private theatricals and other parlor rituals were a resource for role and costume changes. Dickens provided his readers with a theater of social satire within the safety of the home.

Private theatricals form the center of the tenth chapter of *Little Women* (1868) by Louisa May Alcott. Excited by the idea of having a secret club, the girls form the "P.C.": "and as all the girls admired Dickens, they called themselves the Pickwick Club." The girls meet every Saturday in the big garret, each wearing a "P.C." badge around their heads. They conduct a weekly newspaper, *The Pickwick Portfolio*, for which they all write. Meg plays the role of Samuel Pickwick. Jo portrays Augustus Snodgrass. Beth is Tracy Tupman and Amy is Nathaniel Winkle. *The Pickwick Portfolio* begins with a poem by Jo, signed A. Snodgrass. Meg, as S. Pickwick, provides a brief romantic story within the story, "The Masked Marriage—A Tale of Venice." Beth offers "The History of Squash." Amy has N. Winkle apologize for his "sin" of not writing but insists that he will send a French fable. The girls then, in prose and poetry, lament the loss of their pet. Advertisements follow, in which "Miss Oranthy Blummage will deliver her famous lecture on WOMAN AND HER POSITION at Pickwick Hall next Saturday evening, after the usual performances." Acting out the business of their secret society, the girls propose to admit a new member to the club, Theodore Laurence as Sam Weller.[2]

Suggested here is not only Louisa May Alcott's love of the stories of Dickens but also the wide availability and popularity of Dickens's *Pickwick Papers.* *Pickwick* is one text upon which Dickens's readers appear to have drawn their own caricatures. In Alcott's *Little Women,* Dickens stimulates his young readers to write and to imitate him. In their own secret society drama, Dickens serves as the model for their creative efforts as witty humorists in their *Pickwick Portfolio* (Alcott, *LW*, 116–26).

The transformation of Dickens's texts into theater by playwrights like John Broughton or Dion Boucicault, or by Alcott's little women, was a means of democratizing his fiction and making his stories social texts. Dickens's books created a heterogeneous audience: one of working-class, middle-class, and upper-class readers. For Dickens, such rational entertainment was socializing. It touched the affections, brought people together, and was morally uplifting. Consequently, his novels invited audience participation, as Schlicke and others have observed (8). In this way, his fiction supported the democracy that is so much a feature of American national identity.

Samuel Robert Calthrop in 1870 suggests that for some working-class readers Dickens's *Christmas Carol* announced a time for celebration:

> It comes to Mr. Fezziweg at Christmas time, and tells him to let the young men in his shop have a jolly time of it, put by their work, listen to the fiddle, and join the dance [. . . .] Ay, and the dream of those half-forgotten days comes over Scrooge, miserly, miserable Scrooge, and wakes up something like a soul in him. (30)

In Dickens's *A Christmas Carol* we can find the scene to which Calthorp was referring:

> Old Fezziweg laid down, who looked eagerly toward the scene, his pen and looked up at the clock . . .
> "Yo, ho, my boys!" said Fezziweg. "No more work tonight. Christmas Eve, Dick. Christmas, Ebeneezer! Let's have the shutters up!"

Dickens's story signaled a pause in the labor of the young men from the shop. The joining of their voices to the sound of the fiddle and dance reflects a style of entertainment that is social and participatory.

Audience interaction with the stage and actors was part of American folk culture, reflecting a sense of equality, as Kim C. Sturgess has pointed out. He notes that Gustave de Beaumont, who traveled with Alexis de Tocqueville, found American audiences entertaining: "they chat, they argue, they fidget about, they make occasion to drink" (86). While this suggests an American trait, such audiences can be found in *Nicholas Nickleby.* There the British crowd displays a rowdy, participatory style of responding to a performance by Miss Snevellicci. They rise, wave their hats and handkerchiefs, and cheer "Bravo." As they toss wreaths, "the tailor and his family kicked at the panels of the upper boxes till they threatened to come out altogether." Then follows a dramatic duel, a romantic couple's argument, and word of "how the ladies in the audience sobbed." The audience is moved by tantrums and tableaus to applause (*NN* 297–98). They have become melodramatic and theatrical.

> The first scene, in which there was nobody in particular, passed off calmly enough, but when Miss Snevellicci went on in the second, accompanied by the phenomenon as child, what a road of applause broke out! The people in the Borum box rose as one man, waving their hats and handkerchiefs, and uttering shouts of "Bravo!" Mrs. Borum and the governess cast wreaths upon the stage upon the stage, of which, some fluttered into the lamps, and one who crowned the temples of a fat gentleman in the pit who, looking eagerly toward the scene, remained unconscious of the honour; the tailor and his family kicked at the panels of the upper boxes until they threatened to come out altogether; the very ginger-beer boy remained transfixed in the centre of the house; a young officer supposed to entertain a passion for Miss Snevillicci, stuck his glass in his eye as though to hide a tear.

This passage in *Nicholas Nickleby* reminds us that reading Dickens was a social and participatory act, not only a private one. Dickens's readers were expected, like Vincent Crummles' audience in *Nicholas Nickleby*, to participate in the play of an ongoing serial. They often read aloud together, gaining access to what Dickens, in his *Household Words*, called "the amusements of the people." In the serialized *Hard Times*, Sleary's circus, Gradgrindian clowns in the ring, and Stephen Blackpool falling down into a pit, are all parallel to theatrical entertainment. Those who read Dickens's *Hard Times* were guided to its central affirmation of imagination, theater and circus against Gradgrindian fact. In Constance F. Woolson's "A Day of Mystery" which appeared on September 9, 1871, we read:

> One morning on the veranda we had been discussing the romance and reality of modern life. Harry, with the dogmatism of his class, maintained that prosaic reality was all that was left for us and that the increase of knowledge had banished romance, which was only another name for ignorance, from the world forever. But I clinging to my well-loved legends, and remembering any strange adventures on the unknown lake, proclaimed him a rude utilitarian, a living Gradgrind. (292)

Dickens's readers responded to his caricatures, like Gradgrind, who, with their easily identifiable features, reflect the 'types' found in melodrama. The

first words of Vincent Crummles, theater impresario of *Nicholas Nickleby*, are
"There's a picture," as he points to two actors sword-fighting (*NN* 262). This
visual emphasis is underscored as Crummles offers Nicholas the opportunity
to make "signs" for the theater company. "Think what capital bills a man of
your education could write for the shop windows" (*NN* 268). Eventually,
beyond this advertising in the positing of playbills, Nicholas will become
an actor, playing Romeo and other roles. Crummles has suggested to him:
"There's a genteel comedy in your walk and manner, juvenile tragedy in your
eye, and touch-and-go force in your laugh" (*NN* 267).

Caricature, a device familiar to melodrama, may have been a typology that
assisted readers of Dickens in the identification of self and others in society.
"The characters of melodrama are a set of walking cliches who invite snap
moral judgments the moment they appear" (Smith ix). It may have been useful for coding strangers in the city on the basis of appearance and manner. As
Karen Haltunnen points out:

> The anonymity of the antebellum world of strangers was particularly great be-
> cause pre-industrial methods of coding the stranger had become useless before
> modern methods became possible [. . . .] Whenever daily social life is character-
> ized by frequent face-to-face contact with strangers, the fleeting impressions
> made by surface appearances become of great importance. (39)

Dickens's caricatures participated in this coding. We have seen how
Dickens's American readers constructed pictures of people they met, at times
based, in part, upon their previous reading experiences of Dickens. In a
world of cultural objects, Dickens's caricatures were a reference to which they
turned in making sense of the appearances and behavior of people in their
lives. Such readers saw Dickens characters everywhere and enacted Dickens's
style in their own writing and behavior. Dickens's character tags, a device
drawn from melodrama, were repeated by people, who also recorded their
visual impressions of other people in ways similar to the caricatures drawn by
a Union soldier, William Robertson Boggs. As a fellow soldier wrote: "Boggs
preserved three drawings illustrative of West Point, two suggested by characters in Dickens" (Boggs 25).

These visual indicators of personality are matched in Dickens by auditory
cues. These were important for Dickens's audience because they often listened
to his stories read aloud. As Lawrence Levine observes, nineteenth-century
America "remained an oral world in which the spoken word was central"
(36). For example, in their letters between Newport and Charleston, mother
and daughter Eliza Middleton and Mary Hering Middleton recall reading
Dickens aloud (112). Anita Dwyer Wither writes in her journal, "The Captain
is reading Oliver Twist aloud to me" (25). Marion Harland recalls how "*Mar-*

tin Chuzzlewit was read aloud in our family circle" (88). Frederick S. Cozzens, in his novel *The Sparrowgrass Papers*, has his first person narrator, reading aloud to Mrs. Sparrowgrass, say: "and I was just about saying, I meant to read all Dickens' Christmas Stories over [. . .] before the holidays, when we heard something like wheels cheeping through the snow outside, and a muffled crumping, and then a knock at the front door" (Cozzens 198).

Dickens's novels read aloud offered his audience a theatrical interplay of voices, in which a reader or listener encountered many social languages. As in a play, Dickens's readers met with narrative asides and direct address, repetition and shifts in tempo, and a society filled with the voices of many classes of people. These voices are heteroglossia, in Bahktin's sense of the word.

American readers often recognized the voices of Dickens's characters as British and contrasted their own American idiom with them. When these readers encountered voices besides those of their own discourse community, they experienced heteroglossia, or the many-voicedness of society. The reader sensed his or her similarity to Dickens's characters, or a difference from them. Language, says Bahktin, is

> populated with the intentions of others. Forcing it to submit to one's own intentions and accents, is a difficult and complicated process [. . . .] Consciousness finds itself inevitably facing the necessity of having to choose a language. (294–95)

Dickens's narrative voices, the ones he later brought to his public readings, also sustained his audience. The use of contrasts or opposites that unfold in a regular rhythmic pattern ("it was the best of times, it was the worst of times") is characteristic of Dickens's narrative manner. His character descriptions are constructed around a few, selected visual indicators: "There was a king with a large jaw and a queen with a plain face, on the throne of England; there were a king with a large jaw and queen with a fair face, on the throne of France" (*A Tale of Two Cities*). These simple markers provide an anchor for the reader to identify a character. It is this shorthand that some of Dickens's common readers made use of in describing people they met in daily life. For them a Dickensian character apparently was one who was in some way eccentric or visually striking. Just as Dickens typed Mr. Jingles (*Pickwick*) by his way of speaking, so his common readers would type people as being like a Dickens character. Mr. Jingles has his unique manner. "The license," repeated Mr. Jingles. "In hurry post-haste for a license, in a hurry, ding-dong I came back." The sing-song idiosyncracy of his speech is a character tag: "Run on, nothing to the hours, days, weeks, years, where we've united, run-on . . ."

Dickens's common readers appear to have remembered the author's character tags, phrases like Oliver Twist's "please, sir, can I have some more" (*Oliver*

Twist), Mr. Micawber's "in short" and "something will turn up" (*David Copperfield*), or repeated phrases like "Barkis is willing" (*Great Expectations*). These character tags were devices that could be found in melodrama, as in the work of Dickens's acquaintance Douglas Jerrold, in his *Black Ey'd Susan* (1829) and *The Rent Day* (1832). They provided audiences with markers by which figures could be remembered and discussed.

Melodrama, in dialogue with the novel, shows America struggling for what is distinctively American through borrowed forms. In America, sentimental and sensational plots appeared in William Dunlop's *Andre*, Clifton Tayleur's *Horeshoe Robinson*, and William Pratt's *Ten Nights in a Bar-room*. American audiences were treated to the "sensation dramas" of Dion Boucicault, an Irish immigrant who was a Dickens adapter.[3]

The oral and auditory aspects of Dickens's texts suggest how many of his common readers may have experienced them. Dickens, an author who sometimes spoke his character's words aloud before mirrors and who read his work in public on a stage, was often read aloud, or performed in reading circles. When Dickens is read with an ear to verbal patterns and relationships, to follow Vlock's view, "reading is theater, a concert of verbal and physical dramatic gestures gathered up into the frame of a text" (201–03). As Vlock observes: "Much of Dickens criticism has focused on text as written word, literary artifact, and has neglected the layers of extra-textual movement, the vocal and gestural inflection, for example" (198).

The theatricality of Dickens and his audience's responsiveness to oral presentation is evident in his own public readings and in the many public readings of Dickens's stories that took place following his death. A writer in *The Atlantic Monthly* points out how authors imitated Dickens: "The newcomer is of this school of Dickens in treating low life, in copying a few of his names, and in reading from his own works. There the parallel ends." This writer describes Dickens's appearance at Steinway Hall:

> The spell of pathos and humor cast by that somewhat grotesque figure, with its horn-like hair, its bizarre waistcoat and jewelry, and its red face subdued against the maroon screen, would suffice to draw one back to any entertainment that promised a reminiscence of it. (*Atlantic Monthly* [February 1878]: 239)

The imitation of Dickens's public readings was a reminder of his theatricality and his social dimension. Dickens, as a source for public lectures, readings, and theater, drew people together. In 1868, while Dickens was still on his American tour, Charles Eytinge read from "Dickens and Other Authors." James E. Murdock read "Mr. Pickwick and the Lady in Yellow Curl Papers." Augustus Waters read from *David Copperfield*. In 1872, British actor Edmund Yates toured the United States speaking of his recollections of Dickens. In the

1870s, George Vandenhoff, an accomplished actor, was compared to Dickens by the *New York Evening Post* as "a master of elocution" in contrast with "an amateur reader (Dickens)." Theatrical productions of Dickens's stories were plentiful, during his American reading tour and in the years immediately following it. These drew additional readers to Dickens's fiction.

So did lectures, like that of Hiram P. Crozier, who addressed the Atheneum Literary Society November 2, 1876, on parallels between Dickens and Thackeray. Actors for the Chautauqua Institute frequently gave readings from Dickens, some of them portraying the author. The Chautauqua circuit, established in 1874 with some 200–300 local groups, featured performers like William Sterling Battis, billed as an "interpreter of Dickens," and Frank Speight, who did dramatizations. John Kendrick Bangs, the popular humorist and collector of Dickens illustrations, toured the United States, including Dickens material with his own. Across the United States, public readings, joining celebrity and the theatrical, became an important form of entertainment and the manner of Dickens's 1867–68 American readings was imitated.

One of the most successful public lecturers of this time was Mark Twain, whose tour was managed by George Dolby, the manager of Dickens's American reading tour. Samuel Clemens (Mark Twain) had since his youth been an avid reader of Dickens. Twain began his own public lectures soon after the public readings of Dickens. Planning to lecture in Cleveland to the ladies of the Orphan Asylum, Mark Twain alluded to Dickens's *Our Mutual Friend* on January 7, 1869: "it makes you drop into poetry like Silas Wegg" (Twain, *Letters*, 3: 423–24). While on tour in November of that year, he enclosed a newspaper clipping from Boston in a letter to Olivia. In it, a reviewer, writing on Twain's use of rising action, wrote "Mr. Dickens taught us how it might be used to advantage, and Mark Twain, doubtless without borrowing a leaf from Mr. Dickens's notebook, has found out for himself how effective an adjunct it is to humorous speech" (Twain, *Letters*, 3: 528).

In his notebooks, Twain once wrote:

> I have no sense of humor. In illustration of this fact I will say this—by way of confession—that if there is a humorous passage in the *Pickwick Papers* I have never been able to find it. (Twain, *Notebooks* 184)[4]

American audiences laughed at Twain's tales, even as they continued to laugh at Dickens's eccentric characters with their peculiar names. Dickens's texts and phrases, read aloud by public performers, or read in family theatricals, participated in an ongoing social drama.

In the collective imagination of Americans, Dickens served as an imaginary meeting place where oral tradition and theater met and fiction was consumed. Dickens drew upon melodrama and sentimentality and this contributed to his audience's need for both entertainment and stability. He enabled his read-ers to express their emotions, as he would do in his public readings, thereby supporting affective connection between them. Dickens welcomed his audi-ence to become involved in a theater that, like American democracy, was a participatory process. It was one in which melodrama met with the ordinary, romance met with fact, and fancy met with reality.

Notes

1. Dickens's Mr. Pickwick participates in self-performance; he engages in style and parody, as Garret Stewart has demonstrated in *Dickens and the Trials of the Imagina-tion* (Cambridge: Harvard UP, 1974). Pickwick is a character who loses innocence as he comes to terms with the harsh realities of the world. Therein lies the book's com-edy, suggests Barbara Hardy (Hardy, *Moral Art* 73). As Steven Marcus has pointed out, the novel speaks to "the ideal possibilities of human relations in community," the fulfillment of which "extends our awareness of the limits of our humanity" (42).

2. Louisa May Alcott, herself an obvious fan of Dickens, also makes reference to Dickens in her short story "Debby's Debut" which appeared in *The Atlantic Monthly in* August 1870. Her journals and letters include playful "Wellerisms," imitating the verbal mannerisms of Dickens's character in *Pickwick.*

3. Dion Boucicault's *The Octoroon* (1859) was the second most produced anti-slavery play of its time, next to the melodramatic *Uncle Tom's Cabin.* In it a villain sets a riverboat on fire. In *The Poor of New York* (1857), an apartment is set on fire. In *Pauvette* (1858) an avalanche traps a hero in a cabin onstage. In *The Flying Scud* (1866), a horse race is staged by using cut-out horses. In *After Dark* (1868) a hero is drugged and placed on London train tracks.

4. That Mark Twain's public reading career was informed by his acquaintance with the work of Dickens becomes obvious as one reads through his letters. Both Twain and his wife Olivia read Dickens. Recalling Dickens's Tiny Tim, Twain signed a letter from he and his wife to his mother on December 17, 1870: "God bless us everyone" (Twain *Letters*, 4:273–74). Olivia wrote to him on November 28, 1871, sending her letter from Homer, New York, with a mention that she had been reading Dickens.

10

The Public Readings and the American Reconstruction of Charles Dickens

DICKENS, AT LAST, SOUGHT TO MEET HIS AMERICAN PUBLIC face to face. In 1867, he would cross the physical boundary of an ocean and the emotional boundaries of his American readers' love and conflict with him to read aloud to them from his works. Such readings, Dickens believed, were "rational amusement" which nurtured the "sympathies and graces of imagination" ("Amusements of the People" *HW* I [March 30, 1850]: 13–15; *Pilgrim Letters* 9: 58). They also nurtured the reconstruction of Charles Dickens in the minds of his American audience. Indeed, while Charles Dickens, as a public celebrity, was cleverly and systematically exploited for profit by publisher James Fields, who used the public readings as a marketing tool; Dickens's own letters during the American tour express a drive not only for money but for the project of entertaining his audience. Dickens's reading tour was one of the first uses of celebrity for advertising purposes, as Michael Newbury observes (80). However, the quest for income was matched by Dickens's earnest desire to interact with his American public, something that he achieved, as news reports and audience recollections demonstrate. As Kathleen Tillotson and John Butt have pointed out, Dickens's interaction with his audience was the most important "love affair" of his life (12). As Jennifer Hayward puts it, "probably more than any writer of his time he insisted (sometimes against all evidence to the contrary) that his relationship with that public was interactive, even intimate" (39). Dickens said he sought "that particular relation (personally affectionate and like no other man's) that subsists between me and the public" (quoted in Collins 125).

Dickens's American readings were a site for communal imagination. They were a specifically American event in which audience members could match their own imaginings of Dickens's characters with Dickens's portrayal of them. *Galaxy*, in February 1868, said of the readings that it was clear that Dickens was a part of American literary history: "His second visit to America is plainly to be an era in our literary annals as well as in his life" (*Galaxy* [February 1868]: 255).

Dickens's "populist project," as Juliet John has called his work (17), extended to more than sixty American public readings. Dickens observed that America had changed and a new generation of American readers largely overlooked the days of *American Notes* and *Martin Chuzzlewit* some twenty-five years earlier. Some nationalistic resistance to Dickens still remained, but Dickens's humor and theme of sympathy won over his American public. For seventeen years, throughout his journals, Dickens had been constructing "a virtual family, a virtual community, as their imagined audience" (John 90). Now, during his reading performances, Dickens's melodramatic style actualized this connection, stirring sentiment and laughter in city after city.

Much like the fictional theater audience in *Nicholas Nickleby*, the audiences in American cities laughed and cried at the portrayals of familiar characters that many considered fictional "friends." The bond between Dickens and his audience was supported by the interactive theatrical nature of the readings. Centered in entertainment, Dickens's melodrama and sentimentality emphasized the belief that emotional display or "transparency of character is crucial to the survival of community" (John 9). As George William Curtis in *Harper's New Monthly* wrote:

> Why should he try to conceal that which is the very heart of his genius, sympathy—the golden undercurrent of all the writing of Charles Dickens, which has brought him near to so many hearts, and established him in the best seats of the houses of the highest and lowest? (368)

Dickens's readings made a lasting impression on his American audience. Children who attended the readings, who met Dickens, or who heard about the readings from their parents, also read his fiction. In this way, Dickens had an imaginative impact upon America's future.

For many years, nationalistic tensions made it uncertain whether Dickens would ever return to visit the United States. Yet, Dickens's great popularity in America had led to speculation about Dickens's return. As early as September 1862, George Ripley, transcendentalist writer and editor, wrote to H. D. Mayo of rumors of a reading tour (Ripley Papers, Letter [September 8, 1862] American Literary Manuscripts, Morgan Library). However, in June 1866,

Harper's New Monthly was saying that Charles Dickens would never again visit America:

> Mr. Dickens evidently seems so persuaded that Americans are hostile to him, and he has unquestionably for so long a time cherished a feeling toward us which is not exactly friendly, that he is not very likely to cross the sea again to visit us. (*Harper's* [June 1866]: 120)

Park Benjamin, still soured by *American Notes, Martin Chuzzlewit* and the international copyright issue, satirically called Dickens's arrival "the second coming."

Harper's wrote: "Mr. Dickens is now coming to meet a new generation of friends face to face, as he met their fathers. The audiences that he will meet here will be as large as the largest halls any where can hold. But think of his audience in the world of readers!" (*Harper's* [December 1867]: 118).

> his popularity is immense and permanent. There are constant new editions and series of his works issued in England, and after the millions of readers of this magazine have consumed them in this country they are republished in more varieties and editions than any other author has ever known. (*Harper's* [December 1867]:119)

Dickens's American audience eagerly anticipated his readings. Charles Kent reports that George Dolby, Dickens's business manager, sat "all day of November 18th at his desk selling tickets for 13 hours" (68). In America in 1867–68, Charles Dickens read in the company of more than 114,000 people. By Kent's estimate, Dickens averaged about four readings per week in America between December 1867 and April 20, 1868, drawing large crowds. Kent writes of "audiences as numerous as the largest building in each town could by any contrivance be made to contain" (77). He speaks of lines "a quarter of a mile long" in which people waited "in sleet and snow, out in the streets" (76).

While popular, Dickens did not completely shed the nationalistic ambivalence of the American audience. There were disgruntled patrons, ones who said they could not hear the readings, or that they would rather have stayed home. Some audience members wrote that their own interpretation of Dickens's characters was different from the author's. For example, Laurence Hutton, an actor and drama critic, writes:

> When he came here to show his creations as he saw them himself, many of our idols were shattered by the hands of the man who made them [. . .] we were far from being satisfied, in Dickens's interpretations of his own creations, and by these interpretations lost many an old friend forever. Toots and Winkle, Buzfuz

and the Wellers, and many of them as we had known them all our lives, faded into thin air, in the light that Dickens cast upon them at Steinway Hall. (118)

Or, as an editor for *Galaxy* wrote similarly at the time of the readings:

His dramatic power is very great [. . . .] We have, however, not heard of a single instance in which Mr. Dickens threw for his hearer a new light upon any one of his own creations, but of very many in which his presentation of his own personages was found inferior to the ideal in the mind of the hearer. (*Galaxy* [December 1867]: 256)

However, many others, like Ellen Mordecai, were quite enthusiastic. Ellen wrote to her aunt Emma Mordecai from Raleigh, North Carolina:

Aunt Emma! Aunt Emma! Aunt Emma!!! seen Dickens!, shaken hands with Dickens!! sent Dickens flowers!!! RECEIVED A NOTE FROM DICKENS!!!!! OH ME! OH ME! Oh me! That last "oh me!" is to be read in town of (illegible) not selfish tho' for all the big oh's denote my great joy that you have had such an everlasting happiness & couldn't have had one glimpse of that most interesting of mortals. I'm completely bedumbed [. . . .] Where is Dickens now? Are you going to correspond!!!! [. . . .] Don't you feel as if you had seen Oliver, & Dick Snivell, & the Marchioness, & Sully Gross, and Smike, & didn't you feel like asking Dickens about them—just as if they were real people, & getting him to tell you something more of little Nell and the old schoolmaster? I haven't read "Barnaby Rudge" yet. (Ellen Mordecai Letter [April 1, 1842], Mordecai Family Papers, Cadmus Library, University of North Carolina)

The Dickens readings were a public event that brought people together—sometimes in unexpected ways. For example, Samuel Clemens, or Mark Twain as he had become better known to the world, while rooming at the Westminster Hotel in New York on November 19 wrote a letter in which he quipped: "When Charles Dickens sleeps in this room next week, it will be a gratification to him to know that I have slept in it also" (Twain *Letters* 2:104). Joining the family of Charley Langdon for Dickens's reading on December 31, Samuel Clemens sat with Langdon's daughter, Olivia Louise Langdon, whom he had met at dinner a few nights earlier on December 27th. The two fell in love during the next few months and she became Olivia Langdon Clemens. Within a year, Mark Twain would begin a successful reading series of his own, one designed by Charles Dickens's business agent, George Dolby.

Relationships and conversations developed because Charles Dickens reached out to his American audience, creating the occasion for such contact. Dickens built communal imagination in America with readings that were de-signed theatrically. He stripped away much of his satirical edge and he sought to make his audience laugh, to move their emotions. His audience, likewise, was primed by melodrama and prepared by oral reading in school and at home for these presentations. In an 1857 letter to Daniel Maclise, concerning Dickens's play *The Frozen Deep*, the author wrote:

> In that perpetual struggle after an expression of that truth [. . .] the interest of such a character to me is that it enables me as it were, to write a book in company instead of in my own solitary room and to feel its effect coming freshly back upon me from the reader. (Dickens *Pilgrim Letters* 6: 286)

Dickens kept company in America. *Harper's*, recognizing Dickens's theatricality and his rapport with his readers, struck an expectant note:

> There are not many in this country who have heard Mr. Dickens read. Those who have speak of it as a pleasure not less in its kind than that of the first introduction to the world he created. Indescribably he impersonates the characters of the story he reads. (*Harper's* [December 1867]: 120)

Many who attended Dickens's American performances agreed that the public readings were lively pieces of theater. Evert A. Duyckinck, recalling the readings in 1872–74, wrote: "His dramatic skill was here brought into exercise, the 'reading' being, in fact, a thoroughly well-sustained and laborious piece of acting" (397). Louise Bogger, a magazine writer, in an appreciation of Hans Christian Andersen, wrote in July 1871, "To hear Dickens was, in fact, to see a play—one of his own stories dramatised" (45).

With passionate intensity, Dickens evoked feelings. A friend of editor Arthur Benson told him that soon after the readings began, "Five minutes later the whole room was under the spell. Breathless attention, unashamed tears, thrill, irresistible laughter, from one end of the hall to the other! The hour passed like a few minutes." Benson concludes that the reason for this was that Dickens was "a true teller of stories and an actor always" (381). In this account, one can see the enraptured participation of the audience, who were urged by Dickens before his performances to express their emotions.

Dickens's gesture returns us to the notion of stories told around the fireplace, a symbol of communal imagination. With his theatrically enacted stories, Dickens personally entered the theater of oralization of his works. The testing of voices in his own parlor, garden and writing room, the faces he made in private in mirrors while writing his novels, were given a public dimension. This theatrical nature of Dickens's readings in America was observed by Annie Field, who wrote, "He was passionately fond of the theatre, loved the lights and music and flowers, and the happy faces of an audience; he was accustomed to say his love of the theatre never failed" (96). James Fields observed "the delighted crowds that assembled nightly in the Tremont Temple, and no one who heard Dickens, during that eventful month of December, will forget the sensation produced by the great author, actor, and reader [. . . .] He liked to talk about the audiences who came to hear him read" (169).

Audiences were drawn into Dickens's dynamic and interactive readings. The condensed versions of his stories that Dickens prepared suggest that he sought to entertain them. For his readings, he excerpted passages of social criticism and Dickens's little dramas were, as Philip Collins says, "not drawn from the later and more socially critical novels" (Collins, *Public Readings*, xii). They came from his Christmas books and other popular tales. A festive spirit of comedy, laughter, and sentiment was his goal.

This is consistent with Dickens's view of popular entertainment as being culturally inclusive. Dramatic entertainment of Dickens's type provides a communal experience for people of all backgrounds. Dickens, with his popular art, provided for his audience's need for imaginative entertainment. As Philip Collins has said, "He wrote about and defended popular amusements not mainly out of a sense of public duty, or for want of a likely subject, but because he enormously enjoyed them" (Collins, *Dickensian* 61 (1965): 8).

Dickens's public readings corresponded well with America's emergent democracy. His characters were given a voice and his audience was given an opportunity to participate and respond. Reading aloud was natural for a writer who sought living contact with his readers, one who engaged in private and amateur theatricals, and who saw theater and story as necessary amusements of the people. To read for his public was for Dickens a means of expression and contact with his audience. Dickens's corespondence shows that he desired an imaginative bond of sympathy, a community of readers that he believed he was helping to forge. It was not merely a matter of aggrandizing greater fame or monetary fortune, as Hutton contended, or a matter of dark obsessions within him, as Edmund Wilson would later claim. Rather, as Paul Schlicke notes, "He was [. . .] enacting the values which his fiction and journalism had propounded" (245).

America's second look at Dickens came as he entered the city of Boston in late November 1867. James Fields wrote, "On a blustering evening in November 1867, Dickens arrived in Boston harbor, on his second visit to America [. . . .] It was pitch dark when we sighted the Cuba and ran alongside" (168). Dickens's American readings began in Boston on December 2, 1867. They would net the author an estimated profit of 1300 pounds per week. Public curiosity was as intense in 1867 as it had been in 1842. Fields reports that figures on sales for the Boston readings reached the author before he landed in port (165).

Newspaper accounts provide us with some images of Dickens's audience. The *Boston Daily Journal*, December 3, reported:

The reading of the Carol was concluded about half past nine o'clock, and it is no exaggeration to say, afforded unmixed delight to all who heard it [. . . .] To say that his audience followed him with delight hardly expresses the interest with which they hung upon every word [. . .] and eyed every gesture. (*Boston Daily Journal* [December 3, 1867]: 928)

The *New York Tribune* on December 3 observed that the "polished ice of that proper community (of Boston) has seldom cracked so loudly and cheerily." The *Boston Post* wrote that Dickens "means business." The newspaper, on January 4, wrote:

the Dickens fever [. . .] rages here with high unabated virulence [. . . .] Some people say they wouldn't give a quarter in script nor specie to hear the eminent elocutionist a second time. (*Boston Post* [January 4, 1868]: 26)

Henry Wadsworth Longfellow told Charles Sumner in Boston that

the Readings, or rather Actings, have been immensely successful, according to our standards of success; but Boston audiences are proverbially cold. The Gulf Stream would hardly raise their temperature a degree. (Longfellow, *Letters* [December 8, 1867]: 54)

A similar comment came from the *New York Herald*, December 4:

A Boston audience takes nothing for granted. Other audiences would let a man start from his reputation; this audience requires him to start even, and make its reputation under its very eyes. He does it too, and thus his triumph is all the greater. (*New York Herald* [December 4, 1867]: 1)

In New York, Steinway Hall was packed on opening night. *The New York Times*, December 10 reported:

We never have had, and [. . .] never shall have, an entertainment more full of genuine, legitimate and elevating pleasure than those readings of MR. DICKENS. (*The New York Times* [December 10,1867]: 16)

Dickens read *A Christmas Carol*, although *Harper's* writer says, "I must protest against the word *read* in this connection [. . . .] For Dickens is an actor" (ibid.). After Dickens's nearly two hour reading

The audience lingered, after their rounds of applause, until his retreating form finally disappeared behind the screen. I wonder if they, like me, were spooney during that brief pause, and followed Charles Dickens with benedictions for all the happiness and good cheer he has been able to bring into a world never too free of snarlers and sneerers. (*Harper's* [January 1868]: 106)

Dickens's keen awareness of his reputation in America is shown by a response he made to lawyer and editor Richard Grant White, who attended Dickens's first reading in New York and promptly encouraged him to join him in pursuing the copyright question again. Wanting to make amends to his American audience, Dickens, on December 12, wrote to Grant: "even if my leisure were greater, I would rather put the subject aside, in friendship toward the American people." White had also commented to Dickens on *A Tale of Two Cities*. Dickens wrote from his hotel room:

What you say of the Tale of Two Cities is extremely gratifying to me. It may be interesting to you to know, as you mention Mr. Carlyle in the same sentence with it, that he wrote me the highest commendation of the book when he first read it [. . . .] [H]is History inspired me with the general fancy of that story. (NYHS; Dickens, *Pilgrim Letters* [December 12,1867] 11: 230)

Grant had attended the same first reading in New York that an editor from *Harper's* reviewed, with observations of the crowd. The reviewer states his belief that the audience had come to Steinway Hall to hear something about their own lives, or as he put it: "the story of all the experience under other forms of all this audience."

Do you suppose that the sweet white-haired couple who sat before us in Steinway Hall upon the first night of Dickens's readings—that couple of comely age and of lovely deference to each other—believe that there can ever again be such an evening as they knew in the Park Theatre long ago [. . . .] Do we not know, as we look over the humming, happy crowd that fills the tasteless and glaring hall of Steinway, that there are turtle doves here in scores, and all as softly cooing as any that ever flew? A sensitive Easy Chair, in the midst of such a throng as was gathered on that first Dickens evening, positively glows with the consciousness of the amount of hoping and longing, and looking and smiling, and hand-pressing and whispering, and the vast contiguous happiness pervades the hall. Why what have we come to hear but the story of all the experience under other forms of all this audience, written and read by the master? (*Harper's* [January 1868]: 393)

In newspaper accounts, we are given vivid images of the readings and descriptions of audience members. *Harper's* writer notes that as one of the evening readings began, with Dickens's entrance "The steady clapping was prolonged, and Dickens stood calmly, bowing easily once or twice, and waiting with the air of one ready to begin business" (395). Someone seated behind him, he says, was then heard to express "the air of mingled indignation, chagrin, and disappointment. A woman declared that she did not hear a word and added, caustically, that the spectacle alone was hardly worth the money" (394). Another friend stepped forward at this point, saying, "Just let me take your glass, will you? I can't hear a word, but I should like to see how the man looks." The writer concludes that some of the people he overheard will "feel swindled. But let them feel as they may, those who did not hear him are sure to go again, and if they hear the next time, again and again" (395).

The enthusiasm surrounding the readings is typified by one reader, who Kate Field referred to as "Mrs. Jones." Field wrote that the "good woman absolutely adores Dickens, burning a candle under his portrait as Catholics burn candles at the household shrines of the Virgin. She reads nothing but Dickens." Mrs. Jones went to New York and "attended several of his readings and returned home more rabid than ever" (45–46).

The *Brooklyn Eagle*, however, on December 16, insisted that other newspapers were too lavish in their praise of the Dickens readings. The *Brooklyn Eagle*, its writer asserted, would set the record straight.

> The *Eagle* was the first journal in America to expose the fraud practiced upon the people by the newspaper critics, who rivaled each other and exhausted their limited knowledge of our copious mother tongue, in an attempt to show that Dickens was one of our greatest living actors, while as a reader it was not possible to enumerate his excellence. (*The Brooklyn Eagle* [December 16,1867]: 26)

The *Eagle* writer says that "men would have emptied Steinway Hall last night, in ten minutes, if they could read no better than Charles Dickens." While critical of other newspapers and questioning Dickens's ability as a reader and actor, this reviewer appreciated Dickens's writing. He also offered his own positive re-evaluation of Dickens's *American Notes*.

Dickens, meanwhile, offered his re-evaluation of America, as America capitalized on Dickens's readings. From December 27 to January 3, again in New York with a bad cold, Dickens mentioned in a letter to his daughter Mary Dickens that theater versions of his stories were appearing all around the city: "Cricket, Oliver Twist, Our Mutual Friend and I don't know what else, every night," he wrote (Dickens *Pilgrim Letters*, December 30, 1867). Popular as the theater versions were, in January 1868, the editor of *Galaxy* recorded criticisms he had heard regarding Dickens's readings:

> We have heard Mr. Dickens voice spoken of as somewhat weak and husky, but we could have pardoned these blemishes, had we noticed them in any marked degree, much more easily than a certain tone, inflection and manner, which uncomfortably reminded us of a third rate Cockney actor telling us stories at a free-and-easy supper table. (*Galaxy* [January 1868]: 255–56)

William Cullen Bryant, in a letter, pointed to his family's reactions to Dickens's readings, which were no more complimentary:

> Mr. Dickens is here, and everybody is running after him, but I cannot muster up enough curiosity to go. Those of my household here and many of my friends have been disappointed, but the newspapers praise him without stint. They—I do not mean the newspapers—say that his voice is not good, neither strong nor musical and while they admit his comic power as an actor, they call his reading of parts that are not comic monotonous and sometimes, in the pathetic parts, doleful. (236)

Bryant repeated these comments by his household to Miss Jerusha Dewey, to whom he wrote later on March 4, 1868:

> But the winter has been enlivened with the readings of Dickens, none of which have I attended. You have heard, I suppose, all about them—how everybody went, and only one half of every body heard him—how he is a good comic actor, and rather dismal in the pathetic, how he has a bad voice and carries off a good deal of money. (255)

Philadelphia newspapers also reported a mixed response to Dickens's eight readings in the city, across three visits. The *New York Tribune* reported on the Philadelphia reading of January 14:

> It was an audience which, in the words of Sergeant Buzfuzz, I might declare an enlightened, a high-minded, a right-feeling, a dispassionate, a conscientious, a sympathizing, a contemplative, and a poetical jury, to judge Charles Dickens without fear, or favor [. . . .] Mr. Dickens was received coldly. Here was an Englishman who had pulled us to pieces and tweaked the national nose by writing *Martin Chuzzlewit* and *American Notes*. Philadelphia held out as long as she could. The first smile came when Bob Cratchit warmed himself with a candle, but before Scrooge had go through with the first ghost the laughter was universal and uproarious. (*New York Tribune*, January 14, 1868]: 40)

Dickens won over the Philadelphia crowd with infectious emotion and sympathy. The *New York Tribune* writer points to seeing one woman in the crowd who Dickens played to:

> There was a young lady in white fur and blue ribbons, name unknown to the writer, upon whose sympathies Mr. Dickens played as if she had been a piano. A deaf man could have followed his story by looking at her face. The goose convulsed her. The pudding threw her into hysterics; and when the story came to the sad death of Tiny Tim, "my little, little child," tears were streaming down her cheeks. This young lady was as good as Mr. Dickens, and all the more attractive

because she couldn't help it. Then as a joke began to be dimly forseen, it was great to see the faint smile dawning on long lines of faces, growing brighter and brighter till it passed from sight to sound, and thundered to the roof in vast and inextinguishable laughter. (ibid.)

Evidently, many audience members disagreed with the glowing assessments of Dickens's readings, or were unwilling to forget Dickens's criticisms of America of twenty-five years earlier. One irate reviewer would not let copyright controversies of the past go. With nationalistic aggressiveness, Mr. John Wien Forney, a journalist, in *The Philadelphia Press* wrote: "No man has so caricatured, so maligned, so cruelly spoken of us [. . . .] Mr. Dickens has nothing in sympathy with this people" (Moss 126).[1]

Fanny Fern, writer and feminist, who went with her husband James Parton to hear Dickens read at Henry Ward Beecher's Plymouth Church in Brooklyn didn't like it at all. She later wrote to her friend, General Butler, about how she disliked the readings, while her husband loudly applauded them:

I have been to hear the great Dickens. I hate him. No old girl could be vainer [. . . .] Mr. Parton clapped his hands till they were blistered, when he heard him—and turning around to me with glowing face, said, "Fanny, what do you think of that?" "I hate him," I said, with my eyes on his two vests and the obnoxious rosebud. I wanted to see a man. (269–70)

Fanny Fern's animosity toward Dickens may have turned less on nationalistic sentiments than on her feeling spited by press members who had arranged for a dinner for Dickens and excluded women. This exclusion of female journalists, including herself, led to the womens' formation of the Sorosis Club. Fern wrote mockingly in the *New York Ledger* on May 16, 1868:

Perhaps, in justice I should add, that it was suggested that they might perhaps see the animals from "the musician's balcony," or listen to their speeches "through the crack in the door" with the servants.

Fern, the sister of the popular writer N.P. Willis, may also have been jealous of Dickens's popularity. Her husband, James Parton, a Massachusetts-based writer and editor, had written to James Fields, "There ought to be ladies at the press dinner to Dickens." Fanny Fern had applied and was rejected. Recalling the public readings, she was no fan of Charles Dickens.

Dickens made a strong impression upon his audience in Washington, D.C. At Carroll Hall, which held 1,200 people, Dickens's reading was, according to the *National Intelligencer*, "the perfection of art." America's legislators, themselves orators, applauded Dickens, who, in a letter, described "rounds and rounds of applause all through." After the *Carol* was read, the audience "gave a great break out and applauded [. . .] for five minutes," Dickens wrote. Senator Cornelius Cole, who attended all four of the Dickens readings in Washington, described Dickens's approach to the readings. "The book in each case lay open before him, but he paid little or no attention to the text. It was reciting, rather than reading" (Cole in *Dickensian* 38 (1937): 56).

In early March of 1868, the people of Syracuse came to hear Charles Dickens read from his stories. Despite the snow that had fallen heavily around Syracuse, they came from Utica, from Cortland, and from other surrounding towns, curious to see this English writer who had brought into life Pickwick, Oliver Twist, Little Nell, and David Copperfield. The parents of Caroline Lester went to see him. So did the twelve-year-old Robert Chapman and his father. Samuel May, the abolitionist from the Unitarian Church in Syracuse went. So did Aaron Sager of Cortland. These people represent a specific regional community of Dickens's readers.

When Dickens arrived in Syracuse, the upstate farming region was covered with snow. The brick walls of industrial development loomed above these readers of Dickens and the black smoke of the factories rose in a cold wind as they made their way to Wieting Hall. For years, Dickens's stories had been distributed to them in story papers and in book form. They came to Syracuse by rail and coach, from New York, Philadelphia, and Boston. That Sunday afternoon, little Harriet May Mills, playing on a "slushy" streetcorner, stopped her game by the fence and stared. That was her favorite author passing by, someone had just told her: the man who wrote *Little Dorritt* (Harriet May Mills, *Sunday Syracuse American* [March 4, 1934]: 18).

Dickens retired to a hotel, one whose lack of amenities he sharply criticized in letters home. He still felt traces of the cold he'd had since those blustery December days in New York, but by now it had lightened up a bit. What was this God-forsaken place trapped in the snow where his manager George Dolby had booked for a reading? After the busy streets of Boston, New York, and Philadelphia, Dickens wondered to his correspondents, were there even any people here?

In a letter to British actor Charles Fechter, Dickens wrote on March 8:

> I am here in the most wonderful out-of-the-world place, which looks as if it had begun to be built yesterday, and were going to be imperfectly knocked together with a nail or two the day after tomorrow. I am in the worst inn that was ever seen, and outside is a thaw that places the whole country under water. I have looked out the window for the people, and I can't find any people. (Dickens *Pilgrim Letters* 12: 67)

Writing to Georgiana Hogarth, his wife's sister, the same day, Dickens said:

> This is a very grim place in a heavy thaw, and a most depressing one. The hotel
> is also surprisingly bad, quite a triumph in that way [. . . .] We were so afraid
> to go to bed last night, the rooms were so close and sour, that we played whist,
> double dummy, till we couldn't bear each other any longer. We had an old buf-
> falo and an old pig for breakfast, and we are going to have I don't know what for
> dinner at six. In the public rooms downstairs, a number of men (speechless) are
> sitting in rocking chairs, with their feet against the window frames, staring out a
> window and spitting dolefully at intervals. Scott is in tears, and George (Dolby)
> the gasman is suborning people to go clean the hall, which is a marvel of dirt.
> And yet we have taken considerably over three hundred pounds for to-morrow
> night. (Dickens, *Pilgrim Letters* 12: 69)

Indeed there were people in Syracuse, an audience of varied backgrounds
who were fond of Dickens and waiting to see him. The Wieting Hall had been
booked for weeks. An anonymous witness of Dickens's visit to Syracuse in
1868, recalling it in 1909, says:

> In those days, everyone was crazy about Dickens. His stories used to come out
> in *Harper's Monthly* and people could hardly wait for them. I don't think there
> is a writer now or has been in whom everyone took such an interest. The names
> of his characters were household words. (*Syracuse Journal* [June 15, 1909]: 35;
> Onondaga Historical Association)

They came from their homes, some by train, others by carriages, to downtown
Syracuse. Ticket sales in Syracuse had begun on February 24 at Wieting Hall.
Announcements for the reading noted that it would "commence at eight
o'clock and be comprised within two hours." Reserved seats were "$2 each."
The advertisement on the playbill was clear: "The audience is earnestly re-
quested to be seated ten minutes before the commencement of the reading."
All the tickets had been sold.

That first week of March, 1868, a heavy snow storm had fallen upon the
city. On that Sunday afternoon when nine-year-old Harriet May Mills saw
Dickens pass by, she was playing, swinging on the gate of a picket fence near
West Genesee Street and Liberty Street. *Little Dorrit* was Harriet May Mills
favorite book, she later said, "for I had been reading it or hearing it read that
winter" (*Sunday Syracuse American* [March 4, 1934]: 63; Onondaga Historical
Association).

William Thornby was the bellhop at the Syracuse House hotel where Dickens stayed on the second floor. He sat in the wings of the theater the night
that Dickens read from *A Christmas Carol* and *Pickwick*. Years later, in 1911,

Thornby recalled that Dickens handed him a $2 tip and conversed with him about Syracuse:

> He asked who my father was and where he was born. I told him he was from Armagh, Ireland, and he said he had been there: and I told him my father had seen him in England and had read his books and was going to hear him read. Dickens said he would be pleased to meet him.

Dickens mentioned to Thornby that "he wasn't feeling very well." He asked Thornby to carry his manuscripts to the hall.

> He read from his own works and, as I look back at it now, he lived the lives of his characters. The audience was so large, chairs and stools were brought in, and I presume older inhabitants still claim a larger, more cultivated audience was never, before or after, assembled in Syracuse.

However, Thornby gets it wrong. He says that he went back with Dickens to the hotel "which he afterward unmercifully roasted in his *American Notes*." Dickens wrote *American Notes* in 1842–43. Dickens's reactions to the Syracuse hotel were noted in personal letters from the hotel in 1868. They were only made public later by biographers. (*Syracuse Journal* [June 15,1911]: 28); Onondaga Historical Association).

Charles Dickens read in Syracuse on Monday, March 9, 1868, appearing in a black suit and a white shirt, with a red carnation in his buttonhole. He stood at a maroon-covered table with gas jets above it and a dark screen behind it. As the *Syracuse Journal* wrote in "Charles Dickens in Syracuse":

> He made his announcement briefly and immediately commenced the "Christmas Carol." "Marley was dead to begin with," came in a rather rapid, careless tone, and then followed the reading of that wonderful story, so full of human nature, which details the change of the grasping, covetous, old sinner, Scrooge, into the hearty, good humored, lovable old man who believed in Christmas all the year round. (*Syracuse Journal* [March 10, 1868]: 52; Onondaga Historical Association)

Those who attended the reading remembered it well. When she was a little girl, Caroline Lester's parents told her of their experience of hearing Dickens read. She writes:

> My parents with three or four unmarried friends attended the reading of Charles Dickens in March 1868. My parents told of his reading the trial of Pickwick and of the part of the Christmas Carol containing Bob Cratchitt's dinner. One of the facts related to the reading of the Christmas Carol was that when Miss Belvide sweetened up the apple sauce Dickens glanced up and smacked his lips. The fact

that my parents had seen Charles Dickens in the flesh and listened to his voice as he read from some of their favorite parts of his writings was a happy memory throughout their life and a pride to their children. (Caroline Lester [March 3, 1923] Letter to Mr. Durston, Onondaga Historical Association)

Dickens became lodged in memory. Aaron Sager of Cortland, New York, recorded in his diary that he heard Dickens:

> Went to Syracuse in the evening, attended Charles Dickens' reading at Wheaton Hall, the great event of the season for Syracuse. After the reading of Christmas Carol and Pickwick saw Dickens at his room at the Syracuse House. (Sager Diary [May 9, 1868]; Onondaga Historical Association)

K. Frances Hadcock mentioned her mother's recollections of the readings and her sister Gladys Hadcock Petit's collection of Dickens. Hadcock recalled the fondness that she and her sister had for Dickens's novels:

> Our mother was one of the many who attended the Readings of Dickens in the Wieting in 1868 and I have often heard her talk of the charming evening in Syracuse [. . . .] I can only add that when I was twelve years old my mother gave me Dickens novels and I read them all before I was fifteen. My sister also has a set given her by a friend so she and me are interested in the great author. (K. Frances Hadcock Letter to Mr. Dunston [March 4, 1943]; Onondaga Historical Association)

This group of Dickens's readers points to a lasting memory among Syracuse area residents. For the *Syracuse Journal,* even the stage set "established sympathy between audience and reader before he appeared" (*Syracuse Journal* [March 10,1868]: 23). Although sympathy moved through this crowd, again Dickens did not please everyone. The *Syracuse Journal* review the next day stated:

> There are many people who do not admire Dickens's writings, though compared with the numbers counted among his admirers they are few; and such who, out of curiosity to see the man, were in the throng on this occasion, probably did not feel satisfaction with the entertainment. But the feeling of the auditors with these scattering exceptions, was that of pleasure and gratification finally meeting reasonable expectations. (*Syracuse Journal* [March 10, 1868]: 27)

The writer described the evening with the words "sympathy" and "communings":

> But those who get near the great writer cannot fail to sympathize with him, through his literary creations. His hearers last evening, in their communings

with Tiny Tim, Scrooge, the Wellers, Sergeant Buzfuz and Mr. Winkle forgot for a time his snobbery and his reflections upon our nation, and henceforth they will be more charitably inclined toward him. On the whole the fifteen hundred people at the Dickens readings last evening are the better for having been there. No one can hear "The Christmas Carol" interpreted as the audience interprets it, without being made more thoughtful, more considerate, and more humane to his fellows.

An image of the audience is then given to us:

> Throughout the reading the audience was very still and attentive, except when they smiled at the good things which came so often [. . . .] The trial of "Bardell vs. Pickwick" we venture to say was perfectly familiar to the entire audience, and yet it seemed like a new thing as interpreted by its creator. One broad smile commenced with its beginning and continued to its close; often it broke out into hearty yet decorous laughter. The name of "Sam Weller" was enthusiastically cheered as he mounted the witness box—tribute at once to author and character.

The Syracuse reviewer shows us the interactive nature of Dickens's performance:

> Mr. Dickens is a superb actor—a better actor (if we must make the comparison) than reader. He is entirely sympathetic with his audience. (*Syracuse Journal* [March 10, 1868]: 28)

However, there were those who dismissed the reading. An unsigned letter to the editors of *The Herald*, of August 19, 1898 is critical. The writer of the letter, signing it only as "American Boz" writes:

> I sat with Dr. Lyman Clary, listened to Dickens's reading about twenty minutes, heard his poor voice, and commonplace rendition, retired, and gave my pass to Henry C. Leavenworth, who was at the box office, saying, "Take this, Hank, save $3, and sleep soundly, but don't disturb Doctor Clary by snoring." He passed in and wanted to cut my acquaintance after, for the infliction. (*Syracuse Herald* [August 19,1898: 48; Onondaga Historical Association)

The response of E.L.G. to the readings was different. E.L.G. told the *Syracuse Post-Standard* that he "heard Dickens read from a two dollar seat in the gallery." "He seemed to satisfy an immense audience," he wrote. On August 10, 1909, E.L.G. writes:

> Your arraignment of Charles Dickens in the editorial "A Disappointing Hero" is, I think, altogether too severe. In the first place, we must remember that the

letters were intended for the eyes of relatives and intimate friends; there was no thought that they would ever be published to the world, if so, they would never have been written [. . . .] I know that everything said in those letters about Syracuse and the Syracuse House was justified by facts. Accustomed to the trim neatness and solid appearance of English towns, it is not strange after passing through East Washington Street with its wooden structures of all shapes and conditions and landing in the old wooden abomination called depot, little more than a frame of old timbers, dark and dirty, dripping with the melting snow, that Syracuse should strike him as an "out of the world place begun to be built yesterday and was going to be imperfectly knocked together, with a nail or two, the day after tomorrow." Salina Street, especially the approach to the high canal bridge, resembled a barnyard with its cobblestone pavement, in the early spring, those days.

E.L.G. adds that the Syracuse House was "on its last legs as a hotel, and was indifferently conducted." E.L.G. adds a personal belief that

It was his intention and desire to obliterate the ill-feeling produced by *Martin Chuzzlewit*. Had he thought his letters would ever be made public they would not have been written. That he desired the good will of all Americans is shown in George William Curtis' account of his farewell reading in New York. It is good to be criticized, occasionally, to "see ourselves as other see us." Before giving way to indignation, however, be sure that the criticism is in no way deserved. If it is, set about improvement and thank the critic. (ELG, *Syracuse Post-Standard* [August 10,1909]: 23; Onondaga Historical Association)

A *Syracuse Journal* editor emphasized Dickens's reading as a lasting memory:

The presence of Charles Dickens in Syracuse is an event long to be remembered by our citizens. It is our duty, as it is our pleasure, to describe it, if possible, although we fully appreciate our inability to fix in type the varying emotions of joy and respect which filled all our hearts as we looked upon the man whose magic pen has given us so many happy and so many profitable hours, in the days that are gone. (*Syracuse Journal* [March 10, 1868]: 52–53; Onondaga Historical Association)

This editor suggests companionship between Dickens and his audience:

The advent of Mr. Dickens was most affectionately awaited. Curiosity we had in plenty but it was that curiosity which we have in the desire to see a friend whom we have thoroughly known through mutual acquaintances, and whose genial qualities we have tested through intimate correspondence, though one whose face we have not looked upon. It was curiosity blended with recognition. (ibid.)

Significantly, he then points, with italics, to a sense of feeling that connects Dickens with communal feelings and "home":

> Towards him we had the feeling which ever in distant lands takes out thoughts toward home, and which attracts our willing feet thither. *We had the home feeling.* We do not know that we can find fitter expression for it than that. (ibid.)

This community of readers, acquainted with Dickens's characters and stories, would be bound by memories of that night of public readings that seemed so very like reading aloud at home.

Only weeks later, a girl far from her home, aboard a train, met the author as he traveled on his reading tour. Kate Douglas Wiggins recalled this in a chapter in her autobiography that she called "Journey with Dickens." Wiggins recalls the train ride:

> There on the platform stood the adored one. It was unbelievable but he was in the flesh standing smiling breathing like ordinary human beings. There was no doubt then that "angels and ministers of grace" called authors had bodies and could not only write David Copperfields but could be seen with the naked eye. That face known to me from many pictures must have looked in some mysterious way into the face of Dora, of Agnes, of Paul Dombey, of Little Dorritt. My spirit gave a leap and entered a new and unknown world. Dickens's hands were plunged deep in his pockets—a favorite gesture. (3)

Wiggins says that one of Dickens's hands came out to wave away a piece of sponge cake offered by the publisher Mr. Osgood of Boston. Wearing a "squirrel muff" and bonnet, blue ribbon tied under her chin, she went into Dickens's car, "a traveling shrine or altar," when her mother was "occupied by her book." She passed a "popcorn boy" with a ball of molasses and candy and she gazed at Dickens, observing the men exchanging a word of greeting with him. At her first opportunity, she went over to Dickens and sat down in the next seat, as Dickens looked out the window. According to Ms. Wiggins's account, Dickens then turned and said with surprise, "God bless my soul, child. Where did you come from?"

Wiggins says that she was not so frightened as if she had been meeting a stranger. She explains, "You see, I knew him, even if he did not know me." She told Dickens:

> Nora, that's my little sister is left behind in Hollis. She's too small to go on a journey but she wanted to go to the reading dreadfully. There was a lady there who had never heard of Betsey Trotwood and had only read two of your books. (ibid.)

Dickens listened to the child, waving away the seat's former passenger, the publisher Mr. Osgood. She then told Dickens that she had read most of his books, except for two that her family was going to buy in Boston, and that her favorite, *David Copperfield*, she had read six times. Wiggins writes that Dickens was taken aback by this and said: "Those long, thick books, and you such a slip of a thing." Wiggins writes: "Of course," I explained conscientiously, "I do skip some of the very dull parts once in a while. Not the short dull parts, but the long ones." Dickens said that he would like to "learn more about those very long dull parts."

When Wiggins told Dickens that her favorite novel of his was *David Copperfield*, he replied, "I like it best too." She says, "I had almost added *Great Expectations*, I added presently, because that comes next in our family. We named our little yellow dog, Mr. Pip." She explains that a neighbor's dog that visited Pip was named Mr. Pocket, recalling Herbert Pocket, Pip's friend with whom he fights as a child. "They had such a funny fight. It always makes father laugh until he can't read properly." She writes: "Dickens told me little stories about English dogs."

Wiggins appears to have grasped in her own writing Dickens's metaphor for the imagination: the fire from the hearth. She claims that he clasped her hand warmly and she spoke with him "as one talks under cover of darkness, or before the flickering light of a fire." She claims that "all the little details of the meeting stand out as clearly as though it had happened yesterday." Yet, she indicates that someone nearby was taking notes of this and that "a part of our conversation was given to a Boston newspaper the next day by the author himself or by Mr. Osgood and was long preserved in our family archives, while a little more was added by an old lady who sat in the seat next to us."

Sentimentality abounds in Wiggins's account. Upon Dickens's invitation for her to attend a reading, she says that she was about to cry and that Dickens's eyes were "in precisely the same state of moisture" (Wiggins "A Journey" 5–10).[2]

Annie Field said that April in Boston found Dickens "in a wretched state of health."[3] James Edward Root, who attended Dickens's April 3 reading of "Marigold" and "Mrs. Gamp" in Boston, said he thought Dickens was in "better spirits and in more perfect sympathy with his audience." Root's wife said Dickens "never was in better form" (Payne 248–49; Meckier 190).

On April 8, with flowers and palm leaves adorning his reading stand, Charles Dickens bid farewell to his Boston audience and spoke of going away. Recognizing the responsiveness of his audience and the sentiment that connected him with them, he said:

> [I]t is sad to do anything for the last time. But it is my consolation that the spirit of the bright faces, the quick perception, the ready response, the generous and cheery sounds that have made this place delightful to me, will renew, and you may rely upon it that that spirit will abide with me as long as I have sense and sentiment left. (Collins, *Dickens's Speeches* 430)

Dickens next returned to New York City, where on April 18, he was honored at a dinner at Delmonico's Hotel. There Horace Greeley recalled:

> I ran against some sketches from a cheap English periodical which I at once transferred to my paper [. . . .] These sketches were by a then unknown author who wrote under the name of Boz. So I think I can claim to be the first who introduced Mr. Dickens to this country. (Greeley in Wilson 98)

When Dickens rose to speak to the American press, he again struck a communal note, affirming a "loyal sympathy to a brotherhood." Recalling his own days as a journalist, he spoke of "the wholesome training of severe newspaper work," referring his first successes as an author to this.

On April 20, 1868, Dickens gave his final American public reading, at Steinway Hall. Following this reading, Dickens bid farewell to his audience and to America:

> Be assured, however, that you will not pass from my mind. I shall often realise you as I see you now, equally by my winter fire, and in the green English summer, not as an audience, but rather as a host of personal friends, and ever with the greatest gratitude, tenderness, and consideration. (Kent 80)

Notes

1. For an account of the Philadelphia readings, see Frederick Trautmann, "Philadelphia Bowled Clean Over: Public Readings by Charles Dickens" *Pennsylvania Magazine of History and Biography* 98 (October 1974): 215–16.

2. Dickens had canceled four performances in Boston because of the impeachment proceedings. As is the case with other autobiographies, this account is written in retrospect and it is difficult to determine how much Wiggins embellished her account. There is an obvious enthusiasm here in this recollection.

3. Dickens's friend, John Forster, suggests that Dickens was killing himself with his readings, especially with the melodramatic murder in his reading of "Nancy and Sykes." In 1868, Forster advised Dickens against playing the Sikes reading of the murder of Nancy. It was too strenuous for him, John Forster claimed. However, Dickens the actor had long liked melodrama, crime and the murder, as Herman Merivale recollects, pointing out that "melodrama of the higher kind was his pet passion." Herman Merivale, *Pen and Pencil, Supplement* (London, 1885) 30–31.

11

The Afterlife of Charles Dickens

B Y 1870, CHARLES DICKENS, THE FIRST CELEBRITY AUTHOR of the industrial age, had become a literary icon in America. His reputation continued popularly in the life of his audience, by whom he was memorialized, made the subject of numerous tributes, valued by collectors, and further made into a commodity. Dickens was represented in a variety of ways, and served as a focus for interpersonal contact through reading circles, theater programs, and newly emerging Dickens societies. Like many of his characters—Scrooge, Tiny Tim, Little Nell, David Copperfield, and Oliver Twist, to name a few, Dickens became a mass cultural phenomenon. In this way, Dickens manifested America's interest in celebrity, capital and consumerism, and the emerging importance of media and advertising in the United States.

There was a cultural aura around Dickens immediately following his death. Dickens was someone Americans wanted to read about. As Dickens became the subject of biographies and lectures, and a model for public speakers, as well as for writers, he remained a focal point for diverse readers and a fixture in the national imagination. Dickens increasingly became a commodity among consumers who bought his works and collectors who bought Dickens memorabilia. His works, circulated through American libraries, entered schools, and remained valued commercial property in the marketplace for American publishers. At a time of increasing division between high-art and popular mass cultural production, despite professional criticism, Dickens remained popular, sold well, and became a classic. Taking on new life through plays and an ever-continuing stream of editions of his novels, Dickens served as a resource for imagined community and his work remained a living part of American life.

Well before the turn of the century, Charles Dickens's stories had become literary classics. His works appeared in every variety of edition and the reading of his novels extended across gender, race, and class, across every sector of the American public. Dickens was produced in the theater, distributed widely by publishers, and sold in almost staggering quantities on both sides of the Atlantic. According to the *Publisher's Circular* in July 1892:

> A total of close upon seven hundred thousand copies assuredly proves that Dickens is by far the most popular modern writer, with the single exception of Scott. (Patten 330)[1]

That popularity increased following his death in June 1870. Tributes to Dickens in America abounded, reflecting Dickens's importance for American culture. The memorials to Dickens were accompanied by another revival of Dickens reading. Issues of biographies on Dickens quickly appeared and sold rapidly. People were curious to know his story. John Wien Forney (1817–1881), a Philadelphia journalist once critical of Dickens, noted "I am reading with infinite zest, John Forster's second volume of the *Life of Charles Dickens*. Every page is a new pleasure, every chapter a new revelation of the better side of the truest friend of humanity in the literary world" (400).

The British author was claimed by America and represented as a celebrity, as a familiar name, and as a creator of familiar characters.[2] As Oliver Wendell Holmes had put it in Boston on February 1, 1842:

> Thou glorious island of the sea!
> Though wide the wasting flood
> That parts our distant land from thee
> We claim thy generous blood. (Holmes "Song" 172)

Recognizing Dickens's public reception as a luminary in the literary pantheon, Holmes gave an address to Phi Beta Kappa at Harvard University, on June 29, 1870, in which he asserted:

> We are not called to mourn over the frailties of the great storyteller, as we might sorrow in remembering those of the sweet singer of Scotland (Robert Burns). But we all need forgiveness; and there must be generous feelings in every true manhood which it makes Heaven itself happier to pardon. "I am very human," Dickens said to me one of the last times I ever met him. (Holmes, *Mechanism in Thought and Morals* 100–101)

Holmes emphasized Dickens's importance for America. Alluding to the Scottish poet Robert Burns, he went on to say that Dickens had

> vindicated humanity, not against its Maker, but against itself; because he took the part of his frail, erring, sorrowing, dying fellow-creature against the demonologists who had pretended to write the history of human nature, with a voice that touched the heart as no other had done since the Scotch peasant was laid down to slumber in the soil his song had hallowed. (ibid., 99–101)

Other writers memorializing Dickens attempted to take measure of Dickens's significance. Dickens's role as a writer of "the history of human nature" and as a social critic was reiterated on February 22, 1871, by George William Curtis, one of the most popular authors in the country. Curtis offered a retrospective glance at Dickens's *Martin Chuzzlewit* in a lecture at the Adelphi Academy. A *Brooklyn Eagle* writer noted:

> The lecturer gave a beautiful and touching description of the scene at the death-bed of Walter Scott, when he pictured the last great representative of the style of novel writing which Dickens was just then coming to the stage to overturn. (*Brooklyn Eagle* [February 23, 1871]: 68)

Curtis spoke of Dickens as a writer who exposed the masks in society around him and who appealed to the sympathies of the rich on behalf of the poor. According to the *Eagle* reporter, Curtis called the satires of America in *Martin Chuzzlewit*

> one of the most useful series of lessons which the American people ever received, and given at a time when they were most needed. The nation was just getting out of its childhood without having lost the follies of that infantile period, and it was the task of Dickens to show folly in its own form. When he came back again years after, he found that his satire had borne fruit, and he had the manliness to take back all he had said. (ibid.)

Dickens's impact upon America was also suggested in 1897 by Peter Thomas Stanford, the pastor of Mt. Zion Baptist Church in Haverhill, Massachusetts, who was born a slave. Stanford, who was married to an English woman, listed his religious heroes, poets, and three prose writers, "Thomas Carlyle, Ralph Waldo Emerson, and Chas. Dickens" as "men who saw, knew, and taught, and the whole civilized world looks back upon them with admiration and gratitude" (44).

Such tributes were matched by a curiosity about Dickens's personal life that persisted throughout the decade. In 1879, Scribners published two volumes of

The Letters of Charles Dickens "edited by his sister in law and his eldest daughter." On December 12, 1879, a *Brooklyn Eagle* writer speculated on whether Dickens's love letters would become available. The writer was enthusiastic about what the letters might tell about Dickens that was not available in John Forster's biography.[3] The article also had a section on "Dickens's Opinion of America," in which the writer concluded that "Dickens did not like America" (*Brooklyn Eagle* [December 12, 1879]: 48). However, even as traces of the ambivalence about *American Notes* and *Martin Chuzzlewit* lingered, the popularity of Dickens in America increased in the final decades of the nineteenth century.

By 1900, the tensions between American newspapers and Dickens were largely forgotten. Arthur Bartlett Maurice, an editor, in 1903, was saying that times had very much changed:

> There are some Englishmen, for instance, who believe that we are still writhing under the arraignment of our national follies contained in Dickens's *Martin Chuzzlewit* and *American Notes*. They do not realize that the life, the social and economical conditions which Dickens found on his visit to the United States in 1842 seem as strange and remote to the American as they do to the Englishman [. . . .] But these types and eccentricities have so completely passed away [. . . .] Cant and pretence, the love of humbug and the spirit of false democracy are undoubtedly to be found among us now, but their expression is very different. (44)

America was now able to see itself differently and was able to see Charles Dickens differently. Josiah Gilbert Holland (1819–1881), who gave up a career in medicine to write popular novels and essays, pointed to Dickens's quality of sympathy and asserted that Dickens's books would live for many generations:

> [H]e had a heart which brought him into sympathy with all those phases of humanity which were intellectually interesting to him. He loved the rascals whom he painted, and enjoyed the society of the weakest men and women of his pages; and it is this sympathy which gives immortality to his novels. *Pickwick* and *David Copperfield* are as fresh today as when they were written, and are sure to be read by many generations yet to come; yet the learning, the culture, the position of the man—his gifts and acquirements and art—were all inferior to those of Lord Lytton. His superiority was in his heart and his sympathy, and in these he stands far above his titled contemporary in the popular regard. Bulwer is a name whose home is in the catalogues and biographical dictionaries. Dickens is a man whom the people love. One is memory, the other a living and abiding presence. (71)

The American nation had changed greatly since Dickens's 1842 visit. Forgiven what some Americans considered his youthful indiscretions, a reconstructed Dickens was embraced by tens of thousands of American readers. Charles Dickens, the author who was "sure to be read for many generations yet to come," was further commodified. As product, he increasingly became part of America's rising consumer culture. In Dickens's *A Christmas Carol,* Ebeneezer Scrooge's bed sheets and personal items were stolen and sold. In the view of one American newspaper writer in 1878, Dickens's own estate was about to meet with a similar fate. On November 18, 1878, the *Brooklyn Eagle* solemnly posted a notice that Dickens's residence at Gad's Hill was to be auctioned:

> It is a sad commentary on the instability of riches and a mournful reminder of the fleeting nature of earthly possessions that a property intended as an inheritance to be handed down to his children's children and always to be a place associated with his name is to go from his son in less than nine years after his death. (*Brooklyn Eagle* [November 18,1878]: 96)

Anything that had been attached to Dickens soon became a commodity, a collectible, or something of a sacred relic. There was trade in his letters, his reading scripts, his notes to his publishers, his illustrator's drawings, and even his clock. The marketing and collecting of Dickens items proceeded shortly after his death, a sign not only of his popularity but also of America's emerging consumer economy. On September 22 and 23, 1878, the *Brooklyn Eagle* ran an article, "A Dickens Relic" suggesting that Master Humphrey's Clock was undergoing repairs at the establishment of Mr. George N. Joyce at the corner of Fulton Street and Water Street in New York City:

> Lovers of the writings of Charles Dickens must be peculiarly interested in this quaint memento of the great novelist. It has a history which dates far back of the earliest budding of genius of the author of *Old Curiosity Shop* and it had become a favorite acquaintance of his long before that book was ever written. (*Brooklyn Eagle* [September 22–23, 1878]: 16, 114)

Seeking Dickens memorabilia, in the 1890s, were several enthusiastic Dickens collectors who were also avid Dickens readers. Percy Hetherington Fitzgerald (1834–1925), a biographer from Ireland, sought items from Britain and America. On August 8, 1903, upon looking at "the Philadelphia edition of *Pickwick,*" Fitzgerald inquired about obtaining a note (no. 378) between Dickens and his publishers. He sought also "the May bills" and items concerning "the American dinner." F.G. Kitton, the writer of several books on Dickens, traded for items both in Britain and in the United States. On May 8, 1897, Kitton asked of B. and J.F. Meehan, Booksellers in Bath: "Do you still possess the half-bound copy of Edwin Drood recently catalogued by you?" On

December 1, 1897, Kitton, preparing a work on Dickens and his illustrators, sought a letter (No. 366) which "may throw light upon the subject of Cruishank's commission with the novelist." For Kitton, transcontinental trade in what he called "Dickensiana" became a business. For example, on March 14, 1903, Kitton requested Dickens items for a Dickens exhibition:

> Have you any interesting Dickens items—scarce or curious—that you could lend us? We are prepared to effect an insurance on everything entrusted to us and put a star against entries in Catalogue of anything that is for sale. If sold, we ask for 10% commission. (Letters of Fitzgerald, Johnson, Kitton and Dexter, Mortlake Collection, Box 2, Folders 45–46, Rare Books, Penn State University Libraries)

Charles Dickens's texts were put to a variety of other uses. Reformers continued to read Dickens and refer to his texts in unique ways, some of which appear to contradict Dickens's own purposes. For example, the author's embrace of the poor and destitute was inverted in a speech in upstate New York where residents sought to sweep homeless people from their streets. In Saratoga, at a meeting of the American Social Science Association, September 5, 1877, Francis Wayland (1826–1904), the dean of Yale Law School, addressed the audience on the matter of "outdoor relief and tramps." Wayland strikes a note of terror and casts the homeless vagrant as deviant and criminal:

> The innocent little maiden on her way to school, the farmer's wife busied about her household cares, the aged couple living remote from the habitations of their fellow men, are alike the victims of his homicidal or licentious violence [. . . .] As Dickens has said of the English tramp—and many of these cruel and cowardly monsters are contributions from the mother country—the pitiless rascal blights the summer road. (11)

The speaker continues, quoting Dickens, although he has just revealed his negative attitudes toward the otherness or the motherness of Britain. "Do you ask why the aid of the law is not invoked?" he goes on. "I answer [. . .] the difficulty of detection. The tramp has become such a common feature of our daily life, that he excites little remark" (ibid.).[4] W.F. Crafts, a minister from New Bedford, Massachusetts, used Dickens to support his association of disease, blight, and death with the "immoral" practice of drinking alcohol. Speaking at the Centennial Temperance Conference at Philadelphia in June 1876, he correlates wine and fungus:

> There is a superstition mentioned in Dickens's story of "No Thoroughfare" that if any of the fungus fell upon a person it is a premonition of approaching death [. . . .] Under the palace of our Republic, built upon living stones there is the same terrible power of intoxicating drink—evil. (271)

Dickens himself never opposed drinking. Several of his novels spill forth with alcoholic spirits as well as with ghostly ones. Looking at *Pickwick* alone, Margaret Lane accounts for thirty-five breakfasts, thirty-two dinners, ten teas, eight suppers, and the mention of drink 249 times. In *Our Mutual Friend*, she points to drinks such as: "shrub, purl, flip, dog's nose, hot port negus, burned sherry, tea with brandy in it" (166). An Irish-American cook reading *Pickwick* saw only food and drink. Mary Anne Meehan of Brookfield, Massachusetts, who read Dickens before the turn of the century, commented in 1934 on the continual appearance of food in some of Dickens's texts.

> Say girls, did you ever read Dickens' books—*Pickwick Papers?* Well, by gosh, in that book all they do is eat and drink. I read that Pickwick book long ago and on every page there was something about breakfast and lunch and dinner and I started reading the book all over again. I got so curious about it. I just wanted to see just what they did eat [. . . .]
>   Oh, then in *Pickwick Papers* they had hot pineapple rum and hot elder wine rum. I tried 'em out they're good too. *Pickwick Papers* ain't no Temperance lectures, but I guess Dickens didn't mean it to be. (5–6)[5]

While Americans of every class, race, and gender could feast upon Dickens's fiction, not all Americans were invited to the Dickens farewell dinner. Exclusion from the New York dinner reception for Charles Dickens in 1868 became the catalyst for a reform movement begun by female journalists who found themselves shut out of the proceedings. Nellie Roberson, a writer and feminist from North Carolina, describes the formation of the Sorosis Club, a group of female writers and activists:

> One of the pioneer clubs now in existence is the Sorosis Club of New York City, founded in 1868. It had an interesting beginning as sort of an indignation meeting. When Charles Dickens came to America, the Press Club in New York City gave him a dinner which many women active in literary work were anxious to attend but to which they were refused admittance except as spectators. Their exclusion from the celebrated event led them to express their resentment by organizing a club of their own which they called "Sorosis." (50)

Dickens's indirect impact upon this group of women asserting their rights demonstrates the social force that Dickens continued to have in America. This social impact is reflected in the interest in Dickens that brought people of many different backgrounds together in Dickens societies, or literary circles, to read or enact Dickens stories. For example, there was a gathering of Dickens fans in Brooklyn, where a Dickens club dressed up as Dickens characters at the city's roller rink. On April 27, 1877, an item in the *Brooklyn Eagle* noted: "Pickwick will receive The Friends of Dickens at the Rink, Thursday evening next." There was a "Reception of Twenty Dickens Characters" at the Brooklyn Rink. Groups like the Louisville Dickens Society, formed in 1867, put on plays of *Oliver Twist* and *A Christmas Carol* for charity, beginning on February 7, 1872. Such Dickens Society groups were formed across America in each decade following Dickens's reading tour. In South Dakota, Jane Rooker Smith, a social activist, collected news clippings from the Dickens Club in Pierre in the 1880s–90s. The All Around Dickens Club was formed at the Boston Atheneum in 1894. A Dickens Fellowship was founded in Los Angeles in 1902.

Meanwhile, some Americans collected the illustrations of Dickens's stories. For example, while living in Philadelphia and in Brooklyn, Harriet Benson Gustorf and her husband Friedrich Gustorf kept ninety-eight pages of prints depicting scenes from the novels of Charles Dickens, as Friedrich Gustorf noted in his diary (36).[6] The Healey Family of Leadville, Colorado, kept a scrapbook, including editorial comments on Charles Dickens, that was later found in their attic (Healey House Collection, Leadville Historical Association, MS 301). John Kendrick Bangs, a popular humorist who did public readings, was an avid collector of illustrations of Dickens's characters by Felix Octavius Carr Darcy, Solomon Eytinge, and other American artists.

Dickens's wide impact is also demonstrated by the enthusiasm with which America's increasing immigrant population turned to his writings. In 1870, a German language newspaper in Minnesota compared actress Olive Logan (1839–1909) to Dickens, calling her "Miss Olive Dickens" (*Mimic World* 462). This suggests that Dickens, like Logan, whose father was a New York playwright, was viewed as an engaging entertainer by Minnesota's German-speaking immigrants. People of other ethnic backgrounds were also familiar with Dickens. Irish immigrant readers of Dickens are represented in a story that appeared in 1887, "The Boy from Garryowen":

> "You look like Uriah Heep—Dickens' Uriah Heep," he replied maliciously.
> "Well, I don't know the man," said I, for I had never read a novel in my life.
> He stared at me curiously after I had spoken.
> "Didn't you ever read *David Copperfield*?" said he. "Nor *Little Dorrit*, nor *Oliver Twist*, nor any of Dickens?" he added as I shook my head at each name. "Well, you're a queer duck. Brought up in the woods?"
> "No. Brought up in America. American America, which has no woods," said I, nettled. "Perhaps," said I, " you don't know the country I speak of."
> "I read Dickens' *American Notes*," he replied saucily, "which was enough for me." (Smith 390–411)

The evidence of immigrant readers shows that Dickens democratized fiction, as Patten has said (343). Dickens's works reached all classes, races, and sectors of the country, supported by an increase in literacy across socioeconomic classes. The growth of Dickens's public was generated by technological developments which increased the means for distribution of print media, such as newspapers, many of which contained fiction and were read across all classes in the United States. It was further stimulated by educational development, which brought a sharp increase in reading among 6,872,000 public school students in America by 1870. Publisher Walter Hines Page wrote enthusiastically in 1905 of this trend:

> A novel reading democracy—a public-school democracy—is a new thing. It is an impressive thing, It made new and big markets, and we all rushed after it. Cheapness and great editions became the rage. (Page, in Gross 25)

The growth of this reading public and mass consumer market occurred primarily in the decades following the Civil War. In those years, the development of the transcontinental railroad system enabled publishers to better extend their reach across the plains and the mountains to the west. Meanwhile, as the south began a difficult period of reconstruction, northeastern publishers resumed shipping their various editions of Dickens to the south. The publishing trade was slow to regain its presence there, as George Haven Putnam noted: "The resources of the publishing concern and the resources of publishing business generally, had been seriously impaired during four years of war conditions." Businesses faced "the enormous blunders of the reconstruction period which delayed so seriously the restoration of the commercial and industrial life of the South" (G.H. Putnam in Gross 83). However, new Dickens editions made their way.

Key among the northeastern publishers of Dickens immediately following the war was Ticknor and Fields, which had sharply reduced its southern trade before the war. Following his 1867 deal with James T. Fields, Dickens had a new American publisher when he returned to Britain in 1868. When Fields visited Dickens in Britain that year, Dickens told him that he felt bound to an agreement with Harpers to offer the early sheets of his next novel to them. Upon returning to the United States, Fields found a document signed by Dickens granting rights to Ticknor and Fields. Dickens agreed that Ticknor and Fields would have the rights to his books but Harpers would have serial rights. James Fields never had the opportunity to publish a new, completed Dickens novel. What he did produce was a version of Dickens's final, incomplete novel, *Edwin Drood*, which Dickens had begun on April 23, 1870, seven weeks before he died. However, Ticknor and Fields was dissolved within a few years after Dickens's death in 1870 and was absorbed into the Osgood firm. With the economic panic of 1873, Fields' publishing career ended.

Dickens's works were kept before the public eye through advertising. For more than twenty years, T.B. Peterson placed ads for Dickens's novels within the pages of books in the firm's catalog. As early as 1857, a T.B. Peterson advertisement for Dickens quoted *The Syracuse Journal*, which claimed that Dickens's works were "Destined to fill libraries with a kind of literature at once tasteful and choice." It called for people to welcome a new set, "this new candidate for the public favor." Beside this was a quote from the *Auburn Daily Advertiser* which read: "And what is more, the lessons they teach is of the purest morality." Below this, we read that the *Detroit Daily Tribune* said of Dickens's tales that "Each of them is a 'Pearl' of sterling value, and they only need to be read to be admired, by all capable of appreciating high and noble sentiments." Of course, the reader may also have wished to experience fiction in the manner advertised by the O.O. Trade List for Dickens's novels: "the pathetic and humorous happenings compelling the reader first to weep and then to roar with laughter" (Advertisement in Bloss 502). In the 1860s, the company issued *Train's Union Speeches* (1862), which carried two full page ads of Charles Dickens' works and *The Life, Campaigns, and Public Service of General McClellan*, which also carried ads for Dickens's novels. G.W. Carleton and Company, beginning in 1871, issued a Dickens set and advertised it heavily between the covers of its other books. So did A.S. Barnes Company of New York, which also advertised a Teacher's Library, featuring a collection of Dickens's references to education.

Dickens's name was mentioned often in works on literature, or in volumes listing recommended reading. Maria W. Jones wrote of Dickens's novels in *Scribner's Monthly*: "They have become the sources of moral, political, and social instruction, as well as of general entertainment" (*Scribner's Monthly* [February 1875]: 501). Publishers appear to have tried to produce sales by connecting reviews with advertisements, to make these mutually reinforcing. For example, Daniel Appleton, publisher of *The American Cyclopedia* (1874) wrote in that volume of Dickens's Christmas stories: "These stories have met with a popular appreciation not surpassed by his novels; and several of them have been dramatized" (*American Cyclopedia* iv). Appleton, of course, produced their own volume of the Dickens Christmas stories.

Publishers aware of the numerous tributes to Dickens upon his death on June 9, 1870, capitalized upon the public response. Dickens's passing did not slow down the trade in his fiction. In fact, it increased. Despite periods of financial recession, the 1870s and 1880s continued to be a time of growth in the manufacture and sale of Dickens's fiction. In the 1870s, in order to compete with the cheap paperback producers, American publishers created series of cheap fiction paperbacks they called "libraries." Within these series were many British non-copyrighted works that sold for twenty-five cents (Johanningsmeier 14). Dickens was frequently among them.

Dickens remained very popular on both sides of the Atlantic. John J. Curtis of the Bobbs-Merrill Publishing Company in Indianapolis falsely assumed that Dickens was still alive in the 1870s as he recalled:

It was a grand thing in those days, the '70s, for a young man to get in a book-store; at that time Dickens was living, and Bulwer Lytton. Wouldn't it be wonderful now to say, "Here is a new book from Charles Dickens—here is a late book from Bulwer Lytton!" (Curtis in Gross 122–24)

Reminding his American readers of the widespread popularity of Dickens, one enterprising editor at *The Brooklyn Eagle* offered his readers a reflection of Dickens's reputation in the British press:

He was to be met, by those who knew him, everywhere—and who did not know him? Who had not heard him, and who had not seen his photograph in the shop windows? The omnibus conductor knew him, the street boys knew him. (*Brooklyn Eagle* [June 24, 1870]: 17)

That popularity extended across the American continent. Dickens's fiction had firmly made its way into the Old Northwest and into the library catalogs of Indianapolis and Cincinnati in the early 1870s. Already the Chicago book-stores were announcing Ticknor and Fields' Diamond Edition, or the Dickens productions of Harper and Brothers, T.B. Peterson, Lippincott, Little Brown and other publishers.

The pervasiveness of Dickens's posthumous distribution is demonstrated by Harper and Brothers' continuing productions. In 1871, the firm issued an illustrated *Household Edition of Dickens* in sixteen volumes. Now publishing *Harper's Weekly*, the firm continued its distribution throughout the continental United States and Dickens was thought about in connection with the company. In July 1876, an editorial in the *New York Tribune* said that the Harper brothers had "many of the characteristics of Dickens' Cheeryble Brothers," including a Tim Linkinwater in its cashier William H. Demarest (Exman 131). J. Henry Harper, born in the same year as *Harper's Magazine*, recalled "The original Harper brothers, often called 'The Brothers Cheeryble,' were four hard working men, always in perfect harmony with one another" (Harper in Gross 152).

British fiction continued to cross America. With no international copyright law in place until 1891, the works of Charles Dickens and other foreign authors, reprinted by dozens of companies, was marketed to a broad audience. John W. Lovell, in 1878, published and distributed inexpensive editions of Dickens, Thackeray, Coleridge, and Milton, as well as cheap English reprints, and soon became known as "Book-a-Day Lovell." Beginning in 1879, the

American Book Exchange, led by John B. Alden (1879–1908), produced the collected works of Dickens as part of the company's "Library of Choice Fiction." In Boston, DeWolfe, Fiske and Company, beginning around 1880, issued Dickens among its 400 titles. Dickens was everywhere: in books, in periodicals, and occasionally in the new syndicated newspaper fiction.

When the DeWolfe, Fiske and Company stock was later sold to the United States Book Company, it contained English classics, such as the novels of Dickens, Bulwer-Lytton, and Thackeray. The United States Book Company, organized in 1890, continued to print and distribute the works of these authors. *Publishers Weekly* on July 12, 1890 reported that a book trust had been created to overcome price wars and to provide copyright protection and royalties for British authors in the United States. In March 1891, Dickens's dream of an international copyright treaty with the United States was realized when the U.S. Congress passed the Chace Act, connecting United States policy with the Berne Convention of 1886. Now the intellectual property of foreign authors like Dickens was protected when printed in the United States.

Dickens remained popular even as the gulf between "serious" literary publications and popular fiction, or between an elite and a mass audience, widened in the 1880s–90s. While some of this distinction began to appear during his own time, Dickens's career preceded this split. In Jennifer Hayward's view, print served "as social cement, as a focus of discourse" in the nineteenth century (5). She asserts that it was a time of "near idyllic union of high and low culture" (6). Dickens was a major popular author who represents this kind of union and appears to have transcended this high-low dichotomy.

In 1905, Walter Hines Page, in *A Publisher's Confession*, wrote, "If a novel can reach an edition of 100,000 copies there is a good profit in it as matters now stand" (Page in Gross 25). Dickens's novels, with the possible exception of *Edwin Drood*, continued to do so. Patten notes that "Chapman and Hall alone sold 2,000,000 copies of his works between 1900 and 1906" (330). As of 1905, according to Walter Hines Page, who had succeeded S.S. McClure as a partner at Doubleday, "Half the novels advertised during the past few years in big medicine style did not pay the publishers" (Page in Gross 38). Dickens's novels, however, did. They were now popular classics and invariably produced some financial return for their publishers.

The Dickens centenary in 1912 instigated another peak in Dickens sales in America. Along with tributes and displays, like at the Grolier Club in New York City, there was a wide circulation of Dickens, including the appearance of new sets of Dickens's collected works. In addition, many more publications about Dickens were scheduled for the years around the centenary of his birth.

A full page advertisement on the back page of Scribner's *The Book Buyer* in December 1910 announced a publication "in connection with Chapman and Hall of Charles Dickens's Works to commemorate the birth of Charles Dickens in 1811." Charles Scribner's Sons appears to have gotten the date of the Dickens centenary wrong. Or else, they were making an attempt to get a jump on their competition.

In January 1912, *The Bookman* offered its tribute to Dickens with an essay by George H. Casamajor on Dickens's friend and biographer, John Forster. The article, "Charles Dickens and His Biographer" concluded with a photograph of the statue of Dickens with Little Nell in Philadelphia created six years earlier. "The present edition, in honor of the centenary of Dickens's birth, will be a delight to all who love him," *The Bookman* said (643). However, in another section, *The Bookman* firmly stated its opposition to the idea of a Dickens stamp for the financial benefit of his heirs. "We disapproved of them at the beginning, and we disapprove of them now," the trade publication said. "As we have pointed out, the American people paid Dickens very generously for his readings in this country, and the novelist [. . .] left an estate of approximately half a million dollars" (458).

Century Magazine began the year 1912 with a tribute to Charles Dickens in two featured articles, one by editor Harold Begbie and one by William Lyon Phelps, a professor at Yale University (*Century* [January 1912] No. 3). Begbie emphasized the social significance of Dickens's caricatures. "Nevertheless, the magic of Dickens still touches our lives," wrote Begbie, who pointed to people he had met who reminded him of Dickens characters. There were "Charlie the Cornet Player," "The Fantastical Cabman," "the Apple-pitman," "the candid charwoman," "the ex-fighting, ex-drunkard, ex-miserable man," and "the lady who had seen better days." For Begbie, Dickens characters are "portraits" and "oddities." He says, "In fact, steadily contemplated and sympathetically approached, every man and woman has the makings of a Dickens character" (332). Phelps, quoting the comment of a character in an Arnold Bennett story, affirmed that Dickens was a writer who was "engaged in the great work of cheering us all up." The professor wrote, "Such work is sorely needed, and is in truth of enormous importance." Dickens's work, he said, was "of incalculable benefit to humanity." In Phelps's view, "The birth of Charles Dickens in 1812 was one of the best things that happened in the nineteenth century" (334).

"Dickens wanted what the people wanted," wrote G.K. Chesterton in the fifth chapter of his study *Charles Dickens*, in 1906. "There was this vital point to his populism, that there was no condescension in it" (106). As Philip Collins has pointed out: "He wrote about and defended popular amusements not mainly out of a sense of public duty, or for want of a likely subject, but because he enrmously enjoyed them" (Collins, *Dickensian* 61 [1965]: 8). Insisting upon this connection, Dickens participated in significant ways in the life of an American community of readers. As his works circulated among this audience after his death, Dickens passed through several phases of popular and critical reception. A new generation was seeing Dickens differently. By now the initial popular reception of *Pickwick* was a dim memory. The animosity toward *American Notes* was largely forgotten and critical attitudes toward Dickens had also changed. Although his novels continued to sell very well through the 1890s, by the turn of the century Dickens, while popular, was not always in critical favor.

Some of Dickens's sharpest critics had been admirers at one time, with memories of having been affected by his writings. Henry James, for example, remarked that Dickens work was "nothing but figure" and that his characters lacked depth. In 1865, Henry James wrote that Dickens "reconciles us to what is commonplace, and he reconciles us to what is odd" but, in James's opinion, "he fails to see below the surface of things"(157). Yet, as George Ford points out, as a young boy James had a quite different response to Dickens's fiction:

> When *David Copperfield* began appearing as a serial in 1849, one of the many tributes to its potency was paid by a small boy in New York City. One evening, while a relative was reading aloud a chapter about the cruelty of the Murdstones, the seven year old Henry James, hiding under a table to listen, broke into "sobs of sympathy" and was promptly sent to bed. James noted that his family "breathed heavily through *Hard Times, Bleak House* and *Little Dorrit* [. . . .] I was to feel that I had been born [. . .] to a rich awareness." (Ford 203; James 118–19)

Similarly, in writing a tribute on the occasion of the Dickens centenary in March 1912, Arthur Benson, in the *North American Review*, suggests that one's childhood experience of Dickens ought to be distinguished from one's adult reading. He wrote:

> I think it is fair to say that there is not a touch of true poetry in Dickens. There is a vein of pathos, and one ought not be ashamed of having been forced to shed tears over some of his passages, especially when one is young and inexperienced; but as one grows older, one drifts farther and farther away from that possibility and is more and more disgusted at the affected guilelessness, the deliberate ingenuousness of his suffering children and his broken-down old men. (398)[7]

However, other authors, like Thomas Wentworth Higginson, saw considerable merit in Dickens:

> Dickens, for instance, can take a poor condemned wretch like Fagin, whose emotions neither he nor his reader has experienced, and can paint him in colors that seem made of the soul's own atoms, so that each beholder feels as if he, personally, had been the man. (26)

Justin McCarthy, in *Massie—A Romance* (1874), writes of his character Reverend Eustore Massie:

> Dickens, he endured because of his generally commendable morals, although he thought several of his characters terribly vulgar, but he supposed that certain natures needed such entertainments. (60)

The reading of James and Benson also sharply differs from that of common American readers of their own time, or those of a previous period. The Dickens of common readers was one who made them laugh, one who gave them a good story, or who was in some way useful to their needs. He was the Dickens of sympathy and sentiment, an author of memorable characters. They connected Dickens with their own experience, as had Hannah Anderson Ropes of Kansas when she wrote:

> waiting on a muddy levee for us, under a driving rain; thence to a hotel. We were all very much in the condition of David Copperfield, when Mr. Dick suggested a "bath." (24)

Common readers like Charlotte Haven of the Mormon community were not looking for sustained seriousness in the texts they read. Reading *American Notes* in 1846, Haven had said she liked the book. "We admire Dickens," she added. In 1904, Thomas Hughes of Virginia, wrote of being introduced as a child to the "delights of Dickens's works" (94). The response of Dickens's nineteenth-century common readers, like Haven or Hughes, stands in marked contrast with that of some of Dickens's professional readers. It signals the importance of Dickens's texts to Americans engaged in daily pursuits apart from professions of editing, writing, or criticism.

The English world of Dickens spoke to his American readers and contributed to American culture because he was anchored firmly in the world in which his contemporaries lived. While Dickens's English difference prompted the resistance of nationalism that promoted American national identity, the common humanity readers could find in his stories transcended nation and lay close to home for them. Dickens's contemporaries read their own lives and concerns into his stories. Americans of all classes, genders, and races brought his work into their lives. Dickens gave them a language, memorable characters and phrases that became cliches among them. Sustained by his reputation and wide distribution to his American audience, Dickens continued to be read by sophisticated readers and by common ones even as some of the critics began abandoning him because of their preference for realism (Ford 180). When William Rounceville Alger (1822–1905), a minister, gave his words of tribute

at the Boston Music Hall in 1870, he expected a mixed reception for Dickens.
He said:

> Surely, he who felt so keenly for every thing human may well expect that every
> thing human will remember him lovingly now that he is gone. The throng of the
> characters he has created, the marvelous people of his conjuration hover around
> him, holding wreaths over him, with shadowy gestures deprecating any wrong
> offered to him. Surely, every one who speaks of him now will speak in praise of
> charity. (Alger 1–24)

Dickens wrote popularly but he took risks and he maintained his own vision, as Methodist bishop Erastus Otis Haven pointed out:

> When Dickens was publishing in serial numbers several years ago his work then
> entitled "The Old Curiosity Shop" in which he depicts with inimitable power
> that wonderful character "little Nellie," so remarkable for filial affection for
> her old wandering insane father, so intense was the interest awakened in that
> beautiful child, the creature of his fancy, that it is said that he received letters
> from different parts of England and America, even from west of the Mississippi,
> begging him not to kill Little Nell. But the demands of the story were inexorable,
> and little Nell died. (116)

While Dickens's critical reputation declined somewhat following his death
in 1870, the popular reception of his novels continued and the sales of his
novels increased. By an estimate reported by the *Fortnightly Review* in December 1882, one noted by Patten, there were in that year 4,239,000 volumes of
Dickens's works purchased in England. This does not account for an American market filled with Dickens productions, as well as imports from Chapman
and Hall. Patten notes that *Book Monthly* published in 1906 an article titled
"How Dickens Sells: He Comes Next to the Bible and Shakespeare" (330).

Charles Dickens remains an author with a significant reputation in our own
time. However, he has to be viewed within the context of his own age. In the latter part of the century, reviewers tended to overlook the genius of Dickens as a
social critic, as a storyteller, as a comic writer, and as a melodramatist. Yet, he was
all these things to his contemporaries, who despite criticism, kept on reading. As
Louisville's Catholic Bishop, Martin John Spalding wrote in 1875:

> We like Dickens, however, because he has discovered the philosopher's stone;
> he transforms into pure gold everything that he touches. He is the friend and
> advocate of the poor and distressed, and he strikes at tyranny and avarice in high
> places. Besides, he leaves a good moral impression inmost of his works. (526)

Dickens is by no means a lesser writer because he is popular. In fact, he may
be considered greater because that popularity indicates that he knew how to

reach a wide audience. He also became a seminal literary influence for novelists who followed him. Not only his contemporaries drew from Dickens, but so did significant novelists such as Dostoevsky, Conrad, Wells, and Orwell. In America, Dickens was important to Alcott, Harland, Stowe and many lesser known writers of fiction also. Besides this, Dickens was studied by film directors, from D.W. Griffith to Sergei Eisenstein for his visual storytelling and montage.[8]

Critics have argued that Dickens is "sentimental." Reading audiences, however, responded favorably to the sentiment in Dickens's stories, particularly in the late 1830s and 1840s, when the expression of sentiment served to maintain social bonds. Audiences at Dickens's public readings, years later, were moved to laughter and to tears. Dickens's contemporary readers let their emotions be moved. Mary Chesnut wrote on August 17, 1861: "I am reading Oliver Twist. I had forgotten how good it is." Jane T.H. Cross wrote in 1860: "I will read now, I will lose myself in the pathetic story of Oliver Twist, a sense of my own miseries. It is one of the few novels I can read; there are some touches of deep feeling in it" (155).

American readers saw Dickens characters everywhere in their everyday lives. His fiction served to mediate the real, suggesting the possibilities of romance in the ordinary. For readers like southern novelist and poet Jane T.H. Cross, Dickens "saw deeper" into "women that grow up under his hand as they do in nature." Of Nancy in *Oliver Twist*, she wrote: "As you read the sad story of her life, you say: That is how it happened" (48). Dickens juxtaposed the fantastic and the grotesque with the every day to assert the value and powers of imagination, as Robert Newsom has pointed out. Readers like Anna Alice Chapin, who observed a strange light in a Greenwich Village doorway, viewed this peculiarity as Dickensian. Odd people with eccentric habits and odd names struck some readers as very real indeed.

Critics like Henry James and George Eliot faulted Dickens for a lack of psychological inwardness and depth in his characters. However, those were their own goals, ones they accomplished through their own consummate skill and artistry. Dickens was not writing novels in which a complex psychological analysis of character is central. Rather, he tended to create social panoramas and to write a social statement. Dickens developed entertainments in which the character is a figure pointing to social elements. Narrators like David Copperfield and Pip do give us some of their inner life, at times in an ironic manner. But Dickens was not primarily a psychological writer. Rather, Dickens made the outward world vivid. As A.D.T. Whitney wrote:

> Past the walls of old warehouses, that stand up from the dark water, past piers and strands, and the dim city edges that dip drearily and dreggily into the brink; their very dreariness and uncleanness made classic and thrilling to us by the

mysteries and uncleanness of Dickens's stories, that have brought us here in pictured scenes so often, and that have made themselves living presences forever in the land and the city where he wrought them out. (294)

Dickens's use of coincidence to resolve his plots has come under attack by many critics. However, belief in coincidence and a human community of connection was part of his basic insight into the nature of reality. Dickens himself pointed to the fictive community of his characters and his readers:

> It struck me that it would be a new thing to show people coming together, in a chance way, as fellow travelers [. . .] as happens in life; and to connect them afterwards, and to make the waiting for that connection a part of the interest. (Forster 1: 624)

Dickens showed people discovering their hidden connections and brought together readers in common experiences with his stories. His American audience read him together at home, or in literary societies, libraries, military camps, or schools, relating Dickens's fictional worlds to their lives in a variety of ways. For example, Frances Bugg Cheatham, the daughter of the Nashville's mayor during the Civil War years, kept a "Dickens Birthday Book" in her later years, 1910–1918. The red covered book has a Dickens caption for each day of the year and a calendar space in which she entered the names of people she met, or those who were important to her. Under her entry for May 11, she revises the caption by Dickens from *Barnaby Rudge.* The day is assigned to Elizabeth Fry Page: "E.J.P., Your playmate in the kindergarten of God." The Dickens caption reads: "There is little doubt that troubles are exceedingly gregarious in their nature and flying in flocks, are apt to perch capriciously." Cheatham has crossed out "troubles" and has substituted the word "joys," which is handwritten in clear blue ink. Then she revises the caption as: "in their nature and fly in flocks." She crosses out the rest. For Cheatham, Dickens became a keepsake, a record-keeper, a guide to memories.[9]

"It is the quality of Dickens's imagination, after all, that causes people to buy and read his works," Patten concludes (333). Dickens's American audience appears to have responded most to what George Orwell also called Dickens's finest quality, his fertile imagination "which is invention not so much of characters [. . .] and situations, as of turns of phrase and concrete details. The outstanding mark of Dickens's writing is the unnecessary detail" (Orwell 69).[10] Such unnecessary detail emphasized necessary themes. For Alan Wallace, who was interviewed while sitting inside his old Ford in Brookfield, Massachusetts, in the 1930s, reading Dickens at Christmas before the turn of the century was about keeping a "spirit" alive:

If we can always keep the Christmas spirit alive this old world of ours will never go entirely wrong. Always after dinner, on Christmas Day, Father would read Dickens Christmas Carol; we never grew tired of listening to it—we felt the Cratchits, Scrooge, and Tiny Tim were people who belonged to us and came to visit every Christmas. (5)

Charles Dickens engaged America's readers because of that uniqueness which is a property of all great writers. Most of Dickens's American readers in the nineteenth-century do not seem to have minded what literary critics have viewed as his defects. Many liked his sentimentality and the tears he aroused in them just as they enjoyed his humor. There was little bickering about his coincidences. People who lived in a world which did not feel the full impact of Darwinian theory, or secularism, until at least the 1870s, seem to have not felt that a *deus ex machina* was inappropriate. Nor do the soundings of professional critics appear to have slowed the steady sales of Dickens's novels to the general public. The posthumous Dickens, however dimmed in the critical regard, met the popular public and the beginning of the twentieth-century in full stride.

One might look to the example of African American librarian Mamie Brown (Madaline Allan), who drew upon her interest in Dickens, which had begun in her childhood, to share Dickens with a new generation of children. By the 1920s, in Charleston, South Carolina, Mamie Brown was a teacher, librarian, and an assistant cashier at Mutual Bank who read Dickens stories aloud to children in the library. "Mamie held storytelling hours and soon the children were flocking to the library to hear her stories, for Mamie had the knack of making her characters live," says Muriel Mann, who interviewed her in Charleston for the Federal Worker's Project in the early 1930s. Perhaps, in part, she had learned this from Dickens. Or, perhaps her natural inclination to tell stories lay behind her interest in embracing Dickens's books. Mamie Brown sometimes knitted as she read and wove stories. "She and her husband read the classics, Dickens, Scott, Thackeray, while her nimble fingers worked swiftly on delicate fabrics or crocheted many useful articles." In her rooms were "built-in bookcases filled with books, many books" (Brown 44–8).

A look at readers like Mamie Brown may give us a different appreciation of Dickens from that of professional readers. Dickens's novels invited his readers into a social world peopled with peculiar characters and unexpected happenings. Shared feeling and sympathy were a way of keeping people in contact and preserving human values. In the end, Dickens was, for most of his American readers, a writer who forged human sympathy. For all the enemies he may have made with his barbed critique of America in *American Notes* or, more so, with *Martin Chuzzlewit*, he appears to have made many more friends. Charles Dickens and several of his characters became a common property of American readers. His texts became a resource for imagined community.

Dickens meant many different things to his American readers. His books intersected with their lives, sometimes in remarkable and unique ways. They drew from Dickens with considerable individuality and often gained personally from his writings. Charles Dickens's writings shaped American life because they served as familiar texts that drew his American audience together in a common experience of reading. He contributed to American life a language of characters, phrases, and images that became part of a common inheritance. He twice visited America, and each time produced a significant effect upon the nation. Dickens himself was both resisted and celebrated by America. He was a source of income for printers, publishers, and booksellers and a boon to the American publishing industry that appropriated his texts. Likewise, in that unique relationship with his readers that has been called the principal "love affair of his life," Dickens was a storyteller whose stories were an inspiration to many people.

The critical heritage gives us insight into the workings of this memorable author. A recognition of the historical and material context in which Dickens worked and was produced adds to our sense of Dickens and his impact. In an attempt to fill out the picture of Dickens's career and cultural influence, we also seek to locate and to remember the voices and perspectives of his American audience and, when possible, his common readers. They remind us of Dickens's wide social impact in America and suggest a variety of response to his novels. For example, a note in the back pages of a twentieth-century Syracuse newspaper tells us that even one of the darkest and more complex of Dickens's novels, *Little Dorrit*, could be remembered as a "favorite." We recall that in Syracuse, New York, one woman pointed out that at the age of nine *Little Dorrit* was her "favorite" book. Recounting Dickens's visit, she recalled that she had been excited to see Charles Dickens. The response of a little girl who probably heard Dickens's novel read at home and fell in love with its characters suggests that Dickens was very much a part of an American community of readers.

Notes

1. As Robert L. Patten has noted of Dickens's readings, "People more accustomed to the stage than the page were sent back to the printed word by what they had seen and heard" (333). The conditions of publishing also had much to do with Dickens's career (343). Payments from the United States, apart from his earnings through his British publishers and excluding Ticknor and Fields' royalties from the U.S. tour, have been estimated at 10,000 pounds. This amount was made by Dickens through a variety of agreements and funds were paid to him despite the lack of an international copyright agreement.

2. Among the responses to Dickens's death was the appearance of biographies. Along with John Forster's two-volume biography, there were quickly written biographies by John Camden Hotton and R. Sheldon Mackenzie, commentary from Edwin Percy Whipple, and biographies from F.B. Perkins (1870), T. Taylor (1870), and G.A. Pierce (1872). Later there was James T. Fields's *Yesterday's With Authors* (1881). Americans could also read Kate Field's *Pen Photos of Charles Dickens's Readings* (1868), *Charles Dickens as Reader* (1872) by Charles Kent, Richard Henry Stoddard's *Anecdote Biographies of Thackeray and Dickens* (1874), or Dickens' correspondent Mary Cowden Clarke's *Recollections of Writers* (1878). The second volume of Richard Henry Stoddard's ten-volume *Reminiscences* was titled "Thackeray and Dickens."

3. At the time, there was no knowledge of Dickens's relationship with Ellen Ternan. Ellen Ternan (1839–1914) was an actress from a theatrical family and was likely Dickens's mistress, in the years of the dissolution of his marriage. Her sister had acted in the American theater. After some thought, Dickens declined to bring her to America with him in 1867.

4. During the Grant administration, in 1877, the country was experiencing an economic downturn, likely resulting in many of these appearances of "the tramp." By 1850, more than half of the foreign born in the United States lived in New York, New Jersey, Massachusetts, or Pennsylvania. Some of these immigrants, who had wandered from hunger or revolution in Europe, continued to wander in search of self-sustaining work and employment.

5. Particularly popular was the festive Christmas Dickens, for whom holidays, home and hearth, and drink and food came together. Marian Harland associates reading Dickens with a good meal (Harland *Autobiography* 68). Belle Kearney promises to tell Dickens's stories or Scott's, if others will take over her duties as a cook: "If you will cook every time mother gets sick, I will tell you one of Dickens' stories or one of Walter Scott's novels as regularly as the nights stroll around" See Belle Kearney, *A Slaveholder's Daughter* (New York: Abbey Press, 1900), 25. Abram Child Dayton (1818–1877) in *Last Days of Knickerbocker Life in New York* (1882) asserts: "Dyspepsia has always been an American weakness; all the Trollopes and Dickens of the world cannot eradicate this national trait" (44).

6. Sol Eytinge (1833–1905) illustrated the *Diamond Edition of Dickens* for Ticknor and Fields. Of his illustrations, Dickens had said: "They are remarkable alike for a delicate perception of beauty, a lively eye for character, a most agreeable absence of exaggeration, and a general modesty and propriety which I greatly like." F.O.C. Darley (1821–88) was called by F.G. Kitton "Perhaps the best of Dickens's American illustrators." Others have said that he was "an illustrator of the American spirit" and that "His works helped forge our national identity" (Carol Digel, F.O.C. Darcy Society website). Darley's illustrations for the first American "Household" edition of Dickens's works and his work for W.A. Townsend and Company in 1861 and Sheldon and Company (1862–65) in forty-nine volumes of Dickens provided images of Dickens's characters to American readers. Darley's five hundred drawings for the works of James Fenimore Cooper also played a part in visualizing the early American frontier.

7. Benson qualifies his statement: "Dickens did, I think, come near to a sort of poetry in his rendering of great, misty, confused effects of nature, the horror of dark-

ness and broken light, of the rolling eddies of the river and its vast and weltering mud-flats"(Benson 398).

8. Film director Sergei Eisenstein (1898–1948) wrote "Dickens, Griffith, and the Film Today" in *Film Forum,* in which he described D.W. Griffith's use of Dickens's montage. Dickens created a "head-spinning tempo of changing impressions," he said.

9. Frances Bugg Cheatham records among the names of her acquaintances, the birth dates of the Brontes and the birth dates of "Olive Dickens" (January 15), "Elaine Dickens" (August 6), and "Marie Dickens" (December 6). She makes no specific comment about Charles Dickens. She notes the birth dates of Patrick Bronte and his author-daughters but does not record Dickens's birthday, February 7, 1812. She notes the birthday of Bret Harte (August 25), whose "Dickens in Camp" she may have read.

10. George Orwell showed that Dickens was not so radical a spokesperson for the poor as he seemed. He claimed that while Dickens can be merited for his anger at injustice and shown to be an artist who piles up much unnecessary detail, he is writing for a middle-class largely about a shopkeeping and servant class.

Bibliography

Primary Sources

Abbott, Austin. "A Village Library." *Harpers New Monthly Magazine*, Vol. 36, Issue 216 (May 1868): 776.

Adams, Charles F. "A Chapter on Erie." *North American Review*, Vol. 109, Issue 224 (July 1869): 114.

Adams, John G. B. Reminiscences of the 19th Massachusetts Regiment. Letter of June 21, 1863, from Vicksburg, MS. sunsite.utk.edu/civil-war/Mass19.html

Adams, Richard H. Civil War Papers 1862–66. Letter from Fort Delaware, August 7, 1864. Virginia Military Institute Archive. Ms. 00358

Alcott, Louisa May. *Little Women*. New York: Pocket Books, 1994.

———. *Work: A Story of Experience*. Boston: Roberts Brothers, 1875.

Alger, William Roansville. *Sword, the Pen, and the Pulpit*. A Tribute to Charles Dickens at the Boston Music Hall. June 19, 1870. New York Public Library.

Alphabetical and Analytical Catalogue of the New York Society Library. New York: R. Craighead, Printer, 1850. New York Society Library.

Ames, Mary Clemmer. *Ten Years in Washington*. Hartford: A. D. Worthington; Chicago: Louis Lloyd; San Francisco: F. Dewing. 1874.

Andrew, Eliza Frances. *The Wartime Journal of a Georgia Girl*. New York: D. Appleton, 1908. University of North Carolina—Chapel Hill Davis Library, Southern Historical Collection. Documenting the American South. On-line.

Andrews, Sidney. *The South Since the War*. Boston: Ticknor and Fields. 1866.

Antwerp, Amelia van. Commonplace Book 1863–1865. Copied sections of Dickens's *Dombey and Son*. Sallie Bingham Center for Women's History and Culture. NcD 321001 2nd 64:B (Sm. Misc. Vols, Box 1).

Arp, Bill. *From the Uncivil War to Date 1861–1903.* ed. Marian (Arp) Smith. Atlanta: Hudgins, 1903.

Atlantic Monthly. Book Review, Vol. 49, Issue 29 (January 1882): 144.

———. "The Contributor's Club," Vol. 76, Issue 457 (November 1895): 852.

Avary, Myrta Lockett. *Girl in the Civil War.* New York: D. Appleton. 1903.

Avirett, James Battle. *The Old Plantation, How We Lived in Great House and Cabin Before the War.* New York and Chicago: F. Tennyson Company, 1901.

Backus, William Henry. *Some Suggestions on the Principles and Methods of Elementary Instruction.* Albany: J. Munsell, 1862.

Bagby, George William. *Canal Reminiscences.* Richmond: West, Johnston, 1869.

Baker, Isaac Norval. Memoirs. Part I, June 1863. Virginia Military Institute Collection. UMIMS. #0357.

Barnard, Henry. *American Pedagogy—Education, School, and the Teacher in American Literature.* Hartford: Brown and Gross, 1876.

Barnes, W. H. "A Chapter on Self Made Men." *Ladies' Repository,* Vol. 15, Issue 4 (April 1855): 232–35.

Barrow, Mrs. Grand Entertainment. A Reading by Mrs. Barrow at Mechanic's Hall. Saturday, November 15, 1869. Princeton University Library Archives. BDSDS 1869.

Bart, Richard W. Letter from Newark, Ohio July 18,1862. Letter from Vicksburg, June 10, 1863. e-history.com/uscw

Bartlett, Elisha. Letter. Syracuse Library, Gerrit Smith Collection.

Beecher, Bernard Henry. *Scientific London.* Statistical Society XII. 1875.

Bell, Alexander Graham. Letter to Gilbert H. Gosvenor of October 14, 1906. Bell Family Papers. memory/oc. gov/ammon

Benjamin, Park. Letter from New York. *Southern Literary Messenger,* Vol. 16, Issue 6: 373.

Benjamin, William Evarts. 37 letters and a manuscript removed from his copy of *The Childhood Youth of Charles Dickens.* 32 letters to Charles Roach Smith, collector. Columbia University Library Collection.

Bittinger, J. B. "Should We Have a More Readable Bible?" in *Putnam's Monthly Magazine,* Vol. 15, Issue 30 (June 1870): 668.

Blake, John L. *The Modern Farmer, or Home in the Country.* New York, 1854.

Blount, Annie. in *Southland Writers, Biographical and Critical Sketches of Living Female Writers of the South.* ed. Ida Raymond. Philadelphia: Claxton, Remsen, and Hafflefinger. 1870.

Bostsford, Arthur. Interview with 80 year old clockmaker by Frances (Donovan), at Seth Thomas Clock Company, Thomaston, Connecticut. Federal Writers Project. November 1938, p. 13.

Boucicault, Dion. Letter to Mrs. Dickens. February 12, 1863. Morgan Library, New York.

Bourne, William Oland. *History of the Public School Society of the City of New York.* New York: William Wood. 1870.

Boyd, Andrew Kennedy Hutchison. *The Autumn Holidays of a Country Parson.* Boston: Ticknor and Fields. 1865.

————. *Leisure Hours in Town.* Boston: Ticknor and Fields, 1863.

————. *The Recreations of a Country Parson.* Boston: Ticknor and Fields, 1866.

Boyd, Belle (Hardinge). *Belle Boyd in Camp and Prison.* London: Saunders, Otley, 1865.

Branch, Mary Jones Polk. *Memoirs of a Southern Woman.* Chicago: Joseph Brand Publishing. 1912.

Bremer, Frederika. *The Homes of the New World, Impressions of America.* trans. M. Howatt. New York: Harper, 1853.

Brooke, Stopford H. ed. *The Life and Letters of F. W. Robertson.* 1870.

Brooks, Charles Timothy. *Roman Rhymes, Being Winter Work for a Summer Fair.* Newport, Rhode Island, 1869.

Brougham, John. *A Basket of Chips.* New York: Bunce and Brother, 1855.

Brown, David. *The Planter, or Thirteen Years in the South.* Philadelphia: H. Hooker, 1853.

Brown, John. *Spare Hours.* Boston: Ticknor and Fields, 1865.

Brown, Mamie. Librarian Madeline Allen (Mamie Brown) was interviewed in Charleston, South Carolina, by Muriel A. Mann for the Federal Writer's project.

Brown, Moses T. Reading at Tufts of *A Christmas Carol.* (1870). Princeton University Library Archives. BDSDS 1870.

Browne, Henri Junius. *The Great Metropolis, a Mirror of New York.* Hartford: American Publishing Company, 1869.

Brownson, Orestes. *The Spirit Rapper, An Autobiography.* Boston: Little Brown, 1854.

Bryan, Mary Narcott. *A Grandmother's Recollections of Dixie.* New Bern, North Carolina: Own G. Durn. 1912. University of North Carolina—Chapel Hill, Southern Historical Collection, Documenting the American South, on-line.

Bryant, William Cullen. Introduction to *Precaution,* James Fenimore Cooper. New York, 1852.

————. Speech at Metropolitan Hall, New York. February 25, 1852.

Burge, Dolly Lunt. *Diary of 1848–1879.* ed. Christine Jacobson Carter. Athens: University of Georgia Press, 1997.

Burwell, Letitia M. *A Girl's Life in Virginia Before the War.* New York: F. A. Stokes, 1895.

Butler, Henry B. Letters of August 25, 1862. January 11, 1863. March 31, 1863. The Butler Letters Collection. e-history/uscw

Cabell, Margaret Couch. *Sketches and Recollections of Lynchburg by the Oldest Inhabitant.* Richmond: C. H. Wynne, 1858.

Carlyle, Thomas. *Past and Present.* Berkeley: University of California Press, 2006 [1843].

Carroll, John W. *Recollections of an Uneventful Life.* Henderson, TN, 1898.

Cary, Alice. *Ballads, Lyrics, and Hymns.* Boston: Ticknor and Fields, 1874. rpt. 1887.

————. "Dickens," *Personal Papers,* Boston, 1887.

Cary, Thomas Greaves. "Letter to a lady in France, with enquiries concerning the books of Captain Marryat and Mr. Dickens." New York Library Society.

Carey, Henry Charles. *Miscellanea—Works of Henry Charles Carey.* Philadelphia, 1872.

Catholic World. "Elinor's Trial," Vol. 14, Issue 84. (March 1872): 790–802.

———. Letter from D. H. S. of St. Paul, Minnesota to the Editor, Vol. 53, Issue 313 (1891).

Channing, William Ellery. *Works.* 5 vols. Boston, 1841.

Chapin, Anna Alice. *Greenwich Village.* New York: Dodd, Mead, 1917.

Chapman, Robert. Journal. Onandaga Historical Society. Syracuse, NY.

Chase, Lucien Bonaparte. *English Serfdom and American Slavery, Ourselves as Others See Us.* New York: H. Long and Brother, 1854.

Cheatham, Frances Bugg. "The Dickens Birthday Book." (April 26,1910). Verses and Birthday Records of Friends (1901–1928). New York Historical Society.

Chesnut, Mary. *A Diary from Dixie.* New York: D. Appleton, 1905.

Child, Lydia Maria Francis. *The Life of Isaac T. Hopper.* Boston: John P. Jewett, 1853.

Choate, Rufus. *The Works of Rufus Choate, with a memoir of his life.* Samuel Gilman Brown, ed. Boston: Little Brown and Company, 1862.

Clarke, Donald Henderson. *In the Reign of Rothstein.* New York: Vanguard Press, 1929.

Clinkscales, John George. *On the Old Plantation: Reminiscences of Childhood.* Spartansburg: Band and White, 1916. University of North Carolina-Chapel Hill Davis Library, Documenting the American South, on-line.

Coe, Ellen M. Lecture on Childrens' Reading at the New York Library Club. 1902. New York Historical Society Collection.

Conway, Moncure Daniel. *Tracts for Today.* Cincinnati: Truman and Stofford, 1858.

Cooke, Philip St. George. *Scenes and Adventures in the Army.* Philadelphia: Lindsay and Blakiston, 1857.

Cooper, James Fenimore. Letter of August 6,1842 to the editors of the (New York) *Evening Post* concerning Dickens and the copyright issue. James F. Beard, Jr. ed., *Letters of James Fenimore Cooper.* Harvard University Press, 1960–68. Volume IV, pp. 302–5. Letter No. 685.

Copee, Henry. *English Literature Considered as an Interpreter of English History, designed as a Manual of Instruction.* Philadelphia, 1873.

Copway, George. *Running Sketches of Men and Places.* New York: J. K. Riker, 1851.

Cortland Ladies Literary Society, 'Dickens in London' discussion of November 20, 1889.

Cory, Dwight Henry. The Dwight Henry Cory Collection. Letter of June 11, 1865. Journal entry of March 3, 1865. February 26, 1865. e-history.com/uscw

Cotton, Sally Southall Cotton. *History of the North Carolina Federation of Women's Clubs.* Raleigh: Edwards and Broughton, 1925.

Cozzens, Frederic S. *The Sparrowgrass Papers, or Living in the Country.* New York: Derby and Jackson, 1856.

Craig, William S. Letter from camp of August 16, 1864. February 21, 1864. March 27, 1864. e-history.com/uscw

Crane, J. T. "Novels and Novel Reading," *Popular Amusements.* Cincinnati: Hitchcock, Walden and Strove, 1870.

Crosby, Howard. *The Healthy Christian: An Appeal to the Church.* New York: American Tract Society, 1871.

Cross, Jane T. H. "The Incomprehensibility of Woman to Man," *Southland Writers*, ed. Ida Raymond. 1870.

Cruishank, Robert. Robert Cruishank Collection. Letter to his wife Mary of September 21, 1862. e-history.com/uscw

Curry, Jabez Lamar Monroe. *The South in the Olden Time*. Harrisburg, PA: Harrisburg Publishing Company. 1901.

Cuyler, Theodore Ledyard. Letters to Charlotte Morrell Boyer, February 25, 1842; March 11, 1842; May 6, 1842; May 30, 1842; June 24, 1842; September 16, 1842. New York Historical Society, Morrell Collection.

Davis, C. H. *Narrative of the North Polar Expedition, U. S. Ship Polaris*. United States Naval Observatory. Washington, DC: United States Government Printing Office, 1876.

Davis, Rebecca Harding. *Bits of Gossip*. Boston: Houghton Mifflin and Cambridge: Riverside Press, 1904.

Dayton, Abram Child. *Last Days of Knickerbocker Life in New York*. New York: George W. Harlan, 1882.

Derby, George Horatio. (John Phoenix, pseud.) *Phoenix Sketches*. New York, 1856.

DeSaussure, Nancy Bostick. *Old Plantation Days: Being Recollections of Life Before the Civil War*. New York: Duffield and Company, 1909.

Dexter, John F. Letters of Dickensiana collector. Mortlake Collection. Penn State University Paterno Library.

Dickens, Charles. *American Notes*.

———. "The Amusements of the People," *Household Words*.

———. *Barnaby Rudge*.

———. *Bleak House*.

———. *The Chimes*.

———. *A Christmas Carol*.

———. *The Cricket on the Hearth*.

———. *David Copperfield*.

———. *Dombey and Son*.

———. *Great Expectations*.

———. *Hard Times*.

———. *The Letters of Charles Dickens*. Pilgrim Edition. Eds. Humphrey House, Graham Storey, Kathleen Tillotson. London: British Academy.

———. *Little Dorrit*.

———. *Martin Chuzzlewit*.

———. *The Mystery of Edwin Drood*.

———. *Nicholas Nickleby*.

———. *Old Curiosity Shop*.

———. *Oliver Twist*.

———. *Our Mutual Friend*.

———. *Pickwick Papers*.

———. *A Tale of Two Cities*.

———. *The Works of Charles Dickens*. New York: Books, Inc.

Dickens, Charles, Jr. "Glimpses of Charles Dickens." *North American Review,* Vol. 160, Issue 462 (May 1895): I: 525.

Dickens, Henry Fielding. *Memories of My Father.* London: Duffield, 1928.

Dickens, Mamie. *My Father as I Recall Him.* New York: Dutton, 1897.

Dill, Edward Marcus. *The Mystery Solved, or Ireland's Miseries, the Grand Course and Cure.* 1852.

Douglass, Frederick. "Friend of Man," *Frederick Douglass Paper* (January 15, 1852).

———. Letter to Dr. Elisha Bartlett, Gerrit Smith Papers, Rush Rhees Library, University of Rochester. Box 1.

———. Letter to Samuel May. March 18, 1852. E. S. Bird Special Collections, Syracuse University George Arents Research Library.

Downing, Andrew Jackson. *Rural Essays.* New York: Leavitt and Allen, 1856.

Duganne, August Joseph Hickey. *Camps and Prisons, Twenty Months in the Department of the Gulf.* New York: J. P. Robens, 1865.

Duncan, Mary Grey Lundie. *America as I found It.* New York: Robert Carter and Brothers, 1852.

Dupre, Louis J. *Fagots from the Campfire.* Washington, DC: Emily Thornton Charles and Company, 1881.

Duyckink, Evert Augustus and George L. Duyckink, *Cyclopedia of American Literature.* Philadelphia: Baxter Publishing, 1881.

Eastman, Mary H. *Aunt Phyllis' Cabin, or Southern Life as It Is.* Philadelphia: Lippincott, Grambo and Company, 1852.

Edmonson, Belle. Diary entries of February–June 1864. University of North Carolina Davis Library at Chapel Hill, North Carolina, Documenting the American South, on-line.

E. L. G. Letter to the Editor. August 5, 1909. *Syracuse-Post Standard.* Onondaga Historical Society, Syracuse, New York.

Emerson, Nancy. *Diary of Nancy Emerson.* Special Collections, University of Virginia, Charlottesville, Virginia.

Emerson, Ralph Waldo. "Behavior," in *The Prose Works of Ralph Waldo Emerson.* 2 vols. Boston: Fields, Osgood, 1870.

Fairfield, Sumner Lincoln. *The Autobiography of Jane Fairfield.* Letter to W. B. Phillips. Boston: Bazin and Ellsworth, 1860.

Farrar, Mrs. John. *Recollections of Seventy Years.* Boston: Ticknor and Fields, 1865.

Fern, Fanny. *Fresh Leaves, or My Old Ink Stand and I.* New York: Mason Brothers. 1857.

Field, Maunsell Broadhurst. *Memories of Many Men and Some Women.* New York, 1874.

Fields, Annie. *Diaries of Annie Adams Fields.* Massachusetts Historical Society, Boston.

Fields, James Thomas. *Yesterdays with Authors.* Boston: Osgood, 1872.

Finley, James B. *Autobiography of Reverend James B. Finley, or Pioneer Life in the West.* 1853.

Fisher, George Park. *Life of Benjamin Stillman.* Diaries and Correspondence. 1866.

Fiske, Stephen. *Off-Hand Portraits of Prominent New Yorkers.* New York: George Lockwood and Son, 1884.

Fitzgerald, Percy Hetherington. Letters. Mortlake Collection. Penn State University Paterno Library.

Forney, John Wilen. *Anecdotes of Public Men.* New York: Harper and Brothers, 1873–1881.

Foster, George G. *New York in Slices.* New York: W. H. Graham, 1849.

Foster, John. *Life of Dickens.* New York: W. F. Burgess, 1850.

Fowle, William Bentley. *The Teacher's Institute, or Familiar Hints to Young Teachers.* New York: A. S. Barnes, 1867.

Fox, Samuel M. Letters. April 23, 1863; May 8, 1863; Sept. 9, 1863; Feb. 4, 1864; Jan. 30, 1865; April 16, 1865. e-history/uscw.

Francis, Wayland. "Papers on outdoor relief and tramps." Conference of State Charities. September 5–6, 1877. Saratoga, New York Meeting.

Free Public Libraries. American Social Sciences Association. Washington, DC: United States Office of Education.

Gaskell, Peter. *Manufacturing Population in England.* New York: Arno, 1972.

Gibbons, Phoebe Earle. "English farmers." *Harper's New Monthly Magazine,* Vol. 66, Issue 395 (April 1883).

Giddings, Luther. *Sketches, Ohio Volunteers in 1846–1847.* New York, 1853.

Giles, Henry. *Lectures and Essays.* Boston: Ticknor, Reed, and Fields, 1851.

Gladden, Washington. *From the Hub to the Hudson.* Greenfield, MA: E. D. Merriam, 1869.

———. *Working People and Their Employers.* New York: Funk and Wagnals, 1886.

Gow, Alexander. *Good Morals and Gentle Manners for Schools and Families.* Cincinnati and New York: Van Antwerp, Bragg and Company, 1873.

Greeley, Horace. Letter to H. Orober. May 10,1865. Morgan Library, Department of Literary and Historical Manuscripts, Miscellaneous American. New York.

Griffith, A. A. *Lessons in Elocution.* Self-published, 1865.

Gunn, Thomas Butler. *The Physiology of New York Boarding Houses.* New York: Mason Brothers, 1857.

Hadcock, K. Frances. Letters. Onondaga Historical Society, Syracuse, New York.

Harrell, S. C. Letter to the Editor, *Syracuse Post-Standard.* August 5, 1909.

Haesler, Charles A. *A Dream Which Was Not All a Dream.* The American Institute of Homeopathy at the Academy of Music, Philadelphia. June 6, 1971.

Hamilton, Gail. (M. A. Dodge) *Gala Days.* Boston: Ticknor and Fields, 1866.

———. *Twelve Miles from a Lemon.* New York: Harper, 1874.

Hanford, Phoebe. *Life and Writings of Charles Dickens: A Woman's Memorial Volume.* 1871. Princeton University Library Collection.

Harland, Marion. *The Story of a Long Life.* New York: Harper, 1910. *Common Sense.* New York: Scribner and Armstrong. 1874.

Harrison, Mrs. Burton. *Memoirs.* New York: Scribners, 1911. University of North Carolina Davis Library, Documenting the American South, on-line.

Harper Brothers Papers, Columbia University Library. *The Archives of Harper and Brothers,* 1817–1914. 58 reels. Cambridge: Chadwyck-Healey Microfilm Edition, 1980.

Harper's New Monthly Magazine. Vol. 1, No. 1 "A Word at the Start" (June 1850): 2.

———. "A Reading by Charles Dickens" (unsigned), Vol. 18, Issue 107 (April 1859): 702–3.

———. Editor responds to letter to the editor by L. M. L. Vol. 23, Issue 135 (August 1861).

———. Vol. 36, Issue 395 (April 1883).

———. Vol. 38, Issue 224 (January 1869). 'Editor's Easy Chair' comments on a reader of *A Christmas Carol*.

Harrison, Mrs. Burton. *Memoirs*. New York: Scribner's. University of North Carolina Davis Library at Chapel Hill, Documenting the American South.

Hart, Mary. "A Studio Sketch." *Catholic World* (1877).

Haven, Erastus Otis. *The Pillars of Truth. A Series of Sermons on the Decalogue*. New York: Carlton and Porter, 1866.

Hayes, Isaac Israel. *An Arctic Boat Journey, in the Autumn of 1854*. Chapter XXI. Boston: James Osgood and Company, 1871.

Helper, Hinton Rowan. *The Land of Gold, Reality Versus Fiction*. Baltimore: Henry Taylor, 1855.

———. *The Impending Crisis of the South: How to Meet It*. New York: A. B. Burdick, 1860.

Higginson, Thomas Wentworth. *Cheerful Yesterdays*. Boston: Houghton Mifflin, 1898.

———. *Harvard Memorial Biographies*. Cambridge: Sever and Francis, 1866.

———. *The Life of Birds—Outdoor Papers*. Boston: Ticknor, Reed, and Fields, 1863.

Hill, Alonzo. *Secrets of the Sanctum, An Inside View of An Editor's Life*. "A Noted Libel Suit." Philadelphia: Claxton, Remsen, and Haffelfinger, 1875.

Hillard, George Stillman. Letter to Rev. Dr. Peabody. Boston, February 18, 1861. Morgan Library, New York.

Holbrook, James. *Ten Years Among the Mail Bags*. Philadelphia: H. Cowperthwait and Company, 1855.

Holland, J. G. *Every-day Topics, a Book of Briefs*. New York: Scribner, Armstrong, 1876.

Holloway, William Robeson. *Indianapolis: A Historical and Statistical Sketch of the Railroad City*. Indianapolis, 1870.

Holmes, Oliver Wendell. Address to Phi Beta Kappa at Harvard University. June 29, 1870.

———. *Mechanism in Thought and Morals*. Boston: James Osgood, 1871.

Hone, Philip. *The Diary of Philip Hone*. New York: Dodd, Mead, 1889.

Howitt, Ann Mary. *An Art Student in Munich*. New York, 1854.

Hughes, Thomas. *A Boy's Experience of the Civil War*, 1904. University of North Carolina Davis Library at Chapel Hill, Southern Historical Collection. Documenting the American South, on-line.

Hughes, William H. *A Week's Tramp in Dickens Land*. Illustrated by F. G. Kitton. London: Chapman and Hall, 1891. New York Society Library.

Hutton, Laurence. *Plays and Players*. New York: Hurd and Houghton, 1875.

Irving, Washington. Letter to Mr. Wetherell. Morgan Library Department of Literary and Historical Manuscripts, Miscellaneous American. New York.

Johnson, Charles Plumptree. Letters of Dickensiana collector. Mortlake Collection. Penn State University Paterno Library.

Jones, Joseph. Letter, Pineville. September 27, 1842 to Mr. Thompson in *Major Jones Courtship*. 1872.

Jones, Maria W. "A Vision." *Scribner's Monthly,* Vol. 9, Issue 4, (February 1875): 500–501.

Kearney, Belle. *A Slaveholder's Daughter.* New York: Abbey Press, 1900. University of North Carolina Documenting the American South Collection, on-line.

Keep, Austin Baxter. *History of the New York Society Library.* (1911) New York Society Library. Stack 11.

Keiley, Anthony M. *In Vinculis, or The Prisoner of War, Being the Experience of a Rebel in Two Federal Prisons.* Petersburg, Virginia: Daily Index Office, 1866.

Kelly, William Darrah. *House of Representatives, Public Speeches.* Philadelphia: Collins Printers, 1876.

Kent, Charles. *Dickens as Reader.* Philadelphia: J. B. Lippincott and Company, 1872.

Kent, William. *Recollections, Delivered to the Young Men's Association of Albany, New York.* February 7, 1854. New York: Van Norden and Amerman Printers, 1854.

Kirkland, Caroline M. *The Letters of Caroline M. Kirkland,* ed. by Audrey J. Roberts. Madison: University of Wisconsin Press, 1976.

———. *A New Home, Who'll Follow?, or Glimpses of Western Life.* New York: C. S. Francis, 1839.

Kitton, Frederick George. A Dickensiana collector's letters. Mortlake Collection. Penn State University Library.

Knight, Charles. *Passages of the Life of Charles Knight.* New York: G. P. Putnam, 1874.

Knox, Thomas Wallace. *Camp Fire and Cotton Field: Southern Adventure in Time of War.* New York: Blelock and Company, 1865.

Ladies Book of Etiquette and Manual of Politeness. New York: James Miller. (No date)

Ladies Repository. Anonymous letter. Vol. 26, Issue 313.

———. Vol. 8, Issue 4.

———. Vol. 17, Issue 4. Book Sales at Chicago and Cincinnati.

———. Vol. 19, Issue 1.

———. Vol. 23, Issue 4 (April 1863). "Methodist Book Concern."

Lamb, Martha J. and Mrs. Burton Harrison. *History of New York-Its Origin, Rise and Progress.* New York: A. S. Barnes, 1877.

Lanman, Charles. *How-ho-no, or Records of a Tourist.* Philadelphia: Lippincott, 1850.

Laughlin, Clara E. "How Culture Came to the Peterbys." *Harpers,* Vol. 93, Issue 556 (September 1896): 642.

Lester, Caroline. Letter to H. C. Durston of Onondaga Historical Society.

Logan, Olive. *The Mimic World, and Public Exhibitions—Their History, Their Morals, and Effects.* Philadelphia: New World Publishing, 1871.

Lunt, George, ed. *Old New England Traits.* New York: Hurd and Houghton, 1873.

MacMullen, John. *A Lecture on the Past, Present, and Future of the New York Society Library.* 1856. New York Society Library Collection.

Mallard, Robert Q. *Plantation Life Before Emancipation.* Richmond, VA: Whittet and Shepperson, 1892.

Martin, Elizabeth S. "Melopomene." *Ladies Repository,* Vol. 26, Issue 9 (September 1866): 539.

Massett, Stephen C. *Drifting About.* New York: Carleton, 1863.

Matthew, William. *Getting On In the World, or, Hints on Success in Life,* 1874.

May, Samuel J. Diary, 1868. Cornell University Carl A. Kroch Library Rare Books Collection.

McCabe, James Dabney. *Great Fortunes and How They Were Made. The Struggles and Triumphs of Self-Made Men.* Cincinnati and Chicago: E. Hannaford and Company, 1871.

McCarthy, Justin. *Lady Judith: A Tale of Two Continents.* New York: Sheldon and Company, 1871.

———. *Paul Massie—A Romance.* New York: Sheldon and Company, 1874.

McConnel, John Ludlum. *Western Characters.* New York: Redfield, 1853.

McCracken, Stephen Bromley. ed. *Michigan and the Centennial.* The Jonesville Library Association, 1876.

McNary, Martha A. Correspondence with Margarette McNary Spencer. Springfield, Massachusetts. Both wrote poems and discussed Dickens. Contains an appreciation of Dickens. Joseph Downs Collection, Collection 28, Winterthur Library, Winterthur, Delaware.

McPherson, Edward M. *The Political History of the United States during the Period of Reconstruction.* Washington, DC: Solomons and Chapman, 1875.

Meehan, Mary Anne. Interviewed by Louise G. Bassett in Brookfield, Massachusetts, Federal Writers Project. February 6, 1939.

Memorial of Francis Gardner, Late Headmaster of the Boston Latin School. anon., Boston Latin School, 1876.

Menken, Ada Isaacs. *Poems.* Philadelphia: Lippincott. 1873, The book is dedicated to Charles Dickens. Schomberg Collection, New York Public Library.

Messler, Basil H. Diary. Entries of May 16, 17, 20, 28, 1864. June 20, 21, 24 1864. September 20 and 23, 1864. October 2, 1864. January 1, 1865.

Michigan University Magazine. (February 1867): 58. Making of America, University of Michigan, online.

Middleton, Mary Hering and Eliza Middleton Fisher. *Best Companions, Women's Diaries and Letters of the South,* ed. Eliza Cape Harrison. Columbia: University of South Carolina Press.

Mitchell, Donald Grant. *The Lorgette, or Studies of the Town, By an Opera Goer.* New York: Stringer and Townsend, 1851.

Moore, Charles H. *What to Read and How to Read. Classified Lists of Choice Reading.* New York: D. Appleton and Company, 1871.

Mordecai, Ellen. Letter to her aunt Emma Mordecai of April 1, 1842 from Raleigh, North Carolina. Mordecai Family Papers, Southern Historical Collection, University of North Carolina-Chapel Hill.

———. Letter to her aunt Ellen, January 21, 1860 from Raleigh, North Carolina, in Duke University Collection.

Moses, Jefferson. Memoirs, Diary and Life of Private Jefferson Moses. Company G, 93rd Illinois Volunteers. ioweb.com/civil war.

Nack, James. "To Charles Dickens" in *The Romance of the Ring and Other Poems.* New York: De Lisser and Procter, 1859, rpt. 1875.

Nassau, Mabel Louise. *Old Age Poverty in Greenwich Village: A Neighborhood Study.* New York: Fleming Revel, 1915.

New York Historical Society. Proceedings. 1843–1849.

New York Society Library. Collections of the New York Society Library. 1859, 1868.

Nichols, Rebecca S. "Little Nell," in *Poems* 1840–1850.

Noyes, George Freeman. *The Bivouac and the Battle Field, or Common Sketches in Virginia and Maryland.* New York: Harpers, 1863.

Oakley, Henry Augustus, ed. *Outline of a Course of English Reading.* New York: G. P. Putnam, 1853.

O'Brien, Frank Brian. *The Story of the Sun—1833–1928.* New York: D. Appleton, 1928.

O'Connor, William Douglas. *Harrington, A Story of True Love.* Boston, 1860.

Olmstead, Frederick Law. *Walks and Talks of an American Farmer in England.* Chapter XXXIL, Columbus: Jos. H. Riley, 1859.

Osgood, James. Letter concerning American editions of Dickens. Morgan Library, New York. MA 2032, 125310.

Parker, Richard Green. *Aids to English Composition.* New York: Harpers, 1863.

Parker, Theodore. *Sermons of Theism, Atheism, and the Popular Theology.* Boston: Ticknor and Fields, 1861.

Parker, Willie. *The Freedman's Story.* University of North Carolina-Chapel Hill, Southern Historical Collection, Documenting the American South, on-line.

Parsons, Thomas William. *Poems.* Boston: Ticknor and Fields, 1854.

Parton, James. *Topics of the Time.* Boston: James Osgood and Company, 1871.

Pearson, Thomas. *Infidelity—Its Aspects, Causes and Agencies.* New York: Robert Carter and Brothers, 1854.

Penny, Virginia. *The Employments of Women.* Boston: Walker, Wise and Company, 1863.

Perry, Kate. *Commonplace Book.* Morris Parish Collection, Princeton University Library. NjPmss CO 171 Box #4.

Phelps, Mrs. Lincoln. *The Educator, or Hours With My Pupils.* New York: A. S. Barnes, 1876.

"Philadelphia Bowled Clean Over," Public Readings of Charles Dickens in Philadelphia. Pennsylvania Historical Society. Va. 6 v. 98.

Plunkett, Caroline Mordecai. Letter to her brother George Washington Mordecai, or Samuel Mordecai. Jacob Mordecai Papers, Duke University.

Pomeroy, Maron Mills, *Nonsense, or Hits and Criticism on the Follies of the Day.* New York: G. W. Carleton. London: S. Low, Son, and Company. 267.

Pond, James Burton. Letters by lecture manager to order electrotype portraits of Dickens from Harpers. October 11, 1887–November 25,1887. Morgan Library, New York.

Porter, Noah. *Books and Reading, or What Books Shall I Read and How Shall I Read Them?* New York: Charles Scribners, 1871, rpt. 1877.

Putnam, George Palmer. George Palmer Putnam Collection. Princeton University Library. CO 685.

Pycroft, James. *A Course in English Reading.* New York: G. P. Putnam, 1854.

Quint, Alonzo Hall. *The Potomac and the Rapidan and Army Notes, 1861–63.* Boston: Crosby and Nichols, 1864.

Reed, Whitelaw. *After the War, a Southern Tour.* Cincinnati: Moore, Wilstock, and Baldwin, 1866.

Reed, William. *Life on the Border, Sixty Years Ago.* Cornell University Rare Book Collection.

Rhees, William James. *Manual of Public Libraries, Institutions, and Societies in the United States and British Provinces of North America.* Washington, DC: United States Government Printing Office, 1859.

Richardson, Dorothy. *The Long Day: The Story of a New York Working Girl.* New York: Century Company, 1906.

Ripley, George. Letter to Reverend H. D. Mayo concerning rumor of a Dickens reading tour. September 24, 1862. Morgan Library, New York.

Ritchie, Anna Cora Ogden Mowatt. *Autobiography of an Actress.* New York, 1880.

Roosa, Howard. Interviews by Janet Smith. American Life Histories. Manuscripts from the Federal Writer's Project, 1936–1940.

Root, Marcus Aurelius. *The Camera and the Pencil, or the Heliographic Art.* Philadelphia: M. A. Root and J. B. Lippincott, 1864.

Root, Taylor. *School Amusements, How to Make School Interesting.* New York: A. S. Barnes, 1869.

Ropes, Hannah Anderson. *Six Months in Kansas, By A Lady.* Boston: John P. Jewett, 1856.

Rosenkranz, Karl. *Pedagogics as a System.* trans. Anna C. Brackett. St. Louis: R. P. Studley, 1872.

Rusling, James Fowler. *The Great West and Pacific Coast.* New York: Sheldon and Company, 1877.

Russell, William Howard. *My Diary, North and South.* Boston and New York: T. O. H. P. Burnham, O. S. Felt, 1863.

Sagar, Aaron. Diary. Onandaga Historical Society, Syracuse, New York.

Sandrock, Marie Louise. "Another Word on Children's Reading," *Catholic World,* Vol. 51, Issue 305 (August 1890): 677–78.

Sargent, Epes. *Peculiar, a Tale of the Great Transition.* New York: Carleton, 1864.

Saturday Review. "Essays on Social Subjects" (1865): 46–47.

Scribners Monthly. "Topics of the Time." A Tribute to George Eliot, Vol. 21, Issue 5 (March 1881): 790.

Semmes, Raphael. *Memoirs of Service Afloat, During the War Between the States.* Baltimore: Kelly, Piet and Company, 1869.

Seymour, Charles C. B. *Self Made Men.* New York: Harpers, 1858.

Shillaber, B. P. ed. *Life and Sayings of Mrs. Partington.* New York: Derby and Jackson, 1860.

Simms, William Gilmore. "International Copyright." *Southern Literary Messenger* (August 1844) Vol. 10, Issue 8: 464.

Smith, Francis Shubael. "The Young Magdelan," in *Poems,* 1874.

Smith, John Talbot. "A Boy from Garryowen," in *Catholic World,* Vol. 46, Issue 273 December 1887): 390–411.

Smith, Joseph Edward Adams. *Tagconic, or Letters and legends about Our Summer Home.* Printed privately. 1852.

Soldan, Frank Louis. *The Century and the School.* New York: MacMillan, 1912.

Southern Literary Messenger. European Correspondence. Signed "Your Friend": Vol. 11, Issue 5 (May 1845): 323–26.

———. L. L., Letter to the Editor, Vol. 20, Issue 8: 469–70.

———. "Intellectual Culture of Women," Vol. 28 (May 1859): 328.

———. "Scenes Beyond the Western Border," Vol. 17, Issue 9: 564–65.

———. "Note on Charles Dickens' Library," Vol. 4, Issue 81 (October 15, 1870).

Southern Quarterly Review. "Advice on Reading," Vol. 4, Issue 8 (1843): 304–8.

Storrs, Richard Salter. *Preaching Without Notes.* New York: Hodder and Stoughton, George H. Doran Company, 1875.

Stowe, Harriet Beecher. "The Coral Ring" (375–87), *The Mayflower and Miscellaneous Writings.* Boston: Phillips, Samson and Company, 1855.

———. *Sunny Memories of Foreign Lands.* Boston: Phillips, Samson and Company, 1854.

———. *Pink and White Tyranny: A Society Novel.* Boston: Roberts and Brothers, 1871.

———. *Uncle Tom's Cabin.* Boston: J. P. Jewett, 1852. Introduction (1892).

Sumner, Charles. *Orations and Speeches, 1845–1850. 18th Report. The Works of Charles Sumner.* New York: G. P. Putnam, 1870.

Swett, John. *The History of the Public School System in California.* Institute Address. 1876.

Sylvis, William H. *The Life, Speeches and Essays of William Sylvis.* Speech of 1872 on behalf of Iron Moulders Union and the National Labor Union. Philadelphia: Claxton, Remsen, and Haffelfinger.

Taylor, Bayard. *John Godfrey's Fortunes, Related by Himself. A Story of American Life.* New York: G. P. Putnam, 1864.

The Old World Seen With Young Eyes. Anonymous. New York: T. Whittaker, 1871.

The Stars and Stripes (December 27, 1918), Vol. 1, No. 47. Paris.

Thompson, W. V. "Savannah" in *Appleton's,* Vol. 5, Issue 106 (1871): 407.

Thornby, William. Former Syracuse Hotel bellhop interviewed in *Syracuse Journal,* June 15, 1911. Onondaga Historical Society.

Train, George Francis. 1862. *Train's Union Speeches, Delivered in England during the Present American War.* Philadelphia: T. B. Peterson, 1862.

Truxton Club, The Readers Circle, minutes of February 2, 1886; November and December, 1891; March 1892.

Tuttle, Joseph. *The Way Lost and Found.* Cincinnati: The Evangelical Alliance, 1870.

Twain, Mark. *Mark Twain's Autobiography.* ed. Albert Bigelow Paine. 2 vols. New York: Harper and Brothers, 1924.

United States Office of Education, "Free Libraries," U. S. Government Printing Office, 1876.

Valley of the Shadow—Two Communities in the American Civil War. Letters. Franklin, PA: William Heyser notes, 1863; Abraham Essick journal. Rachel Cormay note of June 14, 1863 and July 6, 1863; Adasa Sterrett note of May 8,1861; Harvey Bear letter of March 13, 1862; John D. Hildebrand note of March 6, 1864. valleyvcdh .virginia.edu

Venable, W. H. "Book Love" in *Ladies Repository*, Vol. 24, Issue 3 (January 1864): 166.

Waddel, Joseph Addison. Diaries. 1855. 1857. 1858. 1862. 1863. Valley of the Shadow Letters.

Wallace, Allan. Interviewed by Louise G. Bessett for the Federal Writer's Project. December 1, 1938 in Brookfield, Massachusetts.

Ward, Austin N. and Maria Ward, ed. *The Husband in Utah: Sights and Scenes Among the Mormons.* New York: Derby and Jackson, 1857.

Welch, Samuel Manning. *Recollections of Buffalo.* Buffalo: P. Paul and Brothers, 1890.

Westbrook, Raymond. "Open Letters from New York." *Atlantic Monthly* (February 1878), Vol. 41, Issue 244: 239.

Whitney, Adeline Dutton Train. *Patience Strong's Outings.* Boston: Loring, 1869.

———. *Sights and Insights.* Boston: Houghton Mifflin, 1876.

Wiggin, Kate Douglas. "A Journey With Dickens." *My Garden of Memory: An Autobiography.* Boston and New York: Houghton Mifflin, 1923.

Willis, N. P. *Outdoors at Idelwild, or The Shaping of a Home on the Banks of the Hudson.* New York: Charles Scribners, 1856.

Winthrop, Robert Charles. *Addresses and Speeches on Various Occasions.* 1852 to 1867. Boston: Little Brown, 1867.

Withers, Anita Dwyer. *Diary 1860–65.* Entry of November 1861. Transcript in University of North Carolina Davis Library at Chapel Hill, Southern Historical Collection. Documenting the American South, on-line.

Wood, John George. *Man and Beast, Here and Hereafter.* New York: Harpers, 1875.

Woolsey, Jane Stuart. *Hospital Days. Printed For Public Use.* New York: D. Van Nostrand, 1870.

Wright, Mabel Osgood. *My New York.* New York: MacMillan, 1930.

York, Galutia. Letter of October 8, 1862. Virginia Military Institute online.

Youmans, Edward Livingston. *The Culture Demanded by Modern Life.* New York: D. Appleton, 1873.

Secondary Sources

Ackroyd, Peter. *Dickens.* London: Sinclair-Stevenson, 1990.

Altick, Richard D. "Bleak House—The Reach of Chapter One." *Dickens Studies Annual* 8, New York: AMS Press.

———. *The English Common Reader—A Social History of the Mass Reading Public 1800–1900,* Columbus: Ohio State Press (1957), 2nd edition, 1998.

Anderson, Benedict. *Imagined Communities: Reflections on the Origin and Spread of Nationalism.* London: Verso, 1991.

Andrews, Malcolm. *Charles Dickens and His Performing Selves: Dickens and the Public Readings.* Oxford: Oxford University Press, 2006.

Auerbach, Nina. *Private Theatricals.* Cambridge: Harvard University Press, 1990.

Axton, William. *Circle of Fire: Dickens' Vision and Style and the Popular Victorian Theater.* Lexington: University of Kentucky Press, 1966.

Bakhtin, Mikhail. *The Dialogical Imagination.* Austin: University of Texas Press, 1981.

Barnes, James J. *Authors, Publishers, and Politicians: The Quest for an Anglo-American Copyright Agreement, 1815–1854.* London: Routledge, Kegan and Paul, 1974.

Booth, Wayne. *The Company We Keep—An Ethics of Fiction.* Berkeley: University of California Press, 1988.

Brantlinger, Patrick. *The Reading Lesson—The Threat of Mass Literacy in Nineteenth Century British Fiction.* Bloomington: Indiana University Press, 1998.

Butt, John and Kathleen Tillotson. *Dickens at Work.* London: Methuen, 1957.

Carlisle, Janice. *The Sense of an Audience—Dickens, Thackeray and George Eliot at Mid-Century.* Athens: University of Georgia Press, 1981.

Cavallo, Guglielmo and Roger Chartier. A *History of Reading in the West.* Amherst: University of Massachusetts Press, 1999.

Chartier, Roger. *The Order of Books.* Stanford University Press, 1994.

Charvat, William. *Literary Publishing in America, 1790–1850.* Philadelphia: University of Pennsylvania Press, 1959. rpt. (with an Afterword by Michael Winship) Amherst: University of Massachusetts Press, 1993.

———. *The Profession of Authors in America.* ed. Matthew J. Bruccoli. Columbus: Ohio State University Press, 1968.

Chesterton, G. K. *Appreciations and Criticisms of Charles Dickens' Works.* New York: Dutton, 1911.

Christensen, Allan C. "A Dickensian Hero Retailored: The Carlylean Apprenticeship of Martin Chuzzlewit." *Studies in the Novel* 3 (1971): 18–25.

Collins, Philip *Charles Dickens: The Public Readings.* London: Oxford University Press, 1975.

———. *Dickens and Crime.* Bloomington: Indiana University Press, 1968.

———. *Dickens and Education.* London: Macmillan, 1963.

———. ed. *Dickens: The Critical Heritage* London: Routledge, Kegan Paul, 1971.

———. "Dickens and Popular Amusements." *Dickensian,* Vol. 61 (1965): 7–19.

———. "Queen Mab's Chariot Among the Steam Engines—Dickens and Fancy." *English Studies,* Vol. 42 (1961): 78–90.

———. "The Popularity of Dickens." *Dickensian,* Vol. 70 (1974): 5–20.

Davidson, Cathy N. *Revolution and the Word: The Rise of the Novel in America.* New York: Oxford University Press, 1986.

Davis, Lennard. *Factual Fictions: The Origins of the English Novel.* New York: Columbia University Press, 1983.

Dickens Fellowship 56th Conference, Boston 1962 Cambridge, MA: Charles Dickens Reference Center, Livingston Stebbins Library, Lesley College. A Symposium with George H. Ford, Edgar Johnson, J. Hillis Miller, Sylvere Monod, Moderated by Noel C. Peyrouton, 1962.

Douglas, Ann. *The Feminization of American Culture.* New York: Alfred Knopf, 1977.

Exman, Eugene. *The Brothers Harper.* New York: Harper and Row, 1965.

———. *The House of Harper.* New York. Harper and Row, 1967.

Feltes, N. M. *Modes of Production of Victorian Novels.* Chicago: Chicago UP, 1986.

Fielding, K. J. ed. *Charles Dickens: A Critical Introduction,* 2nd ed. Boston: Houghton Mifflin, 1965.

———. *Speeches of Charles Dickens,* ed. K. J. Fielding. Oxford: Clarendon Press, 1975.

Fields, James T. *Yesterdays with Authors.* Boston: Osgood, 1872.

Flint, Kate. *The Woman Reader 1837–1914.* Oxford: Clarendon Press, 1993.

Ford, George. *Dickens and His Readers: Aspects of Novel Criticism Since 1836.* Princeton UP, 1955.

Forster, John. *The Life of Charles Dickens (1872–1874).* Everyman's Library, ed. A. J. Hoppe. London: Dent, 1966.

Frye, Northrop. *Anatomy of Criticism: Four Essays.* Princeton University Press, 1957.

Garis, Robert. *The Dickens Theater: A Reassessment of the Novels.* London: Oxford University Press, 1965.

Gilmore, William J. *Reading Becomes a Necessity of Life—Material and Cultural Life in Rural New England, 1780–1835.* Knoxville: University of Tennessee Press, 1989.

Gissing, George. *Charles Dickens,* New York: Dodd, Mead, 1924.

Goldberg, Michael. *Carlyle and Dickens.* Athens: University of Georgia Press, 1972.

———. "From Bentham to Carlyle: Dickens' Political Development." *Journal of the History of Ideas* 33 (1972): 61–76.

Greenspan, Ezra. *George Palmer Putnam.* University Park: Penn State University Press, 2000.

Haltunnen, Karen. *Painted Women and Confidence Men.* New Haven: Yale University Press, 1983.

Hardy, Barbara. *The Appropriate Form—An Essay on the Novel.* London: University of London, Atholone Press, 1964.

———. *The Moral Art of Dickens.* New York: Oxford University Press, 1970.

———. *Tellers and Listeners: The Narrative Imagination.* London: Atholone Press, 1975.

Hayward, Jennifer. *Consuming Pleasures: Active Audiences and Serial Fictions from Dickens to Soap Opera.* Lexington: University of Louisville, 1997.

Henkle, Roger B. *Comedy and Culture—England 1820–1900.* Princeton: Princeton University Press, 1980.

Hollingsworth, Keith. *The Newgate Novel, 1830–1847.* Detroit: Wayne State University Press, 1963.

Holloway, John. "Dickens and the Symbol," in *Dickens 1970,* ed. Michael Slater, New York: Stein and Day, 1970.

———. "The Life of Carlyle's Language," in *Thomas Carlyle,* ed. Harold Bloom, New York: Chelsea House, 1986, pp. 17–32.

Horton, Susan R. *The Reader in the Dickens World.* Pittsburgh: University of Pittsburgh Press, 1981.

House, Humphrey. *The Dickens World,* 2nd ed., London: Oxford University Press, 1960.

House, Madeline, Graham Storey, and Kathleen Tillotson. *The Pilgrim Edition of the Letters of Charles Dickens.* Oxford: Clarendon Press.

Hughes, Winifred. *The Maniac in the Cellar: Sensation Novels of the 1860's.* Princeton: Princeton University Press, 1980.

Iser, Wolfgang. *The Implied Reader: Patterns of Communication in Prose Fiction from Bunyan to Beckett.* Baltimore and London: Johns Hopkins University Press, 1974.

Jackson, T. A. *Charles Dickens: The Progress of a Radical.* New York: International Publishers, 1938.

James, Louis. *Fiction for the Working Man 1830–1850.* Harmondsworth: Penguin, 1974.

Johnson, Edgar. *Charles Dickens: His Tragedy and Triumph.* London: Gollancz, 2 vols. 1953.

———. *Charles Dickens—An Introduction to His Novels.* New York: Random House, 1969.

Kaplan, Fred. *Charles Dickens: A Biography.* New York: Morrow, 1988.

———. *Dickens and Mesmerism.* Princeton: Princeton University Press, 1975.

Kaser, David. *The Cost Book of Carey and Lea, 1825–1838.* Philadelphia: University of Pennsylvania Press, 1963.

———. *Mssrs. Carey and Lea of Philadelphia: A Study in the History of the Booktrade.* Philadelphia: University of Pennsylvania Press, 1957.

Keating, P. J. *The Working Classes in Victorian Fiction* New York: Barnes and Noble, 1971.

Keating, Peter. *A Social History of the English Novel 1875–1914.* London: Secker and Warburg, 1989.

Kenny, Blair. "Carlyle and Bleak House." *Dickensian* 66 (1970): 36–41.

Klancher, Jon P. *The Making of English Reading Audiences 1790–1832.* Madison: University of Wisconsin Press, 1987.

Kucich, John. *Repression in Victorian Fiction: Charlotte Bronte, George Eliot, Charles Dickens.* Berkeley: University of California Press, 1987.

LaCapra, Dominick. "Rethinking Intellectual History and Reading Texts," in *Modern European Intellectual History.* Ithaca: Cornell University Press, 1982, pp. 47–85.

Leavis, Q. D. *Fiction and the Reading Public.* London: Chatto and Windus, 1939.

Lehuu, Isabell. *Carnival on the Page: Popular Print Media in Antebellum America.* Chapel Hill: University of North Carolina Press, 2000.

Lettis, Richard. "Dickens, Drama and the Two Realities." *Dickens Study Annual,* Vol. 16. New York: AMS Press, 1987, pp. 149–188.

Levine, Lawrence W. *Highbrow/Lowbrow: The Emergence of Cultural Hierarchy in America.* Cambridge: Harvard University Press, 1988.

Lukacs, George. *The Historical Novel* (1937). Boston: Beacon Press, 1963.

Lyons, Martyn. "New Readers in the Nineteenth Century: Women, Children, Workers," in *A History of Reading in the West,* ed. Cavallo and Chartier. Amherst: University of Massachusetts Press, 1999.

Marcus, Stephen. *Dickens: From Pickwick to Dombey.* New York: Simon and Schuster, Clarion Books, 1968.

Mayhew, Henry. *London Labour and the London Poor*. 4 vols. New York: Dover, 1968.

McAleer, Joseph. *Popular Reading and Publishing in Britain 1914–1950*. Oxford: Clarendon Press, 1992.

McGill, Meredith. *American Literature and the Culture of Reprinting, 1834–1852*. Philadelphia: University of Pennsylvania Press, 2004.

McHenry, Elizabeth. *Forgotten Readers*. Durham: Duke University Press, 2000.

Miller, J. Hillis. *Charles Dickens: The World of His Novels*. Cambridge: Harvard University Press, 1965.

———. *The Form of Victorian Fiction*: Thackeray, Dickens, Trollope, George Eliot, Meredith, and Hardy, South Bend: University of Notre Dame Press, 1968.

Mitch, David. *The Rise of Popular Literacy in Victorian England: The Influence of Private Choice and Public Policy*. Philadelphia: University of Pennsylvania Press, 1992.

Mitchell, Sally. *The Fallen Angel: Chastity, Class and Women's Reading, 1835–1880*. Bowling Green University Press, 1981.

Monod, Sylvere. *Dickens the Novelist*. Norman: University of Oklahoma Press, 1967.

Moss, Sidney P. *Charles Dickens's Quarrel With America*. Troy, New York: Whitston, 1984.

Newsom, Robert. *Dickens on the Romantic Side of Familiar Things: Bleak House and the Novel Tradition*, New York: Columbia University Press, 1977.

Oddie, William. *Dickens and Carlyle: The Question of Influence*. London: Centenary Press, 1972.

Ong, Walter J. *The Presence of the Word*. New York: Simon and Schuster, 1970.

Orwell, George. "Boys Weeklies," in *The Collected Essays, Journalism and Letters of George Orwell*. Vol. 1. Ed. Sonia Orwell and Ian Angus, London: Seker and Warburg and New York: Harcourt Brace, 1968–70.

———. "Charles Dickens." *Critical Essays* (7–56). London: Secker and Warburg, 1946.

Palmer, William J. *Dickens and the New Historicism*. New York: St. Martin's Press, 1997.

———. "New Historicizing Dickens." *Dickens Studies Annual*, Vol. 28. New York: AMS Press, 1999, pp. 173–196.

Patten, Robert L. *Charles Dickens and his Publishers*. London: Oxford University Press, 1978.

———. "A Surprising Transformation: Dickens and the Hearth," in *Nature and the Victorian Imagination*. Ed. U. C. Knoepflmacher and G. B. Tennyson. Berkeley: University of California Press, 1977.

Pawley, Christine. *Reading on the Middle Border*. Amherst: University of Massachusetts Press, 2001.

Pemberton, Thomas. *Dickens and the Stage* (1888). London: Kessenger, 2008.

Peterson, Carla L. *The Determined Reader: Gender and Culture in the Novel from Napoleon to Victoria*. New Brunswick: Rutgers University Press, 1986.

Radway, Janice. *Reading the Romance: Women, Patriarchy, and Popular Literature*. Chapel Hill: University of North Carolina Press, 1984.

Reed, John R. *Victorian Will.* Athens: Ohio University Press, 1989.

Romano, John. *Dickens and Reality.* New York: Columbia University Press, 1978.

Rose, Jonathan. *The Intellectual Life of the British Working Classes.* New Haven: Yale University Press, 2001.

———. "How Historians Study Reader Response, or, What Did Jo Think of Bleak House?" *Literature in the Marketplace: Nineteenth Century British Publishing and Reading Practices,"* ed. John O. Jordan and Robert C. Patten. Cambridge: Cambridge University Press, 1995.

———. "Reading the English Common Reader: A Preface to a History of Audiences." *Journal of the History of Ideas* (1992): 47–70.

Ruskin, John. *Fiction, Fair and Foul.* In *The Works of John Ruskin,* ed. E. T. Cook and Alexander Wedderburn. 39 vols. London: George Allen; New York: Longmans, Green 1908; 34: 264–397.

Schlicke, Paul. *Dickens and Popular Entertainment.* London: Allen and Unwin, 1985.

Schlicke. Paul and Michael Slater. *Oxford Reader's Companion to Charles Dickens.* Oxford and New York: Oxford University Press, 1999.

Schor, Hillary. *Dickens and the Daughter of the House.* Cambridge: Cambridge University Press, 1999.

Siegel, Jules P., ed. *Thomas Carlyle: The Critical Heritage.* London: Routledge and Kegan Paul, 1971.

Slater, Michael. "Dickens (and Forster) Work on The Chimes." *Dickens Studies* 2 (1966): 106–40.

———. "The Christmas Books." *Dickensian* 65 (1969): 17–24.

———. ed, *The Christmas Books by Charles Dickens,* 2 vols. Harmondsworth: Penguin, 1971.

———. ed. *The Dent Uniform Edition of Dickens' Journalism,* Vols. II-III. Columbus: Ohio State University Press, 1996, 1999.

Small, Helen. "A Pulse of 124: Charles Dickens and a Pathology of the Mid-Victorian Reading Public." in *The Practice and Representation of Reading in England,* ed. James Raven, Helen Small, and Naomi Taylor. Cambridge: Cambridge University Press, 1996, 271–81.

Stewart, Garrett. *Dear Reader: The Conscripted Audience in Nineteenth Century British Fiction.* Baltimore and London: Johns Hopkins University Press, 1996.

Stern, Madeline B., ed. *Publishers for Mass Entertainment in Nineteenth Century America.* Boston: G. K. Hall, 1980.

———. *Books and People in Nineteenth Century America.* New York: Bowker, 1978.

Stoehr, Taylor. *Dickens: The Dreamer's Stance.* Ithaca: Cornell University Press, 1966.

Stone, Harry. *Dickens and the Invisible World: Fairy Tales, Fantasy and Novel Making.* London, 1979.

———. *Dickens's Working Notes for his Novels.* Chicago: University of Chicago Press, 1987.

Sutton, Walter. *The Western Book Trade: Cincinnati as a Nineteenth Century Publishing and Book Trade Center.* Columbus: Ohio University Press, 1961.

Tambling, Jeremy. *Bleak House. New Case Books.* New York: St. Martin's Press, 1998.

———. *Dickens, Violence and the Modern State.* London: St. Martin's Press, 1995.

Taylor, Jenny Bourne. *In the Secret Theatre of Home: Wilkie Collins, Sensational Narrative, and Nineteenth Century Psychology.* London: Routledge, 1988.

Tebbel, John. *A History of Book Publishing in the United States.* New York: R. R. Bowker, 1972.

Thomas, Deborah. *Dickens and the Short Story.* Philadelphia: University of Pennsylvania Press, 1982.

Thomas, Ronald. "Double Exposures: Arresting Images in Bleak House and The House of Seven Gables." *Novel* 31 (1997): 87–113.

Tillotson, Geoffrey and Kathleen Tillotson. "Writers and Readers in 1851," in *Mid-Victorian Studies.* London: Athlone Press, 1965.

Tillotson, Kathleen. *Novels of the Eighteen Forties.* Oxford: Clarendon Press, 1954.

Timko, Michael. "Dickens, Carlyle and the Chaos of Being." *Dickens Study Annual,* Vol. 16. New York: AMS Press 1987, pp. 1–16.

Vincent, David. *Bread, Knowledge and Freedom: A Study of Nineteenth Century Working Class Autobiography.* London: Methuen, 1982.

———. *Literacy and Popular Culture: England 1750–1914.* Cambridge: Cambridge University Press, 1989.

Vlock, Deborah. "Dickens, Theater and the Making of a Victorian Reading Public." *Studies in the Novel* 29 (1997): 164–90.

———. *Novel Reading and the Victorian Popular Theatre.* Cambridge: Cambridge University Press, 1998.

Watt, Ian. *The Rise of the Novel.* Berkeley: University of California Press, 1957.

Webb, R. K. *British Working Class Reader, 1790–1848: Literacy and Social Tension.* London: Allen and Unwin, 1955.

Welsch, Alexander. *From Copyright to Copperfield: The Identity of Dickens.* Cambridge: Harvard University Press, 1987.

Williams, Raymond. *Culture and Society: 1780–1954.* New York: Harper and Row, 1958, rpt. New York: Columbia University Press, 1983.

Wilson, Angus. *The World of Charles Dickens.* London and New York: Viking, 1970.

Wilson, Edmund. "Dickens: The Two Scrooges," in *The Wound and the Bow.* London: W. H. Allen, 1941.

Winship, Michael. *American Literary Publishing in the Mid-Nineteenth Century—The Business of Ticknor and Fields.* Cambridge University Press, 1995.

———. "The Transatlantic Book Trade and Anglo-American Literary Culture in the Nineteenth Century," in *Reciprocal Influences: Literary Production, Distribution, and Consumption in America,* ed. Steven Fink and Susan S. Williams. Columbus: Ohio State UP, 1999, pp. 98–122.

Wittmann, Reinhard. "Was There a Reading Revolution at the End of the Eighteenth Century?" in *A History of Reading in the West.* Cavallo and Chartier eds. Amherst: University of Massachusetts Press, 1999, pp. 284–312.

Zabel, Morton Dauwen, ed. *Charles Dickens' Best Stories.* Garden City: New York: Hanover House, 1959.

Zboray, Ronald J. *A Fictive People: Antebellum Economic Development and the American Reading Public.* New York: Oxford UP, 1993.

Index

Abbot, Austin, 85
Abbot, Hamlin, 126
Abbot, John Stevens, 127
Abbott, Josiah Gardner, 22
Agnew, Samuel Andrew, 146
Alcott, Louisa May, 96, 136–37, 165–66, 172n2
Alden, John B., 204
Alger, William Rounceville, 207
Altick, Richard, 3
American Book Exchange, 204
American Literary Gazette, 60
American Whig Review, 46, 116
Ames. J.G., 95
Ames, Mary Clemmer, 27–28, 134
Andersen, Hans Christian, 177
Anderson, Benedict, 6–7, 12, 14, 44
Andersonville prison, 149
Andover House Library (Boston), 88
Andrews, Sidney, 29
anti-slavery novels, 125
Archer, A.O., 94
Arcturus, 49
Arthur, T.S., 145
A.S. Barnes Publishing Company, 202
Astor Place Theater riot, 159–60

Atheneum Library (Boston), 94, 200
Atlantic Monthly, 25, 61, 88, 170, 172
autobiographies, 16–17, 39, 63n7
Avary, Myrta Lockett, 30
Axton, William, 3, 8, 109, 162

Bagby, George W., 102
Bakhtin, Mikhail, 8, 169
Baldwin, Joseph Glover, 26
Bangs, John Kendrick, 171, 200
Bangs (distributor), 59
Barker, Harriet, 92
Barnard, Henry, 110–12
Barnes, W.H., 116
Barthes, Roland, 16
Bartol, Cyrus Augustus, 127
Battis, William Sterling, 171
Beard, Ida May, 104, 118n3
Becker, Bernard Henry, 112
Beecher, Henry Ward, 183
Begbie, Harold, 205
Bell, Bill, 142
belles letters, 48, 164
Benjamin, Park, 44, 51, 63n5–6, 64n10, 80, 175
Bennett, Arnold, 69

— 235 —

Benson, Arthur, 207
Blount, Annie R., 105, 136
Bobbs-Merrill Publishing Company, 203
Book Buyer, 203
Book Monthly, 208
Bookman, The, 205
Bogger, Louise, 177
Boggs, William Robertson, 168
Boston Daily Journal, 178–79
Boston Music Hall, 208
Boston Post, 179
Boston Public Library, 83
Boston Transcript, 60
Boucicault, Dion, 166, 172n3
Boyd, Andrew Kennedy Hutchison,
    113–14, 122–23
Bradbury and Evans, 53, 62n1, 66
Bremer, Frederika, 52, 71
Briggs, Charles, 54
Brooklyn Eagle, 15, 126, 181, 195–97, 203
Broome, Richard E., 17
Brother Jonathan, 43, 68
Brougham, John, 93, 166
Brown, David, 128, 135
Brown, John (physician), 124
Brown, Mamie (Madaline Allan), 211
Browne, Junius Henri, 24
Brownson, Orestes, 22
Bryan, Mary Narcott, 113, 130
Bryant, William Cullen, 46, 80, 89, 182
Bulwer Lytton, Edward, 20, 52, 55–56,
    90–91, 144–45, 148, 150, 196, 203–4
Bunyan, John, 104
Burns, Robert, 195
Burt, Richard, 147
Burwell, Letitia M., 129–30
Bushman, Richard L., 18, 164

Cabell, Margaret, 19, 24–25
Cairo (Illinois; in *Martin Chuzzlewit*),
    75, 78, 82n8, 143
Calthrop, Samuel Robert, 166
Cameron, J.D., 150
camp, soldiers in, 145–49, 157

Carey, Henry, 4, 45, 49–50, 55, 58, 62n1,
    63n9, 64n10
Carlyle, Thomas, 3, 90–91, 195
Carroll Hall (Washington, DC), 183–85
Casamajor, George, 205
Catholic World, 106
Centennial Temperance Conference
    (Philadelphia), 198
Central Park (New York), 103
Century Magazine, 205
Chapin, Anna, 109–10, 209
Chapman and Hall, 49–50, 53, 59, 61,
    62n1, 66, 80
Chapman, Robert, 184
Chartier, Roger, 3
Chase, Lucien Bonaparte, 129
Chautauqua Institute, 171
Cheatham, Frances Bugg, 210
Chesnut, Mary, 150–55, 164, 209
Chesterton, G.K., 205
Child, Lydia Marie, 28, 74, 132
Cincinnati Commercial, 126
Cincinnati Daily Times, 95
Cincinnati Mercantile Library, 96
Cincinnati Public Library, 95–96
Civil War (American), 12–13, 22,
    138–41, 150–58
Clark, Lewis Gaylord, 63n7
Clay, Henry, 45, 52, 133
Clemens, Olivia Langdon, 172n4, 176
Clemens, Samuel. *See* Mark Twain
Colclough, Stephen M., 13
Cole, Cornelius, 184
Coleridge, Samuel Taylor, 203
Collins, Wilkie, 39n2, 159
Columbian Reading Union, 103
Commager, Henry Steele, 39n1
communications circuit, 13, 43, 63n2
Connelly, James A., 148
Cooke, Philip St. George, 67, 71
Cooper, Anna J., 127
Cooper, James Fenimore, 15, 46, 56, 86,
    88–92, 143, 145, 148
Copee, Henry, 73, 117

Copway, George, 17
copyright, 15, 46, 202. *See also* international copyright
Cortland (New York), 36, 41n14, 184
courtesy of trade, 49, 58, 81
Cozzens, Frederick S., 169
Crofts, W.G., 198
Cross, Jane Tandy, 20, 135–36, 209
Curry, Jabez Lamar Monroe, 75
Curtis, George William, 54, 64n14, 174, 189, 195
Curtis, John J., 203
Cutter, Charles Ammi, 94
Cuyler, Theodore Ledyard, 77, 82n7

Dana, Richard Henry, 48–19, 56, 92
D. Appleton Publishing, 61, 66, 202
Darcy, F.O.A., 200
Darnton, Robert, 16, 43
Davis, C.H., 102
Davis, Jefferson, 134
Dawson, Sarah Morgan, 151
Delmonico's Hotel (New York), 192
Demilt Apprentices Library (New York), 87, 192
democracy, 11, 44, 49, 52, 63n4, 101, 121
Derby, James Cephas, 62
De Quincey, Thomas, 17
Detroit Daily Times, 202
De Wolfe, Fiske and Company, 204
Diblee, William, 92
Dickens, Charles, subjects of: caricatures, 168; catchphrases, 21–22, 169–70; coincidence, 210; collaborations with Wilkie Collins, 177, 198; film, 209; hallucinative imagination, 109, 118n4; in America (1842), 67–82; in America (1867), 173–92; memorabilia, 197–98; public readings, 173–92; slave named after, 127; statue of, 205
Dickens, Charles, works of: *All the Year Round*, 56, 94, 108, 144, 158n1;

American Notes, 6, 13, 17, 45, 50–52, 62, 66, 69, 72–75, 79, 82n5, 116, 119n5, 129, 160, 163, 182, 186, 206–7, 211; "Amusements of the People," 173; "Bardell and Pickwick" (*Pickwick Papers*), 61; *Barnaby Rudge*, 50, 96, 107; *Bleak House*, 9, 38, 57, 62, 86, 108, 122–29, 131, 133, 139n2, 151, 153, 162, 206; "Bob Sawyer's Party" (*Pickwick Papers*), 61, 146; *Child's History of England, A*, 36; *Christmas Books*, 50, 59, 178; *Christmas Carol, A*, 20, 163, 166, 179, 185–86, 188, 197; *David Copperfield*, 30, 42n14, 53, 61, 103–6, 118, 131, 144, 149, 152, 170, 184, 190–91, 206–7; *Dombey and Son*, 35, 41n13, 50, 53, 63n8, 64n12, 80, 102, 123; *Frozen Deep, The* (with Wilkie Collins), 177; "George Silverman's Explanation," 61; *Great Expectations*, 38, 126, 144, 146, 150, 153, 157, 170, 191; *Hard Times*, 55, 110–13, 132–33, 167; "Holiday Romance, A" 61; *Household Words*, 9; *Little Dorrit*, 132, 148, 154, 184–85, 206, 212; *Martin Chuzzlewit*, 50, 52, 67–70, 72–74, 79–80, 82, 116, 126, 133, 142–43, 151–53, 184, 197, 208; *Master Humphrey's Clock*, 96, 197; "Mrs. Lirriper's Lodgings," 153; "Mugby Junction," 108; *Mystery of Edwin Drood, The*, 196, 201; *Nicholas Nickleby*, 25, 107, 113–13, 117, 130, 137, 152–54, 166–68, 174; *No Thoroughfare* (with Wilkie Collins), 198; *Old Curiosity Shop, The*, 18–19, 50, 64n11, 123–24, 146, 152–53, 184, 197, 208; *Oliver Twist*, 21–25, 33, 59, 63n9, 67, 90, 115, 124, 127, 152, 160–61, 168, 181, 209; *Our Mutual Friend*, 108, 150, 155–57, 181; *Pickwick Papers*, 37, 42n15, 44, 49, 61–62, 63n4, 67, 70, 124, 144, 161, 184, 188, 196, 199; *Pictures of*

Italy, 152; *Sketches by Boz*, 63n9; *Tale of Two Cities, A*, 11–12, 17, 34, 142, 148, 157, 179, 185–86, 188, 197
Dickens, Kate, 104
Dickens societies, 193, 199–200
dime novels, 145
Disraeli, Benjamin, 90, 128
Dodge, Mary, 20, 27
Dolby, George, 171, 175–76, 184–85
Douglas, Ann, 39n3
Douglas, Henry Kidd, 149
Douglas, Stephen, 133
Douglass, Frederick, 122, 125
Downing, Andrew Jackson, 70
Drew, John M.L., 144
Duganne, August Joseph Hickey, 148
Duncan, Mary Grey Lundie, 104
Dunlop, William (*Andre*), 170
Duyckinck, Evert A., 49, 63n8, 177
Dwight, Timothy, 15

Eggleston, George Cary, 146
Eisenstein, Sergei, 209
Eliot, George, 209
Elmira (New York), 26; prison, 149
Emerson, Ralph Waldo, 76, 90, 116, 195
Erie Canal, 5
Etinge, Solomon, 200
Everett, Edward, 127
Examiner, The, 146
Exman, Eugene, 58, 64n10

factories, 94, 136
Fahs, Alice, 13, 40n1, 143
fancy, 110
Farman, Ella, 134
Farrar, Mrs. John, 28–29
Fawle, William Bentley, 115
Feather, John, 63n4
Fechter, Charles, 184
Federal Writer's Project, 17
Felton, Rebecca Latimer, 151
Fern, Fanny, 20, 65n16, 183
fictive community, 12–14
Field, Annie, 177, 181, 191

Field, Maunsell Broadhurst, 134
Fields, James, 61,127, 133, 173, 177–78, 201
Fillmore, Millard, 55
film, 209
Fitzgerald, F. Scott, 2
Fitzgerald, Percy Hetherington, 197
Flint, Kate, 3, 7
Ford, George, 2, 68, 79, 81, 206
Forney, John Wien, 183, 194
Forster, John, 17, 67, 81n3, 95, 97, 192n3, 194, 196, 205
Fortnightly Review, 208
Fourth of July orations, 82, 160
Frederick Douglass Paper, 125–26
Freedley, Edwin T., 58
French Revolution, 36
Freud, Sigmund, 9
Fuller, Margaret, 91
Fulton, David (John Thorne), 126–27

Gad's Hill, 41n14, 197
Galaxy, 174, 176, 181
Garis, Robert, 8, 162
Garvey, Ellen Gruber, 138
Gaskell, Peter, 162
Giddings, Luther, 122
Gilman, Arthur, 25
Gilmore, William, 4, 15
Godey's Lady Book, 143
Godwin, Parke, 54
Gordon, George H., 144
Gorving, Mrs. D.H., 36
Gould, Samuel Shelton, 17
Gow, Alexander Murdoch, 117
Graham's Magazine, 56, 143
Grant, Ulysses S., 21
Grattan, Thomas Colley, 76
Greeley, Horace, 192
Green, Wharton Jackson, 75
Greenspan, Ezra, 83
Griffith, D.W., 209
Griswold, Rufus, 46, 57
Gustorf, Harriet and Friedrich, 200
G.W. Carleton Publishing Company, 83

Hadcock, K. Frances, 187
Haltunnen, Karen, 40n5, 41n11, 164
Hare, Mrs. H.R., 32
Harland, Marion, 94, 143–44, 168–69, 213n5
Harper Brothers, 4, 9, 50–51, 54, 58, 64n10, 203
Harper, J. Henry, 203
Harper's Monthly/Harper's Weekly, 9, 12, 54–57, 60, 64n14, 65, 68, 131, 141, 144, 147, 150–52, 155, 157–58, 158n1, 167, 174–75, 180, 203
Harper's Priority List, 57
Harrison, Mrs. Burton, 149
Hart, Abraham, 45
Hart, Mary, 106
Harvard University Library, 194
Haven, Charlotte, 76, 207
Haven, Erastus Otis, 208
Hawthorne, Nathaniel, 51, 56, 90, 124
Hayes, Israel Isaac, 30, 40n7
Hayward, Jennifer, 7, 173
Helper, Hinton Rowan, 23
Hemingway, Ernest, 2
Higginson, Thomas Wentworth, 17, 206
Hogarth, Georgiana, 185
Holbrook, James, 23
holidays, reading Dickens during, 166, 169, 210
Holland, Josiah Gilbert, 196
Holloway, William Robeson, 26
Holmes, Oliver Wendell, 194
Hone, Philip, 70
Honey Moon (play), 163
House of Seven Gables (Nathaniel Hawthorne), 124
Household Words, 91
Howells, William Dean, 80
Howitt, Mary Ann, 30
Hughes, Linda and Michael Lund, 7, 31–32, 41n12
Hughes, Thomas, 149
Hurd and Houghton Publishers, 83
Hutton, Lawrence, 175, 178
Huxley, T.H., 112

illustrations, 175
imagined community, 6–7, 14, 211
imitating Dickens characters, 167
Indianapolis Public Library, 96–97
Infelicia (Adah Menken), 126
international copyright, 45–49, 55–56, 62n1, 63n8, 133
Irving, Henry, 159
Irving, Washington, 18, 50–51, 56, 88, 95, 98, 148

Jackson, Andrew, 133
James, Henry, 206–7, 209
J. Applegate Publishing, 61
Jerrold, Douglas, 162, 170
Joanningsmeier, Charles, 7
John, Juliet, 174
Johnson, Edgar, 64n11, 159, 163
Johnson, Paul, 5
Jones, Emma, 36
Jones, William Alfred, 49
Jonesville Library (Michigan), 37
Jordan, John O., 63

Kearney, Belle, 150–51, 164–65
Keiley, Anthony M., 149
Kelly, Emma Dunham, 125–26
Kelly, William Darrah, 133
Kent, Charles, 175
Kent, William, 48
Kitton, F.G., 197–98
Knox, Thomas Wallace, 79

Ladies' Library Association (Kalamazoo, MI), 37
Ladies Repository, 58, 116
Lea and Blanchard Publishing, 49–50, 52, 59, 63n9, 67
Le Conte, Emma, 154
Leigh, Frances Butler, 151
Lester, Caroline, 186
Lewes, G.H. (George Henry), 109, 118n4
libraries, 8–9, 13, 18, 83, 211
"Library of Choice Reading" (Wiley and Putnam), 47, 49

Library of Congress, 95
Lincoln, Abraham, 133, 146
Lippincott Publishing, 54, 59, 61, 66, 126, 203
literacy, 108–9
Littel's Living Age, 54
Little Brown Publishing Company, 54, 59, 203
Liverpool, England, 49
Logan, Olive, 200
London, England, 24, 38, 79, 122, 156, 162
Longfellow, Charles Appleton, 145
Longfellow, Henry Wadsworth, 56, 133, 160, 179
Loring, Ellis Gray, 74
Lunt, George, 34
Lyons, Martin, 18

Macauley, Thomas Babington, 17
Maclise, Daniel, 117
Macready, William Charles, 159–60, 163
Mallard, Robert Q., 123
Manchester Public Library (England), 99
Marcy, William L., 134
Marryat, Frederick, 51, 91, 143
Martin, Elizabeth S., 161
Martineau, Harriet, 115
Marvel, I.K., 65n16
Massett, Stephen, 162
Matthews, Cornelius, 49
Matthews, William, 116
Maurice, Arthur Bartlett, 196
May, Samuel J., 122
McCabe, James Dabney, 117
McCarthy, Justin, 112, 206
McConnel, John Ludlum, 27
McElrath, T.L., 58
McGill, Meredith, 7, 44–46, 51–52
McGuffrey's Readers, 131
McHenry, Elizabeth, 125
McKinley, William, 26, 83
Meckier, Jerome, 68, 78–79. 81
Meehan, Mary Anne, 199
Megda (Emma Dunham Kelly), 126

melodrama, 3, 64n11, 126, 162–64, 167–68, 174
Melville, Herman, 122, 124
Mencken, H.L., 2
Menken, Adah Isaacs, 126–27, 139n3
Methodist Book Concern, 137
Miall, David S., 23–24
Middlesex Mechanics Association Library (Lowell, MA), 88
Middleton, Eliza and Mary, 168
Mills, Harriet May, 184–85
Milton, John, 203
Milwaukee Public Library, 88
Mitchell, Donald Grant, 64, 161
Mitchell, Sally, 7
Mordecai, Ellen, 25, 142, 176
Mordecai, Samuel, 128, 142
Mormons, 18, 76, 207
Mortlake Collection (Pennsylvania State University Library), 9
Moss, Sidney, 69
Mott, Frank Luther, 63n6, 64n11
Mount Zion Baptist Church (Haverhill, MA), 195
Murdock, James E., 170

Nack, James, 123
Nadal, E.S., 131
Nascher, Ignatz Leo, 25
Nassau, Mabel Louise, 26
Nation, The, 60
nationalism, 43, 51, 62, 129, 159–60, 175, 183
National Review, The, 133
New England Magazine, 83
Newsom, Robert, 109, 118n6, 119
New World, 44–46, 51–52, 64n10
New York Courier and Enquirer, 69
New York Evening Post, 46, 171
New York Herald, 45, 68, 179
New York Historical Society, 8
New York Mercantile Library, 83
New York Mirror, 143
New York Observer, 144
New York Society Library, 83 90–91, 99n8

New York Sun, 45–46
New York Times, 179
New York Tribune, 60, 160, 179, 182
New York World, 68
Niagara Falls, 46, 75
Nichols, Rebecca S., 20
Niles, Jason, 148
Nisbet, Ada, 79
North American Review, 206
North Star, 122
Noyes, George Freeman, 145

O'Connor, William Douglas, 138
Okker, Patricia, 7, 41n10, 44n10, 64n14, 118n1, 139n1
Olmstead, Frederick Law, 63n7, 103
Onondaga Historical Society (Syracuse, NY), 6, 35
O.O. Trade List, 202
Orphan Asylum (Cleveland), 171
Orwell, George, 209–10
Osgood, James R., 190–91
Oswego System, 111
Outlook, The, 126

Page, Thomas Nelson, 74
Page, Walter Hines, 201, 204
Panic of 1837, 64
Park, Robert E., 149
Parker, Willie, 25, 126–27
Paroissien, David, 122
Parton, James, 183
Parsons, Thomas Williams, 132
Parton, James, 183
Patten, Robert L., 8, 50, 52, 56, 58, 62n1, 63n3, 64n12, 65n17, 68, 83, 208, 210
Pawley, Christine, 4, 6–7, 33
Pearce, George, 95
Peckham, Walton H., 92
Pell, Clarence, 91
Pell, George, 91
Pennel, Mary H., 91
Pennsylvania System, 133
Phelps, Almira Hart Lincoln, 115–16
Phelps, William Lyon, 205

Philadelphia Mercantile Library, 89
Pickwick Club (in Alcott, *Little Women*), 165
Pickwick Society (Deposit, NY), 37
Pierce, Ann, 91
Pierce, Franklin, 55, 134
Pilgrim's Progress, 104
Plymouth Church (Brooklyn, NY), 183
Poole, William, 96n3
Porter, Noah, 161
Potter, David, 39n1
Potter, Edward, 91
Pratt, William (*Ten Nights in a Barroom*), 170
Presbyterian, The, 144
private theatricals, 165
Providence Atheneum (Rhode Island), 94–95
public readings, 173–92
publishers, 13, 43–48, 50–55, 62, 62n2, 69, 202–4
Publisher's Circular, 194
Putnam, George Palmer, 4, 48–49, 56, 59, 62
Putnam's Monthly, 54–57, 64n14, 138
Pycroft, James, 73

Quakers, 24
Quincy, Josiah, 67
Quint, Alonzo Hall, 147

Radway, Janice, 7
Railton, Stephen, 125
Raleigh (North Carolina), 176
reading circles, 14, 32, 34, 36–38, 41n14
readers and audience: abolitionists, 28, 74, 132; African Americans, 125–27; at sea, 17, 30–31, 104; children, 165, 184, 186–87, 207, 190–91; clerks, 123; educators, 15, 25, 71, 73, 110–13, 115–16, 119n5; farmers, 23; German Americans, 25; Irish Americans, 103; Jewish Americans, 25, 142, 176; landscape designers, 70, 102; mailmen, 23; miners, 22; ministers,

73, 77, 79, 95, 113–14, 122–23, 166, 207–8; Mormons, 18, 76; Native Americans, 17; soldiers, 21, 27, 122, 141, 144–49; Southerners, 30, 74, 122–23, 127–31, 141–42, 145–46, 148–49, 174; spiritualists, 23; theater patrons (public readings), 173–92; women, 134–39, 140n5
reform, 112, 122–24, 134, 139n4
Reid, Whitelaw, 29
Repplier, Agnes, 88
reprinting, 7–8, 15, 44–46, 50–52
Rhees, William Jones, 87, 99
Richardson, Dorothy, 137
Richmond, Virginia, 12
Ripley, Eliza Chinn McHatten, 26
Ripley, George, 82n6, 174
Ritchie, Anna Cora Ogden, 163
Riverside Press, 25
Robertson, Nellie, 199
Robinson Crusoe, 104, 108
Rochester (New York), 5, 125
Rose, Anne C., 41n10, 118n1
Rose, Jonathan, 3–4, 17, 40n8, 62n2, 98n2, 102, 118n3
Roosevelt, James, 90
Roosevelt, R.B., 23
Roosevelt, Theodore, 80
Root, James Edward, 191
Root, Taylor, 116
Rosenkranz, Karl, 25
Rozwenc, Edwin C., 41n11
Ruskin, John, 90
Rusling, James Fowler, 22
Russell, William Howard, 79

Sadlier, Michael, 58
Sager, Aaron, 184, 187
San Francisco libraries, 97
Sargent, Epes, 52, 147
Saturday Evening Courier, 143
Schlesinger, Arthur, 48
Schlicke, Paul, 3, 112, 178
Schomberg Collection (New York Public Library), 126

Scientific American, 135
Scott, Sir Walter, 48, 56, 65n19, 85–86, 88, 90, 92, 94–95, 144–45, 147–50, 195
scrapbooks, 137–38, 210
Scribner's Monthly, 202, 204
Scribner's Sons Publishing, 66, 195, 204
Sedgwick, Catharine Maria, 56
sentimentalism, 19, 64n11, 123–24, 139, 141, 163–64
serialization, 31–34, 57, 62, 64n11, 71, 101, 123, 141, 150, 155–57
Seward, William, 133
Sewell, Elizabeth Missing, 107
Seymour, Charles C.B., 116
Shakespeare, William, 8, 14, 17, 36, 41, 94, 159–60, 163
Sigourney, Lydia Huntley, 39n3
Simms, William Gilmore, 122
slavery, 45, 121, 125–30, 141
Smiles, Samuel, 116
Smith, Augustus F., 83
Smith, James L., 164
Smith, Jane Rooker, 200
Smithsonian Institution, 83
Sorosis Club, 199
Southern Literary Messenger, 101–2, 128, 131
Southern Quarterly Review, 46–47, 122, 129
Spalding, Martin John, 208
Spiller, Robert, 14
Stanford, Peter Thomas, 195
Stanton, Edwin, 133
Starrs, Willie, 137
Steinway Hall (New York), 170, 176, 180, 192
Stephen, Alexander H., 29
Sterling, Edward, 19
Stewart, Garret, 172n1
Stillman, Benjamin, 71
Stoddard, Richard, 63n7
Stowe, Harriet Beecher, 22, 83, 122, 124–26, 129, 132, 153
Strong, George Templeton, 76

Sturgess, Kim, 7, 14, 160, 166
Sumner, Charles, 132–33, 179
Sweet, Elizabeth, 23–24
Swett, John, 111
sympathy, 101, 123, 187
Syracuse (New York), 5–6, 32, 35–36, 41n14, 110, 184–88
Syracuse American, 184
Syracuse House Hotel, 185–85, 189
Syracuse Journal, 186–87, 189, 202
Syracuse Post Standard, 188

Tauchnitz Publishing (Leipzig), 83, 94, 96
Tayleur, Clifton (*Horseshoe Robinson*), 170
Taylor, Bayard, 63n7, 77
Taylor, Zachary, 34
T.B. Peterson Publishing, 54, 58–60, 201–2
Tebbel, John, 59, 61
Tennyson, Alfred Lord, 17, 89, 91, 155
Thackeray, William Makepeace, 89–92, 94, 98, 124, 129, 131, 145, 148–49, 162, 202–4
Thornby, William, 185–86
Ticknor and Fields Publishing, 54, 59–61, 65n18, 66, 201, 203–4
Ticknor, George, 48
Tillotson, Kathleen and John Butt, 7, 32, 81, 173
tobacco, spitting, 71
Tocqueville, Alexis de, 81n4, 166
Train, Enoch, 105
Train, George Francis, 82n6, 76
travel narratives, 15, 17, 51, 74
Tremont Temple (Boston), 178
Trollope, Frances, 17
Truxton Club (Cortland, NY), 36–37, 42n15
Tucker, Mary E., 126–27
Tuckerman, Henry, 73
Twain, Mark (Samuel Langhorne Clemens), 96, 142–43, 147, 171, 172n3, 176

Uncle Tom's Cabin, 56, 124–25, 139n2, 142, 146, 153, 171, 172n4, 176
United States Book Company, 204
urban population growth, 32–33
U.S. Congress, 133
U.S. Democratic Review, 11, 47, 101

Van Antwerp, Amelia, 102
Vanderhof, George, 171
Venable, W.H., 96, 107
Vincent, David, 3, 63n2
Vlock, Deborah, 8, 170

Wallace, Alan, 210
Ward, Austin, 18
Warfield, Catherine Ann, 13
Warner, Susan, 65n16, 100, 186
Washington, DC, 27, 134, 183
Washington, George, 19
Washington Tribune, 29
Waters, Augustus, 170
Wayland, Francis, 198
Webb, James Watson, 69
Wednesday Club (Syracuse, NY), 32, 35–36, 41
Weedon, Alexis, 62
Weisbuch, Robert, 7, 14, 124
Weiting Hall (Syracuse, NY), 5, 184–87
Welch, Samuel Manning, 75
Western book trade, 83, 95–96
White, Richard Grant, 180
Whitman, Walt, 15, 101–2
Whitney, A.D.T (Adeline Dutton Train), 38, 105, 209
Wiggins, Kate Douglas, 20, 191,92
Wilbur, Hervy Backus, 110
Wiley, John, 63n8
Wiley and Putnam, 47
Willard, Frances E., 15–16
Williams, Raymond, 133, 139n4
Willis, N.P. (Nathaniel Parker), 29, 113, 132, 183
Wilson, Edmund, 178
Winship, Michael, 62n2, 83
Winsor, Justin, 83

Winthrop, Robert Charles, 93
Wise, John Sargent, 148
Wither, Anita Dwyer, 107, 168
Wittmann, Reinhard, 3, 14, 18
Wolfe, John D., 90, 92
Woolf, Virginia, 2
Woolsey, Jane Stuart, 144
Woolson, Constance Fenimore, 134, 167
Wright, Laura M., 143

Wright, Louise Wigfall, 151
Wyeth, Mary F., 92

Yates, Edmund, 170
YMCA libraries: Augusta (Georgia), 86; Milwaukee, 88
Youmans, Edward Livingston, 112

Zboray, Ronald, 6–7, 12–13, 41n10, 92, 99n8, 143